DISRUPTING
SAVAGISM

Intersecting Chicana/o,

Mexican Immigrant, and

Native American Struggles

for Self-Representation

Arturo J. Aldama

DUKE UNIVERSITY PRESS

Durham & London

2001

D1021844

© 2001 Duke University Press

All rights reserved

Printed in the United States

of America on acid-free paper ♾

Designed by Amy Ruth Buchanan

Typeset in Scala with Officina Sans display

by Tseng Information Systems, Inc.

Library of Congress Cataloging-in-

Publication Data appear on the

last printed page of

this book.

DISRUPTING SAVAGISM

A book in the series

LATIN AMERICA OTHERWISE

Languages, Empires, Nations

Series editors:

Walter D. Mignolo, Duke University

Irene Silverblatt, Duke University

Sonia Saldívar-Hull, University

of California at Los Angeles

About the Series

Latin America Otherwise: Languages, Empires, Nations is a critical series. It aims to explore the emergence and consequences of concepts used to define "Latin America" while at the same time exploring the broad interplay of political, economic, and cultural practices that have shaped Latin American worlds. Latin America, at the crossroads of competing imperial designs and local responses, has been construed as a geocultural and geopolitical entity since the nineteenth century. This series provides a starting point to redefine Latin America as a configuration of political, linguistic, cultural, and economic intersections that demand a continuous reappraisal of the role of the Americas in history, and of the ongoing process of globalization and the relocation of people and cultures that have characterized Latin America's experience. *Latin America Otherwise: Languages, Empires, Nations* is a forum that confronts established geocultural constructions, that rethinks area studies and disciplinary boundaries, that assesses convictions of the academy and of public policy, and that, correspondingly, demands that the practices through which we produce knowledge and understanding about and from Latin America be subject to rigorous and critical scrutiny.

Arturo J. Aldama's *Disrupting Savagism: Intersecting Chicana/o, Mexican Immigrant, and Native American Struggles for Self-Representation* is the first book in our series that displaces the idea that "Latin America" is a bounded, existing entity, in which things happen and which Latin Americanists study. "Latin America" has moved to the U.S. and *is* also reinscribed in the world at large. In Aldama's book, Mexican anthropologist and indigenista, Manuel Gamio enters into a critical dialogue with Gloria Anzaldúa, which refashions his previous connections with Robert Redfield and U.S. anthropology. Norma Alcarcón and other Chicana cultural critics are placed in conversation with "white" and "third world" feminism; while Chicana Gloria Anzaldúa is put in dialogue with Laguna writer Leslie Marmon Silko. And a new reading of Gloria Anzaldúa's *Borderlands/La Frontera* is offered through the work of Sonia Saldívar-Hull.

In this groundbreaking study, familiar terms are defamiliarized. Mestizaje, neocolonialism, and internal colonialism, of common currency in Latin American scholarship, are redefined. Subalternity and postcolonialism, of common currency in Commonwealth scholarship, are recast from the racial and gender experiences of Chicana/os (and more generally, Latina/os), and thereby revealing the color and gender of epistemology.

Aldama's book is not only of interest because of its novel interpretation of Chicana/os' texts and experiences but also, and perhaps mainly, because it opens up the possibilities of dialogues with the rich tradition of social and philosophical thinking in Latin America. Indirectly, the book is an invitation to imagine Latin America otherwise, that is to say, to critically examine the imaginary of French "Latinity" and U.S. "area studies" in which "Latin America" is still being mapped today.

Contents

Acknowledgments, ix

Preface, xi

PART I
Mapping Subalternity in the U.S./México Borderlands

1. The Chicana/o and the Native American "Other" Talk Back: Theories of the Speaking Subject in a (Post?) Colonial Context, 3

2. When Mexicans Talk, Who Listens? The Crisis of Ethnography in Situating Early Voices from the U.S./ México Borderlands, 35

PART II
Narrative Disruptions: Decolonization, Dangerous Bodies, and the Politics of Space

3. Counting Coup: Narrative Acts of (Re)Claiming Identity in *Ceremony* by Leslie Marmon Silko, 71

4. Toward a Hermeneutics of Decolonization: Reading Radical Subjectivities in *Borderlands/La Frontera: The New Mestiza* by Gloria Anzaldúa, 95

5. A Border Coda: Dangerous Bodies, Liminality, and the Reclamation of Space in *Star Maps* by Miguel Arteta, 129

Notes, 145

Selected Bibliography, 159

Index, 175

Acknowledgments

This book would have not been possible without the support, mentorship, and encouragement of so many colleagues and friends. My work on this manuscript was finished at the Center for Chicano Studies at UC Santa Barbara, with a generous postdoctoral fellowship and research support. I am especially grateful for how the Chicana/o Studies faculty made me feel so welcome to the UC Santa Barbara community. I very much appreciate that María Herrera-Sobek, Carl Gutiérrez-Jones, and Chela Sandoval took time from their busy schedules to read parts of my manuscript and offer sensitive and thorough commentary on the material. I am also grateful for Pat Richardson's efficient administrative support. At Arizona State University I am truly thankful for the personal and intellectual support of so many colleagues and friends. First, I want to thank Vicki Ruiz, a fearless scholar and historian and wonderful department chair. I also want to thank Cordelia Candelaria for her professional mentoring; Eduardo Escobar, Lisa Magana, and Ray Padilla for providing a collegial and interdisciplinary environment; Alejandra Elenes for her theoretical insights to my work; and Manuel de Jesus de Hernandez-Gutiérrez for his warm intellectual camaraderie. My gratitude also extends to Tey Diana Rebolledo for reading my chapter on feminist theory and for her struggles to make the MLA more welcoming to scholars in Chicana/o literatures.

I also want to acknowledge my mentors and friends from UC Berkeley. First, I want to thank Norma Alarcón, my dissertation chair, who has constantly inspired me to do the best work possible. Alfred Arteaga has not only challenged me to do the best work possible, but also he has been a great, great friend and role model whose advice and support have proven invaluable. José David Saldívar has done judicious readings of my work and given the generosity of his time and professional advice; he is a great mentor and friend. Pat Hilden's advice and support are exemplary.

I am also indebted to Deena Gonzalez for her meticulous readings of my earlier work at the Tomás Rivera Center. I also want to acknowledge graduate students, especially the keen editorial support of Delberto Dario Ruiz, along with Sarah Ramirez, Perlita Dicochea, and Lisa Flores whose work on Maria Elena Lucas is groundbreaking. At Duke University Press, I want to acknowledge Reynolds Smith for his belief in my work and Sharon Parks Torian for her warm commitment to detail.

A much earlier version of chapter 2 appeared in *Discourse: Journal for Theoretical Studies in Media and Culture* (1995–1996): 122–46. An early version of chapter 3 appeared in *Cross Addressing: Resistance Literature and Cultural Borders,* ed. John Hawley (New York: SUNY Press, 1996), 157–81. Some of the ideas on resistance, violence, and decolonization that shape this book were also explored in the following articles: "Millennial Anxieties: Borders, Violence, and the Struggles for Chicana/o Subjectivity," *AZ Journal of Hispanic Cultural Studies* (1998): 42–62; and "Visions in the Four Directions: 500 Years of Resistance and Beyond," in *As We Are Now,* ed. W. S. Penn (Berkeley: University of California Press, 1997), 140–68.

I wish to thank *mi padre* Luis, whose brilliance, struggles, and persistence have always been my true inspiration; and *mi hermano* Federico, whose love of writing is infectious. Also, I want to remember the ancestors, the spirits, and the animals—all those who have come before us—who speak in dreams, whose presence I feel, and who truly inspire my sense of wonder. Finally, I want to dedicate this work to Dulce, *mi compañera por vida,* whose wisdom, humor, and unconditional love is the motivating force in my life.

Preface

Contemporary debates in comparative transethnic cultural studies challenge Anglo-America's protected status as the exclusive holder of cultural and literary value. Chicana/o, Native American, feminist, and postcolonial literary and cultural studies provide a series of crucial challenges to patriarchally driven Anglo-American and Eurocentric theoretical assumptions and literary practices. These textual, theoretical, and inherently political interventions rupture or at least problematize the hermetic seals that have surrounded the uncontested dominance of Eurocentric literary and cultural canons and their ties to the colonial imposition and neocolonial maintenance of social privilege in the political economy of the United States. The disruption of these seals of privilege provides alternate spaces for the articulation of subaltern voices whose "identities in difference" (mestizaje, race, class, gender, sexuality, immigration status, and indigenous land claims, to name a few) [1] challenge the discursive economy of a nation-state legitimized through the imperial and genocidal practices of "manifest destiny." Crystallized by the militarized rubicon of the U.S./Mexico border, the rise of Chicana/o, Mexican émigré, and Native American voices opens epistemic spaces that allow the emergence of subjectivities that are "old"—even ancient—in their linkages to the diverse cultural and historical genealogies of the Americas and yet also are radically "new" in terms of cultural and linguistic hybridity.

Driven by 508 brutal years of material and psychic colonialism, the questions of *mestizaje* (racial, ethnic, and cultural mixing), the insidious processes of internalized colonialism, and the negotiation of identity are complex. What aspects of our hybrid (mestiza/o) identities are celebrated and suppressed, and in what terms? How do we decolonize ourselves without returning to a static and utopic precolonial past?[2] How do these decolonial practices (re)claim and create enunciative spaces (Mignolo 1995) that challenge the violence-driven technologies of imperial and patriarchal subjection? How do we decolonize gender and sexuality from patriarchal and heteronormative practices in the United States, Mexico, and the Chicana/o community (Peréz 1999)? What strategies of decolonization allow our struggles for identity to engage in nonbinary, nonhierarchic, and non-hegemonic articulations of mestiza/o consciousness (Anzaldúa 1999)?

In engaging with these crucial questions, this study is concerned with how Chicanas/os, Native Americans, and *recién llegados* (newly arrived Mexicanas/os) in what José David Saldívar in *Border Matters* (1997) calls the *"transfrontera* contact zone" of the U.S./Mexico borderlands contest symbolic orders in the U.S. nation-state imaginary to represent themselves/ourselves in textual and social spaces. By analyzing how these subaltern subjects disrupt colonially imposed master-narratives that savagize, criminalize, and pathologize our diverse subjectivities, this book seeks to understand the complex politics of racialized, subaltern, feminist, and diasporic identities; the epistemic logic of hybrid and mestiza/o cultural productions; and the reclamation of decolonial space.

Informed by poststructuralism, cultural studies, ethnic studies, gender studies and critical race theory, as well as by revisionary historiographic practices, this study seeks to intersect Chicana/o cultural studies with an Americas-centered postcolonial studies, expanding the critical dialogues set forth by the growing body of critical works devoted to the study of literary, cultural, filmic, and the practices of everyday resistance (in the words of de Certeau) in the militarized borderlands.[3] The interdisciplinary exigencies of my critical framework allow me to analyze the politics of subject-formation within the intersections of literature, language, ethnography, film, history, culture, legal discourses, and philosophy, framed by a critical sensitivity to the differences of race, ethnicity, class, gender, and sexuality in the sociohistoric contexts of colonialism in the Americas and neocolonialism in the United States.

Although my work is purposefully set against traditionalist methods of scholarly writing where a study unfolds according to a logical *telos* set by this statement, a simple set of questions generates my interrogation of the politics of representation and subjectivity throughout the study: How are subaltern subjects formed in colonial patriarchal nation-state imaginaries? How do these subjects inscribe themselves in various types of narrative forms or genres? The issues of representation take urgency regarding subjects who are otherized, marginalized, and criminalized by apparatuses of representation by the dominant culture (media, literature, and history and sociology textbooks, for example) and by institutions that maintain and comprise the hegemony of the dominant culture (legal, educational, immigration, and correctional). In this sense, the questions of self-formation versus formation by processes of representation that are out of our control also become these questions: How are otherized subjects spoken by cultures and institutions of dominance? How do otherized subjects speak, and in what terms?

In pursuing the complex issues of representation and agency for subaltern subjects, I do not want to posit some pure and authentic space of "otherness" or alterity that marginalized peoples occupy. Inspired by Emma Peréz's crucial challenge in *The Decolonial Imaginary* (1999) "to decolonize notions of otherness to move into liberatory terrain" (110), my interest is to chart how Chicanas/os, as subjects of the Americas, create counterdiscourses to the master-narratives of the United States.[4] In this desire to chart counterdiscursive autorepresentational practices, my specific interest is to analyze the politics of identity and difference among Mexican *recién llegados,* Native Americans, and Chicanas/os in various types of narrative practice — the ethnography, the novel, the autobiography, and the film. Chicana/o counterdiscursive practices in the realms of the creative, the theoretical, the revisioning of histories, or the actual political manifestations are acts of resistance that signal our historically rooted presence and diverse identities to each other and to others who care to listen and learn.

Because of my interest in exploring the relationship between different genres and the inscription of subaltern subjectivity, my work departs from a single genre analysis. Instead, I interrogate the politics of identity along with representation vis-à-vis the tensions between the speaking and spoken subject across different sites in narrative. Specifically, I examine the politics of subjection and resistance in the following texts: the ethnographic transcription *The Mexican Immigrant: His Life Story* (1931) by Mexican anthropologist Manuel Gamio; *Ceremony* (1977) by crossblood Laguna Pueblo writer Leslie Marmon Silko; *Borderlands/La Frontera: The New Mes-*

tiza (1999) by Chicana Gloria Anzaldúa, recently reprinted with a scholarly introduction by Sonia Saldívar-Hull; and the film *Star Maps* (1997)
cowritten and directed by Miguel Arteta. By examining the power relations as well as the historical and cultural context in each narrative site, I
consider how a subject is spoken and how a subject speaks. The arrangement of the texts challenges the viability of differing narrative forms to
inscribe "self-formed" subjectivities. Chapter 1 examines theories of the
Chicana/o subaltern speaking subject, chapter 2, the ethnographic subject,
chapter 3, the literary subject, chapter 4, the autobiographical/testimonial
subject, and chapter 5, the cinematic subject. By unraveling the power relations in each narrative site I show how they are tied and tie themselves
into the larger networks of ideology that are central to the maintenance of
nation-states where imperial patriarchal subjects regulate dominance by
disciplining subjects positioned along axes of race, class, gender, ethnic,
and sexual differences.

Part I of this book, "Mapping Subalternity," attempts to understand
how mestiza/o subjects and postcolonial contest and resist their formation in colonial imaginaries as fierce and noble savages, traceable to the
medieval social constructions of the "Wilde Man" and "Wilde Woman"—
originary representations that unfortunately continue to have enormous
resonance in the dominant imaginaries of the early twenty-first century in
film, media, literature, and popular culture. After tracing the geneaology
of how native peoples are "spoken" of as savages in the anthropology of
the "Indians" of the "New World," the model that I use to understand the
tensions of the speaking and spoken subject derives directly from theories
of the speaking subject vis-à-vis Emile Benveniste, Louis Althusser, Kaja
Silverman, and Julia Kristeva.

Chapter 1 brings these scholars' theories to bear on subaltern peoples
struggling against sociocultural marginalization, critiquing their tendencies to reproduce bourgeois, culturally homogeneous subjects. To understand postcolonial subjectivities, I compare Kristeva's notion of the
"subject-in-process" with the third-world-women-produced theories of
subjectivity of Chandra Mohanty, Chela Sandoval, and Norma Alarcón.
Mohanty's and Alarcón's models of oppositional and relational consciousness bridge the analysis of subalternity in the United States, Latin America,
and the third world. They enable a politics of identity that responds to colonialism and neocolonialism, empowering subjects inferiorized along the
axes of race, ethnicity, class, gender, and sexuality. Specifically, Chicana/o

struggles for identity overlap with people of color in the United States and
subaltern peoples in decolonizing and industrializing countries. Because
what sustains my study is the articulation of speaking subjects, I also address my own processes of representation while deconstructing at points
my own presence as a speaking subject writing about the interplay of the
speaking and spoken subject in the texts of my study.

Chapter 2 traces diasporic politics of liminality in south-to-north border crossers in the foundational ethnographic study *The Mexican Immigrant: His Life Story* (1931), a collection of Mexican émigré testimonies by
Manuel Gamio, the pioneer of modern *indigenismo*. Although these testimonies provide the first major opportunity to view the violent effects
that the U.S./Mexico border produces for Mexicans, Gamio frames these
narratives with racial typologies that link to racist ideologies circulating
in the United States and Mexico. Gamio privileges the "white" Mexican
males, depreciating the "Indian" subjects as more "ignorant." Chapter 2
analyzes the tensions between Gamio's ethnographic project and the autobiographic impulses of the Mexican immigrants.

To discuss the politics of the ethnographic subject, I consider Bahktin's
notion of "centrifugal-discourse" as well as poststructural theories of "writing culture," highlighting narratives that testify to the violent historical
forces at play. In the social and historical climate, the Mexican Revolution
of 1910 caused massive upheavals of Mexicans. In the United States, the
race-based congressional decisions of the Race and Labor Immigration Debates of the 1920s "pulled" Mexicans up to service U.S. agricultural and
industrial needs. The immigrants were forced to live and work in "internal" colonies as second-class citizens, until 1931 when ethnic scapegoating
(similar to that of today) led to the first mass deportation that even included
fifth-generation residents.

Gamio, in collusion with Robert Redfield, deploys a racialist ethnographic apparatus that determines "the worth" of the informants based on
how "white" or "Indian" they appear. Part 2 of this book, "Narrative Disruptions," however, considers how writing and speaking subjects of the
Americas use epistemologies of subject-formation whose symbolic orders
and signifying practices engage in plays of *différance* that emerge from
such cultural matrices as matrifocal tribal stories that predate the conquest
of the Americas, along with multilingual language plays (Caló, Nahuatl,
Spanish, English) in the U.S./Mexico borderlands (Arteaga 1997). Reflect-
ing contemporary Native American mixed-blood and mestiza/o identities,

Silko and Anzaldúa invoke precolonial signifying forces into postmodern forms of representation to resist neocolonial forces of subjection and containment. Silko and Anzaldúa inscribe an Americas-based epistemic space that radically decolonizes the enunciation of subjectivities by recovering and hybridizing Nahuatl (Anzaldúa) and Laguna (Silko) "writing" practices denigrated by the colonial imposition of logocentrism (Mignolo 1995). What I find so subversive and empowering about *Ceremony* is the way that agency—even the colonial conquest of the Americas—is given to "Indian" stories of witchery; in *Ceremony* stories generate the universe. In the case of Anzaldúa, *Borderlands* (re)articulates a politics of decolonial sexuality that resists patriarchal and heterosexist social orders in nationalist, nation-state, colonial, and neocolonial imaginaries and grounds the inscription of identity to the materiality of bodies violated by colonial and male violence.

Chapter 3 considers how Silko's *Ceremony* problematizes issues of blood quantum and racial essentialism where blood quantum is putatively tied to issues of ethnicity. To paraphrase the vulgar logic of racial essentialism in the imaginary of the West of manifest destiny, mixed-race native peoples are seen as "halfbreeds": even though halfbreeds are not "real" Indians, you can't trust them because they are half breeds and therefore part savage. In *Ceremony* it is Tayo, a Laguna Pueblo, Mexican, and Anglo "mixedblood," who undertakes the painful process of decolonization, rather than the "full-blood" characters of Rocky and Emo. Tayo is reclaimed by a worldview that emerges from the heterogeneous language play of Puebloan matri-focal tribal stories. I contrast the status of Tayo with the status of mixed-bloods to an actual legal case that determined entitlement (authenticity) based on blood quantum and tribal out-marriage. This case, *Santa Clara v. Julia Martinez*, ruled against the recognition of a child born outside of the tribe because the mother married outside of the tribe. As a counterhistory, *Ceremony* reclaims links between the Pueblos and the central valley of Mexico and creates a literary sentience of the Americas. In this sense I argue that *Ceremony* is a counterdiscourse that reconceptualizes the politics of identity as a ritual that seeks to embrace and resolve the contradictions imposed on mixedblood peoples negotiating their mestizaje in codifying and conflictive cultural and legal systems of binary logic.

Chapter 4 examines *Borderlands/La Frontera: The New Mestiza*, a multi-genre autobiographical historical testimony by Gloria Anzaldúa. *Borderlands* negotiates the real and the discursive in ways that chronicle and challenge the multiplicity of oppression that impinges on Chicana/o and

Mexicana/o communities along the U.S./Mexico border; oppression that travels across the registers of race, class, gender, and sexuality. In the first part of the chapter, I examine how subaltern and feminist autobiographical writings challenge the bourgeois, Eurocentric, and male-dominated field of autobiography and autobiographical studies. I survey such feminist, Latin American, and Chicana interpretive models as the "Out-law Genre" by Caren Kaplan, "Autobiographic Manifesto" by Sidonie Smith, "Testimonio" by John Beverley, and "Border-Feminism," the introduction by Sonia Saldívar-Hull to *Borderlands*. Then I examine how *Borderlands* challenges the practices of internalized colonialism and offers strategies of decolonization that provide an epistemic and political space that embraces the contradictory fullness of mestiza/o identity. Anzaldúa reconceptualizes Chicana/o identity to embrace the Mesoamerican past as a living cultural and psychic force that informs and sustains the present. *Borderlands* bridges the separation between Chicana/o and Native American autobiographic, literary, and historical expression, articulating a consciousness of the Americas that confronts sexism and homophobia in these communities.

In chapter 5 I consider how the film *Star Maps* (1997) by the new-generation filmmaker Miguel Arteta provides dramatic insight into the power relations that drive the racial and (as we shall see) the sexual commodification of *recíen llegado* and first-generation immigrant Latina/o bodies in contemporary Los Angeles. *Star Maps* dramatically shifts the politics of Chicana/o representation in mainstream film by directly indicting the racialized hegemony of the Hollywood Film and Television Industry and by critiquing pathological gender/power relations in the traditional Mexican family reconstituting itself as part of the emergent immigrant class in the United States. In this chapter I analyze how the film critiques the transmission of nascent heterosexist norms of the patriarchal family structure by how a father justifies prostituting his son as part of the macho ritual of teaching him to be a "real man." By illustrating the elasticity of the U.S./Mexico border, where Mexican and Central American south-to-north border crossers (or those perceived as such) continually negotiate violence-enforced borders/barriers through everyday resistances, *Star Maps,* as a cinematic border text, grounds the struggle for decolonizations to the materiality of racialized bodies in the urban ethnoscapes of Los Angeles.

My interest in mestizaje, neocolonialism, and the decolonization of identity across the various ethnographic, literary, autoethnographic, and social texts is not only academic and theoretical but also comes directly from negotiating a decolonization of my own subjectivity, as well as from an exploration of my family history and the various lineages and heritages that form me as a speaking subject. In a simple and direct sense these texts and theories, especially those by Silko and Anzaldúa, enrich the understanding of my own identity and that of other mestizas/os whose presence and genealogies are conveniently denied and erased in the national citizenry of the United States. Moreover, by investigating Gamio and the racial attitudes that were deployed across his ethnographic apparatus and their complicity with Mexico's racial pyramid I am able to gain insight and historical compassion into the generation of my *abuelas* (grandmothers) who suppress and are ashamed of their Otomie, Mayan, and African lineages of their mestizaje.[5]

I was born in Mexico City. My father is Mexican and my mother is Guatemalan and Irish. I came to California, first San Francisco and then Sacramento, when I was eight. I was born *güero,* blondish with light skin. My family loved that I was the first to have blue-green eyes. They thought I looked "less" Mexican (whatever that means?); less than my *prieto* (dark-skinned) father, and more *güero* than my mother who is light skinned with dark brown hair and coffee-colored eyes.

I remember the first couple of years of school in the States. Having just arrived from Mexico, I did not speak English. My blond-haired teacher with perfect teeth loved Chinese kids because they were so "quiet and studious," and she wished Latino kids were more like them. She did not know what to do with me, so for at least a semester and a half I was put in the back of the class and told to play with blocks, clay, and make scissor cutouts. From the second day of school on I became very nervous, starting at the last fifteen minutes of class. My goal was to get home without getting my ass kicked by a group of white, mainly Irish American, marauding second graders who hated "greasers, spics, and dirty Messicans, who don't speak American." *They wanted to kick me back to Mexico, and I wanted to go.* One day, when I could not walk to school because there were shootings in the Golden Gate Park, I asked my mom why everybody hated me so much, and why nobody understood me. She told me that I had it easier than my brother because he is darker, like my father, and that all I needed to do was learn English as fast as I could. I told her I did not like the sound of English, and she got mad at me.

According to my *abuela* (grandmother) on my father's side, I am a descendent of Otomie, Chichimeca, African (four generations back), and Basque peoples. The Chichimeca and Otomie territories are the areas where my Mexican family originated. They come from Guanajuato, which in Otomie means "the place of frogs." This was a center for the 1810 Revolution of Mexican Independence led by some of my ancestors, the brothers Juan and Ignacio Aldama.[6] The basket in which counterrevolutionary forces hung the head of Juan Aldama is still mounted on the northeast corner of the great granary of the *Alhóndiga* in Guanajuato. In the other corners hang the baskets of the other revolutionary leaders: Captain Ignacio Allende; Father Miguel Hildago, whose "Grito de Dolores" inspired the revolutionary uprising where *gachupines* (members of the Spanish bourgeoisie) were ransacked and killed by the masses of Indian and mestizo peoples; and Mariano Jiménez, who led many successful insurrections against the Spanish royalists. Descendants of the Aldama family eventually moved to Mexico City.

My mother is Guatemalan (Spanish and Mayan) and Irish, and she was born to migrant farm workers in Los Angeles. My Guatemalan grandmother came to Los Angeles as a refugee. Along with her seven brothers and sisters, she was raised by her mother who sewed for people and never learned English. My Irish American grandfather, a lanky man who when wearing his cowboy boots is over six feet tall, must have married my grandmother, who is less than five feet tall, because he thought that she would never question his authority. However, she divorced this violent man, himself orphaned by parents who fled hunger and persecution in Ireland. My Irish grandfather once chased me and my brother out of his trailer because he didn't want *"no damn thieving Mexicans in his house."* Being a mixblood Chicano I learned to negotiate contradictions early on in life.

This recognition of my own historicity in this continent, as well as the contradictions of negotiating mestizaje (further complicated by my specifically mixed genealogy) in a transnational context at the interstices of the United States and Mexico, drive the questioning of mestizaje, identity, decolonization, and resistance throughout this book.

PART I

Mapping Subalternity in the

U.S./México Borderlands

1

The Chicana/o and the
Native American "Other"
Talk Back: Theories of the
Speaking Subject in a
(Post?)Colonial
Context

In 1508 Puerto Rican Indians decided to determine whether Spaniards were mortal or not, by holding them under water to see whether they could be drowned.
—Lewis Hanke, *Aristotle and the American Indians*

In the actual era of postmodern neocolonial social relations, the issues of identity are urgent ones for peoples positioned as "Others" or subalterns by the violent histories of colonialism.[1] In the case of Chicanas/os and Native Americans, we cannot discuss who "we are now" without understanding the continued legacy of imperial violence and our strategic and spontaneous resistance to the forces of material and discursive colonialism.[2] In *Abya Yala,* renamed the Americas, we have the diverse nations of indigenous peoples renamed "Indians" through a geographical error and imagined and treated as savages (noble and fierce) by the colonizing cultures.[3] On a material level, looking back over five hundred years of history, we see full-scale invasions, genocide, rapes, usurpation of lands, broken treaties, and our stratification as social and cultural inferiors to the civilizing culture.[4] On a level of discourse, we challenge the violent practices of representation that reify our positions as barbarians, exotics, illegal aliens, addicts, primitives, criminals, and sexual deviants; the essentialist ways we are invented, simulated, consumed, vanished, and rendered invisible by the dominant culture; as well as the insidious processes of internalized colonialism in our understanding of ourselves and of others.

October 12,1992, marked the quincentenary of the "discovery" of Abya

Yala, renamed the Americas. In San Francisco, however, there was a series of events that held the quincentenary accountable to five hundred years of colonial genocide in the Americas. Marches, tribunals, testimonies, and ceremonies, broadly named Resistance 500, transformed San Francisco and other cities in the Americas into an urban center of resistance and renewal for native peoples of the Americas, whatever their "Indian" blood quantum. The events testified to and called for retribution for the physical acts of violence on native peoples, and, further, they provided opportunities to learn from each other's diverse histories and to form oppositional alliances across the differences as people(s) of the Americas affected by imperialism, colonialism, and neocolonialism.

My participation in these social reclamations of decolonial space inspires the ways I understand, live, and theorize resistance, borders and borderland cultural productions, as well as the ways I analyze, practice, and celebrate the possibilities of new and old oppositional alliances between indigenous and decolonizing mestiza/o peoples across the Americas. The liberatory possibilities of anticolonial alliances profoundly shape the methods and goals of my work to understand how Chicanas/os, Mexicanas/os, and Native Americans engage in strategies of resistance, opposition, and decolonization to colonialist practices of imperial patriarchal subjection.

Reports in the Real: Five Hundred Years of Resistance and Beyond

The 1992 Tribunal for Columbus was staged to hold accountable the legacy of colonialism and violence in the Americas. Diverse grassroots groups were present, such as The Chicano Moratorium Coalition and the Mexican labor solidarity group Regeneracíon, which called for the dismantling of the U.S./Mexico border and recited a litany of treaty violations in Aztlán—the U.S./Mexico borderland that includes Texas, California, Arizona, New Mexico, and Colorado. Hawaiian anticolonialists formed coalitions with Puerto Rican nationalists, African American and American Indian activists, as well as Latin American groups fighting for self-determination against CIA- and multinational-backed oppressive regimes.

On October 5, 1992, the Chasqui (a Peruvian Quechua word meaning "messenger" or "prophet") March and Rally started at Dolores Park and ended at La Raza Park in the Mission barrio in San Francisco. The march was led by teenagers from such diverse tribal affiliations as California Pomo, Lakota Sioux, Chippewa, and Nez Perce, and was followed by the Gay and Lesbian Native American Alliance (People of Two Spirits), the Chicano Moratorium, and El Grupo Maya, among many others. Along the way, the parade stopped at several street corners, parks, and schools where performance art events, ceremonies, and dances were performed.

One particular installation took place on 24th Street near the Church of St. Peter, the central street of the Mission barrio, a predominantly Latino and Mexicano neighborhood. Performance artist Gerardo Navarro and mission activist and poet Katia Aparicio along with several others ritualized the conquest, colonialism, and struggle for liberation in the Americas. Katia Aparicio, dressed in chains and burlap covered with clay, screamed "I am the Americas," while Gerardo, wrapped in tubing and wires with a white death-face mask, created a cacophony by reciting in a rapidly spoken combination of Spanish and English a litany of the atrocities of the conquest throughout the Americas: the rapes, the murders, the deceits, the broken treaties, the destruction of the rain forests, and the construction of nuclear power plants on tribal lands in New Mexico and Nevada.

This performance was a postcontact anticolonial exorcism where historicized bodies mark ideological spaces; an event that dramatizes the original colonial assaults on indigenous sovereignties, indigenous women, and the resource-rich continent. Navarro's fluid use of Spanish, English, and Caló and the wrapping of wires and tubing across his body metaphorizes, speaks to, and forebodes how NAFTA, neoliberalism, and globalization has further eroded the land and human rights of indigenous peoples, especially women, in Mexico and the Americas.

The installation drew many onlookers from the busy street, and the shift in consciousness caused by the event was palpable. People from the barrio, Latinas/os, Chicanas/os, Filipinas/os, and street people cried out chanting "she's right, she's right, she's right." The passing parade merged with the onlookers near the installation. During a momentary reflection of shared historical space, a Lakota warrior, a Chicana feminist, a young Cherokee woman, and a middle-aged Latina with her shopping cart cried and acknowledged our diversity, our overlaps, our affiliations, and our alliances in opposition to the forces of colonialism. We entered a liminal zone: Our borders crossed into each other.

The Resistance 500 events culminated on October 12, 1992, in a march that went from Aquatic Park to Civic Center. This march, with its event-high number of participants (4,800), was comprised of coalitions of Chicanos and tribal peoples from every region of the Americas, including

Bolivians, Filipinos, African Americans, Chicanos, Brazilians, and African Caribbeans, as well as Anglo-based solidarity groups of political persuasions ranging from militant Maoists to nonaffiliated anarchists. This postmodern anticolonial microcosm of the mestizaje of the Americas marched in oppositional alliance.

The rally following the march became a site where the monologues and master-narratives of history were disrupted: No, the Indian wars are not over! No, we Indians, the fierce and noble savages of your colonial imagination, have not succumbed to the inevitable march of civilization! And no, we have not vanished! On the stage, various representatives testified to the struggles of their tribal nations, their political coalitions, their *raza*, and their countries. Dolores Huerta addressed the struggles for worker, human, and health rights for the Mexican campesinos (farm workers), as well as the lack of educational opportunities for migrant children. The stories of the Navajo elders of Big Mountain made the listeners feel the high-intensity intimidation of U.S. army helicopters flying in the late night and early morning—their deafening noises, shredding windstorms, and blinding floodlights—and the slaughter of their sheep. Reports were read aloud about the run to the Valley of Teotihuacan where Inuits from what is now called Alaska met tribal peoples from Peru or Ecuador for the first time. Tribal representatives from Ecuador and Oaxaca, Mexico, testified to their fights against the federal appropriation of their ancestral lands, the auctioning off of timber and mineral interests, and the systematic murders of their tribal leaders and activists. Puerto Rican nationalists condemned the false imprisonment of their leaders, and the litany of testimonies continued. On a macro level, the unifying theme of resistance temporarily disrupted the borders between the diverse peoples of the Americas who share a history of resistance and survival against colonial violence.

These contemporary events highlight how the diverse peoples of the Americas—the descendants of original inhabitants and those transported by force and slavery—have survived and resisted the genocidal onslaught of the colonial invasion of the Americas. They (we/I) have formed alliances across difference. These alliances of difference attest to the vitality of tribalized and detribalized peoples. They affirm and reaffirm *communitas*, a coming together of peoples who as individuals or in their respective families, tribes, and nations are challenging attacks that threaten their material existence. Their very presence and testimonies disrupt the master-narratives that guided the official celebrations of Columbus as the "discoverer" of America and herald of "civilization" and "progress" to the savages, whether fierce or noble.

Interestingly, a parade of Maoists and revolutionary anarchists, dressed in hooded black robes and cassocks with white-painted, expressionless faces, resembling in their austerity the parade of priests that would announce the Inquisition trials of the sixteenth century, broke off at a key intersection and headed toward the North Beach neighborhood. The official parade celebrating the discovery of America by Columbus marched on Broadway Avenue, passing a quixotic combination of Italian pizzerias, Chinese restaurants, blues bars, and pornographic sex palaces. There the participants physically clashed with Italian Americans celebrating their cultural hero, Cristobal Colón. Their banners struck each other: "Columbus: the genocidal rapist of the Americas, imperialist, and herald of capitalism" smashed against "Columbus: the great explorer and herald of civilization, science, and progress." This almost comical semiviolent clash symbolizes the conflict between the master- and discounted minor-narratives of history; it illustrates how historical figures are used for opposing agendas— the hero and the scapegoat. Unfortunately, the brief violence of the clash was the only report of Resistance 500 events presented by the mainstream media—it received a thirty-second sound bite in the evening news.

Peoples "subjectified" by colonialism in all its phases, from contact to the complicated social situation of these new millenia, have resisted the hegemony of imperialism. We have survived colonialism, and, in the instance of Resistance 500, we created unity, learning though our diversity and our commonalties. Through recognition of shared historical roots of struggle, this event became a zone of inclusiveness that challenged the imposed divisions of nation-states and the alienation of capitalism. There was a type of "political spirituality"—a feeling of "how-mi-tak-y-san" (the Lakota concept of "all of my relations")—that reinforced the sense of connectedness and community without homogenizing difference. This palpable feeling of connectedness inspired people to cross the borders of nations, language, and ethnicities to enter a shared historical space of resistance; a space where an Ecuadorian *activista* gives a Chatina activista from Oaxaca, Mexico, a cigarette, an orange, and words of recognition and encouragement to continue the struggle against the dispossession of neocolonialism. *The ancestors were present.*

Transdisciplinary Methodologies: Tracing the Savage in the Colonial Imaginary

Inspired by social events of resistance and public expressions of oppositional alliances, my aim is to analyze the forces that form colonized subjects in general and Chicanas/os and Native Americans in particular, as well as to examine the strategies of resistance to these colonialist forces of subjection. *Siting Translation* (1992) by Tejaswini Niranjana, a critic of colonial discourse, summarizes the need for interdisciplinary approaches to understand and counter the intersection of power and violence in the formation of colonial discourse: "Since the practices of subjection/subjectification implicit in the colonial enterprise operate not merely through the coercive machinery of the imperial state but also through the discourses of philosophy, history, anthropology, philology, linguistics and literary interpretation, the colonial 'subject'—constructed through technologies or practices of power/knowledge—is brought into being within multiple discourses and multiple sites" (1). Instead of working along a predetermined interrogative *telos,* my interdisciplinary and comparative approach culls together a constellation of critical terms and their genealogies that shapes and informs the generative dialectic of this project: How are subjects formed in colonial discourse? How do subaltern subjects resist their subjection to enunciate themselves in textual and social space?

Teaching the Postmodern (1992) by Brenda Marshall offers a creative and generous approach to my critical project. Marshall sprinkles in an uneven pattern on page 1 such key referents to postmodern discourse as historiography, genealogy, context, Althusser, and ideology and argues for a way to write that allows critical interventions into localized power relations of textual and social space. Marshall's description of the "postmodern moment" informs my critical enterprise to cross the borders of disciplines and genres to analyze the lived, the spoken, and the written in their full and unwieldy selves: "The postmodern moment is not something that is to be defined chronologically; rather it is a rupture in our consciousness. Its definition lies in change and chance, but it has everything to do with how we read the present, as well as how we read the past. It is of this world and thus political" (5). Key elements that "shuffle un-comfortably in a shared space" for this particular postmodern intervention into my analysis of colonial subjection and decolonial resistance may be different from Marshall's; other elements are shared with her. The critical terms that I

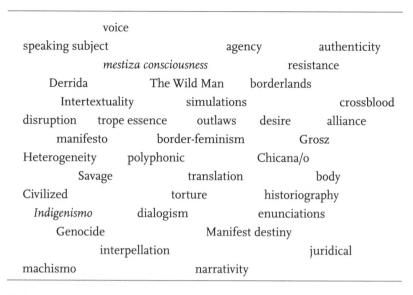

voice

speaking subject   agency   authenticity

mestiza consciousness   resistance

Derrida   The Wild Man   borderlands

Intertextuality   simulations   crossblood

disruption   trope essence   outlaws   desire   alliance

manifesto   border-feminism   Grosz

Heterogeneity   polyphonic   Chicana/o

Savage   translation   body

Civilized   torture   historiography

Indigenismo   dialogism   enunciations

Genocide   Manifest destiny

interpellation   juridical

machismo   narrativity

Fig 1

bring into the zone of the disruptive with a sense of "the limited, local, pro-visional, and always critical. Self Critical" (2) are thrown into the *mezcla*, or mix seen in figure 1.

Following these methodological cues coupled with Foucauldian pre-rogatives (1972) to uncover the intersection of power and knowledge in discourses normalized through colonial dominance, I attempt to trace here how the genealogy of colonialist discourse in the Americas has spoken and speaks and has represented and represents indigenous peoples in terms that inferiorize, infantilize, criminalize, and savagize their diverse subjec-tivities. As "The Other Question" (1994) by Homi Bhabha reminds us, "the objective of colonial discourse is to construe the colonized as a population of degenerate types on the basis of racial origin, in order to justify conquest and to establish systems of administration and instruction" (70).

In the case of the Americas, colonial discourse is dispersed in a way that labels the original inhabitants as "Indians" through geographical error and understands them as *savages*. Robert Berkhofer, in *The White Man's Indian* (1978), argues that the term "Indian" must be a white conception because "it does not square with how those peoples called Indians lived and saw themselves" (1). Berkhofer argues that the term "Indian" was coined and circulated from "erroneous geography" by Columbus, who thought he had discovered the Indies (6). Even though the first colonists realized that they were not in the Indies, the term "Indian" became the predominant way of referring to the inhabitants of the Americas by the colonizing cultures: England, France, Spain, Portugal, and Holland. Berkhofer states: "The first residents of the Americas were by modern estimates divided into at least two thousand cultures and more societies, practiced a multiplicity of customs and lifestyles, held an enormous variety of values and beliefs, spoke numerous languages mutually unintelligible to the many speakers, and did not conceive of themselves as a single people—if they knew about each other at all" (4). Berkhofer argues that Europeans and Euro-Americans classified these people(s) into a single identity, thus simplifying and homogenizing their diversity into an inferior racial type: the *savage*.

In his voluminous work *Dispute in the New World* (1973), Antonello Gerbi argues that the concept of the "savage" was imagined and deployed to all non-European peoples in general and to the peoples of the Americas in particular. Gerbi carefully traces the centrality of the idea of the savage, which was "freely applied to the peoples called the Indians," as the counterpart to the "civilized" in the work of such major European philosophers as Kant, Nietzsche, Hegel, and Locke.

According to *The Myth of the Savage and the Beginnings of French Colonialism in the Americas* (1984) by historian Olive Patricia Dickason, the word *savage* comes from the Latin *sylvaticus,* which means the "woods" or "forest." Interestingly, in Mexican Spanish the adjective *silvestre* is still commonly used to refer to something that exists outside of any human cultivation. Dickason states when the term *savage* is "applied to man, it denotes a person who lives away from society, beyond the pale of its laws, without fixed abode; by analogy one who is rude and fierce" (63). In addition, Dickason argues that Europeans "arrived at the consensus that Amerindians were in a state of pre-civilization," and that they were capable of rising from the lower, more animal rank to become "fully men" (58). Hence, the French used the verb *humaniser* when referring to teaching and evangelizing Amerindians. "There was never any doubt as to the meaning of *humaniser:* it signified the transformation of savages into Europeans" (59). The implications of this idea for contemporary critiques of the humanities and the Western humanist project are immense (an issue that I discuss in detail in chapter 3). In light of the legacy of the savage/civilized discourse, what then is the practice of the humanities? Are humanities a way to civilize the savage? How deep do colonialist tropes lie in the practice of academic discourse?[5]

Likewise, in *Tropics of Discourse* (1978), cultural historian Hayden White convincingly traces the view of the "savage" to the medieval European traditions of the "Wilde Man" and the "Wilde Woman." In his chapter "The Forms of Wildness: Archeology of an Idea" White summarizes the conceptualization of Wild Men and Women: "But to speak of a Wild Man was to speak of a man with the soul of an animal, a man so degraded that he could not be saved even by God's grace itself" (164). In a later chapter, "The Noble Savage Theme as Fetish," White argues that these imaginative creatures served the cultural function of symbolizing all that was "base," "carnal," and "bestial" within the rational, civilizing (imperial) subject.[6]

Wild Men in the Middle Ages (1952) by Richard Bernheimer argues that in medieval philosophy the human being is defined through the hierarchical tension between the divine and the animal; the Wild Man and Wild Woman are at lower stages in the "Greate Chaine of Being."[7] In Christian medieval as well as neoplatonic thought, the great chain of being positions all of "God's Creation" in a hierarchy that proceeds from divine to human to animal to plants, to rocks, and so on. In the same way that the human is dialectically defined in the tensions of divine and animal, the Wild Man exists in a liminal space between animal and human. These imaginative figures (precursors to the gothic aesthetic) are represented as hybrids of bears, goats, and human beings. Based on rationalizations that stem from medieval Christian thought, White argues that "savages were *either* a breed of super animals (similar to dogs, bears, or monkeys), which would account for the violation of human taboos and their presumed physical superiority over men; *or* they were a breed of degenerate men (descendants of the lost tribes of Israel or a race of men rendered destitute of reason and moral sense by the effects of a harsh climate)" (188).

The ideas of the savage and of evolution through the hierarchies of the great chain of being manifest themselves in *Ancient Society* (1877) by Lewis Henry Morgan. This work was made famous by its impact on key social analysts of the nineteenth century such as Frederick Engels and Karl Marx.[8] According to the introduction to the 1982 edition, which was published in India, Morgan bases his theories of social evolution on his observations of the Iroquois peoples that he defended in court for land claims. He locates these "savages" at a state of evolution much lower than the

European and Euro-American—as distant relatives in the "Great Family of Man." For Morgan, native peoples of the Americas represent what European civilization once was: "It follows that the history and experience of the American Indian tribes represent, more or less nearly, the history and experience of our own remote ancestors when in corresponding conditions" (xxvi).

Morgan characterizes the conditions of human society as evolutionary phases of savagery, barbarism, and civilization. He argues that the human family has societies in all phases of the evolution: "As it is undeniable that portions of the human family have existed in a state of savagery, other portions in a state of barbarism, and still other portions in a state of civilization, it seems equally so that these distinct conditions are connected with each other in a natural as well as necessary sequence of progress" (3). In each phase of evolution, which he calls "ethnical periods," Morgan distinguishes between lower, middle, and upper states of savagery, barbarism, and civilization. He creates charts of observable human activity to distinguish the periods; characterizing each by their use of fire, pottery, domestication of animals, and metal smelting (12). For Morgan, the Zunis, Aztecs, and Cholulans are in a "Middle Status of barbarism" because they manufacture "pottery in large quantities" (13). The Iroquois, Choctaws, and Cherokees are in a "Lower Status of barbarism" because they produce less pottery and do so in a "limited number of forms" (13). However, in the lowest state of savagery, the period of infancy of the human race, are the Athapascans and the California Indians, both nonhorticultural producers (14). Conversely, Morgan labels the period from the "Invention of a Phonetic Alphabet, with the use of writing to the present time" (12), as the observable feature of a fully civilized society.[9]

Using notions strikingly similar to the great chain of being, Morgan claims in the final chapter that the savage and barbaric cultural groups will evolve toward civilization by the "good providence of God." Morgan justifies his claims by citing other pioneering classics of anthropology such as the *Researches into the Early History of Mankind and the Development of Civilization* (1865) by Edward Tylor and the 1805 travel narratives of Lewis and Clark. However, how much of his observations on tribes other than the Iroquois are based on any direct contact and discussions with tribal members is not clear, nor is it clear the extent to which such direct interface might have been channeled into prescribed models of racial evolutionism.[10]

The *savage* is the predominant way that native peoples of the Americas were seen by the imperial nations—Spain, Portugal, England, Holland, and France—that invaded that land. However, there is a split between the ways in which the peoples of the Americas were conceptualized in colonialist imaginations: Indians were conceptualized as either "fierce" or "noble" savages. In *Aristotle and the American Indians* (1959), Lewis Hanke argues that the best example of the dichotomy in the discourse of the savage is seen in the 1550–1551 debate at Valladolid, Spain, between Juan Ginés de Sepúlveda and Dominican bishop Bartolomé de Las Casas. For Sepúlveda the "vile and rude" Indians had no souls. They needed to be violently enslaved and then exterminated.

In *The Conquest of America* (1984), Tzvetan Todorov argues that Sepúlveda believed that "hierarchy not equality, is the natural state of human society," a society characterized by the following operations of power: "The domination of perfection over imperfection, of force over weakness, of eminent virtue over vice" (Sepúlveda, qtd. in Todorov: 152). For Sepúlveda, Indians, like women, were living examples of what Aristotle calls the "natural slave." [11] Sepúlveda based his arguments on a simplistic system of binary oppositions to distinguish perfect Spaniards from the imperfect Indians. Todorov summarizes Sepúlveda's distinctions as follows: "The Spaniards are adults, men, and human beings; and the Indians are children, women, and animals (monkeys) without souls" (153).

In demagogic contradiction to the absolute brutality of the Conquest, Sepúlveda saw the Spaniards as distinguished by such attributes as "moderation," "reason," and "moral goodness," in contrast to the baseness, lack of moral control, and propensity for violence attributed to the Indians. In the speech at Valladolid, Sepúlveda, who never even went to the "New World," laid out the four principal arguments to legitimize war against the Mesoamerican peoples. War against these peoples was justifiable if carried out for the following purposes:

1. To subject by force of arms men whose natural condition is such that they should obey others, if they refuse such obedience and no other recourse remains.
2. To banish the portentious crime of eating human flesh, which is a special offense to nature, and to stop the worship of demons instead of God, which above provokes His wrath, together with the monstrous rite of sacrificing men.
3. To save from grave perils the numerous innocent mortals whom

these barbarians immolated every year placating their gods with human hearts.

4. War on the infidels is justified because it opens the way to the propagation of Christian religion and eases the task of the missionaries. (154)

By contrast, the Dominican bishop of Chiapas, Bartolomé de Las Casas, a slaveowner of African peoples, argued in favor of the peaceful colonization of the Indians.[12] Las Casas based his arguments on two related fronts: the universality of the Christian faith, and the "docile," "passive," and "innocent nature" of the Indians. For Las Casas, the Indians were noble savages who were living examples of Christian virtue. As such, they needed the benevolent Christian father to mold them into true Christians who would dutifully serve God, the Church, and the King of Spain (Todorov 1984: 163–67). However, in the concluding chapter to *The Myth of the Savage*, Olive Patricia Dickason aptly summarizes how the savages of the Americas, whether *bons* or *cruels*, were never officially accepted as anything other than inferior and animal-like beings: "Like the Wild Men of the Woods, Amerindians represented anti-structure, man before the acquisition of culture had differentiated him from animals" (273).

Furthermore, Dickason argues that the denizens of the New World "were living metaphors for anti-social forces (273)" that needed to be evangelized and assimilated, or in agreement with Sepúlveda, exterminated. In sum, the savage represented all that was not culture, civilization, and European. The savage was akin to what critic and scholar Julia Kristeva in *The Powers of Horror* (1982) calls the "abject." The savage is the "abject" of the civilizing subject. The abject is the "horror" and the "defilement" of the imperial overculture. The death and mutilation of these symbolic and real "bodies" generate and regenerate the imperial "I's" knowing of itself.

The material effects of Europe's encounter with the Other, the "savage," are devastating. The genocide that occurred is by any standards a violence unmatched by the brutality of all the world wars and civil wars in the history of human societies. However, neither the intensity of colonialism in the Americas nor the intensity of resistance has ever fully been addressed in an official history of a nation-state. In the master-narratives of the United States, Canada, and Mexico, America was discovered by Europe and its inhabitants were either lost to diseases or to manifest destiny, or subsumed into the dominant culture. Todorov summarizes the genocide that occurred in the first hundred years of colonial contact: "Without going into detail, and merely to give a general idea (even if we do not feel entirely justified in rounding off figures when it is a question of human lives), it will be recalled that in 1500 the world population is approximately 400 million of whom 80 million inhabit the Americas. By the middle of the sixteenth century, out of these 80 million, there remains ten. Or limiting ourselves to Mexico: on the eve of the conquest, its population is about 25 million; in 1600, it is one million" (135).

Todorov argues that the Spanish are no more cruel and effective than the English and French colonists farther north; rather their expansion was "not on the same scale" as the French and English, "hence the damages they can cause are not on such a scale either" (133).[13] Furthermore, Todorov summarizes the factors that determined this horrific genocide, still unprecedented in the violent history of human societies, as follows:

1. By direct murder, during the wars or outside them: a high number, nonetheless relatively small; direct responsibility.
2. By consequence of bad treatment: a higher number; a (barely) less direct responsibility.
3. By diseases, by "microbe shock": the majority of the population; an indirect and diffused responsibility. (133)

In terms that illustrate the practices of colonial male violence on indigenous subjects in Mexico, Todorov recalls Vasco de Quiroga's description of the slave traffic during the first years after the 1521 Conquest and the practice of branding indigenous peoples first by the royal seal of Spain, and then by the individual brands of the Spanish *encomendados:* "They are marked with brands on the face and in their flesh are imprinted the initials of the names of those who are successfully their owners; they pass from hand to hand, and some have three or four names, so that the faces of these men who were created in God's image have been, by our sins, transformed into paper" (137).

The ideology of the fierce savage promoted by Sepúlveda and put into practice by the Spaniards and Anglos during the conquest causes subjects to turn others into objects. Indians, then, become literal "hunks of flesh" whose "blood" should be "used to irrigate the fields. . . . Enslavement, in this sense of the word, reduces the other to the status of an object, which is especially manifested in conduct that treats the Indians as less than men; they are killed in order to be boiled down for grease, supposed to

cure the wounds of the Spaniards: thereby they are identified with animals for the slaughterhouse; all their extremities are cut off, nose, hands,
breasts, tongue, sexual organs, thereby transforming them into shapeless
trunks" (175).

Colonialist discourses of inferiority are oppressive violent forces that
engrave subjects. This discourse bases itself on a closed system of significations, meaning that these significations were defined by and within the
imperial civilizing subject, without input from, or room for contradiction
by, the tribal peoples themselves. The epistemic violence that determines
subjects in absolutist and inferior terms mirrors and works to rationalize
the material violence committed on the bodies of these colonial subjects.
Bodies, as much as territories and resources, became the site of colonial
dominance where the scripts of logocentrism allowed the conquistadors
the ability to transcend the brutality of their slaughterhouse violence, setting patterns of denial and amnesia that continue to resonate in the militarized U.S./Mexico borderlands of the early twenty-first century (an issue
I discuss in greater detail in chapter 4).

Postcolonialism and De/colonization: Recentering America as Empire

Having briefly traced the "genealogy" of how indigenous peoples (as all
non-Western peoples) are represented in colonialist imaginaries as either
fierce or noble savages, in the following section I will try to clarify further
the psychic and material effects of colonialism in the global borderlands
between the imperial centers and the wealth-producing peripheries. *Siting
Translation* (1992) by Tejaswini Niranjana helps us to understand how colonialism, postcolonialism, and decolonization overlap in the postmodern
realm of global power relations, and how this overlap provides an important analytical framework. Niranjana acknowledges the "dispersed nature"
of the "post-colonial," arguing that we must understand this state of social truth as "nodes of intersection" between the "history of domination"
and the "formation of colonial subjects": "In beginning to understand the
post-colonial, we might reiterate some of the brute facts of colonialism.
Starting with the period around the end of the seventeenth century and
continuing beyond World War II, Britain and France, and to a lesser extent Spain, Portugal, Germany, Russia, Italy, and Holland, dominated—
ruled, occupied, exploited—nearly the entire world" (6–7). Niranjana clarifies that the initial process of decolonization began around World War I

by arguing that "national liberation struggles" were a "transfer of power" from the "reigning colonial power to an indigenous elite" (7).

For Niranjana, nationalist struggles do not mark the end of colonial discourse: "By colonial discourse I mean the body of knowledge, modes of representation, strategies of power, law, discipline, and so on, that are employed in the construction and domination of 'colonial subjects'" (7). In considering the term "neocolonial," Niranjana argues that the term "postcolonial" is more appropriate, because she does "not want to minimize the forces against colonial and neocolonial domination in these societies" (8). In the postcolonial phase of supposed liberated nations, the condition of "absentee colonialism" reproduces "colonial relations of power." Countries (excolonies) are still economically and politically dependent on the "ex-rulers of the West" (8). Niranjana argues that the struggle in contemporary postcolonial societies is between "absentee colonialism" and "decolonization" on material and cultural levels.

I argue further that these struggles are made more complex by the proliferation of transnational global capitalism dependent on super-cheap labor and natural resources. To apply this analysis to Mexico and other Latin American countries, how do we understand this tension of absentee colonialism and decolonization to countries whose empire center, Spain, is no longer a major player in the control of global economies? [14]

In terms of cultural and aesthetic production, Niranjana argues that decolonization is the slowest in "making an impact," and she points out how excolonials "hunger for the English book" as avidly as their ancestors did (7). In this sense, Niranjana's work on the complex issues of postcolonialism is key to understanding the politics of identity. She drives a simple but crucial point as it relates to issues of identity: the colonialist needs not to be present to execute colonialisms! [15] However, Niranjana, in an otherwise brilliant study, fails to take into consideration the case of the United States: a colony in the process of turning imperial nation-state. In the field of literary study, issues of colonialism, neocolonialism, and postcolonialism are limited mainly to English, and to a lesser degree French, excolonies, revealing an overriding Anglophone centrism. [16]

The tendency in postcolonial studies to relegate the struggles against neocolonialism to a place "over there somewhere" denies the complex power relations of internal colonies and the complexities of racial, class, and gender oppression in the United States, along with the devastating neocolonial effects of U.S. imperialism in Latin America, the Philippines, and Guam.[17] For example, the *Post-Colonial Studies Reader* (Ashcroft et al. 1995), a voluminous collection of mainly essay reprints on decolonization in India and Africa (Fanon, Memi, Bhabha, and Spivak, to name a few) contains only two essays that deal with postcoloniality in the United States and the Americas. The first is the now-famous "Race for Theory" by African American Barbara Christian, which eloquently argues against the theoretical commodification of multiethnic, especially African American, cultural, artistic, and literary practices. The second, "Columbus and the Cannibals" by Peter Hulme, is a five-page essay on how the word "cannibal" was defined in sixteenth-century Europe "as an original inhabitant of the Caribs," now called the Caribbean. Surely, the Americas, I hope, deserve more than five pages.

Mixblood Messages (1998) by critic and novelist Louis Owens responds to the refusal by major postcolonial critics and studies to consider the anticolonial vitality of Native American literary voices by asking: "Is writing by an American Indian less post- or neocolonial than that by a native Nigerian or by those Indians from India? . . . The authors might have made the very interesting point that in fact Native American writing is not postcolonial but rather colonial, that the colonizers never left but simply changed their names to Americans?" (51). In similar terms, the first of the two introductory essays to *Cultures of United States Imperialism* (Kaplan and Pease, eds., 1993), "'Left Alone with America': The Absence of Empire in the Study of American Culture" by Amy Kaplan, argues that there are "three salient absences which contribute to the ongoing pattern of denial across several disciplines" (11). These are: "Absence of culture from the history of U.S. imperialism; the absence of empire from the study of American culture; and the absence of the United States from the postcolonial study of imperialism" (11). Likewise, in the second introductory essay, "New Perspectives on U.S. Culture and Imperialism," Donald Pease argues: "Although the United States' imperial nationalism was predicated on the superiority of military and political organization as well as economic wealth, it depended for its efficacy on a range of cultural technologies, among which colonialist policies (exercised both internally and abroad) of conquest and dominion figured prominently" (22).

So, by recentering America as empire, I ask: What are the Native American, Chicana/o and Latina/o, and African American communities, tribes, and nations' struggles against U.S. imperialism and Anglo-American hegemonic culture? Are Native American peoples in the United States and Canada not survivors of Spanish, English, French, and, later, U.S. and Canadian colonialism/neocolonialism? In the case of Chicanas/os, are not the territories we live in as marginals originally Mexican and Native Mexican annexed as a result of a war driven by U.S. manifest destiny? Also, what are the Asian American communities, especially those Asian peoples exiled by wars (Vietnamese) with the U.S., the internment of Japanese Americans, or whose countries are in a "protectorate" or statehood status with the United States as seen with Hawaii and Guam? Are they not colonies and "excolonies" of the United States? Are Native American peoples not struggling for what was stolen or swindled from them by the U.S.-colonizing culture? Are Chicana/o and Mexicana/o peoples not struggling for their human rights as protected by the Treaty of Guadalupe Hidalgo (1848), as well as other Latina/o peoples who have fled U.S.-backed wars and dictatorships such as those in El Salvador, Chile, Guatemala, or Nicaragua, to name a few? In regard to the specific indigenous territories that are now called the United States, *Inventing the Savage* (1998) by Luana Ross argues that in Euro-American legal practices "genocide against Native people was never seen as murder. Indeed, in the Old West the murder of Natives was not seen even a crime. . . . Those not exterminated faced dire consequences . . . it allowed white people to simply take Native children, those orphaned or supposedly with parental consent, as indentured slaves" (Hurtado qtd. in Ross 1988: 15).

Speaking Subjects and the Negotiation of Decolonial Space

This book speaks directly to the politics of identity and difference among some liminal occupants of the *transfrontera*/transfrontier border space, specifically a politics of subject-formation for Mexican immigrants, Chicanas/os, and Native American crossbloods of what is or was northern Mexico and what is now the southwestern area of the United States. How are these subjects marginalized and otherized along axes of race, class, gender, and sexuality in the social and political economy? And how do these subjects seize, reappropriate, subvert, and (re)invent the means of representation to inscribe themselves in their own terms? To answer some of these questions I consider various models of the speaking subject. I argue that the nexus for the speaking subject is the drive toward self-consciousness on the edge of being sentient of the historical ideologies that form one's identity, and then the drive toward self-liberation by activating this awareness. The continual interplay of how we are invented, demonized, and vanished by the colonizing culture, and how we form ourselves as a result, is an effective way to understand the struggle for identity for peoples caught in historical and contemporary displacements of colonial and neocolonial violence. In the case of Native Americans and Chicanas/os, peoples are being written or spoken about in terms of repression and containment, and they are writing/speaking/acting themselves into a particular narrative and political terrain with a history of over five hundred years of colonially embedded racial and sexual violence with what Louis Owens (1998) states is an insistance "upon the freedom to reimagine themselves within a fluid, always shifting frontier space" (27).

The Subject of Semiotics (1983) by Kaja Silverman summarizes aspects of the genealogy of the speaking subject (43–54). Her reading traces conceptions of subjectivity in the famous *Problems in General Linguistics* (1971) by Emile Benveniste. Silverman argues that subjectivity is formed through the discontinuities between the pronouns "I" and "you" in acts of speaking: "In the space between two discursive events, subjectivity, like the pronouns which sustain it [I and You], falls into abeyance. Benveniste emphasizes the radical discontinuity which characterizes the condition of subjectivity, its constant stops and starts" (45). Silverman argues that the formation of the subject occurs in acts of "discourse as a signifying transaction between two persons, one of whom addresses the other, and through the process defines him or herself" (48).

Silverman links this concept of address to the way that philosopher and theorist Louis Althusser discusses subjectivity and the transfer of ideology in his now famous essay, "Ideology and the State" (1971). She summarizes Althusser's discussion of this exchange as a transfer of ideology, "a person and a cultural agent, i.e., a person or a textual construct which relays ideological information" (48). Furthermore, Silverman distinguishes the act of exchange or relay and considers the act of interpellation to be a determining force in the formation of the subject: "The agent addresses the person, and in the process defines not so much its own as the other's identity. In 'Ideology and Ideological State Apparatuses,' Althusser refers to the address as 'hailing' and its successful outcome as 'interpellation.' Interpellation occurs when that person to whom the agent speaks recognizes him or herself in that speech, and takes up subjective residence there" (48–49). To clarify further the specifics of this interpellative exchange, one needs to go back into Althusser's original essay. There he argues that this ideological exchange is unidirectional in the sense that it derives from a given source. The exchange not only affects a subject or citizen of a particular nation, says Althusser, but also determines or forms that subject: "Assuming that the theoretical scene I have imagined takes place in the street, the hailed individual turns around. By this mere one-hundred-and-eighty-degree physical conversion, he becomes a subject. Why? Because he has recognized that the hail was "really" addressed to him, and that "it was really him who was hailed" (and not someone else)" (174).

But how can we reframe our analysis of the hailing process in the increasingly diverse and ethnically conflicted metropoles of the twenty-first century, where subaltern subjects may not have a command of the dominant language of the state and a shared semiotics of cultural meaning between the dominant culture and their own? For example, how does hailing function with Turkish workers or Congolese, Algerian, and Vietnamese peoples emigrating from their excolonies to the French-only, English-only, German-only, and Spanish-only metropolitan centers to negotiate their survival and identity as second-class citizens, scapegoated for all economic woes in ways similar to Mexican and Latin American peoples in the United States? What happens when someone from a diasporic community does not understand that they are being hailed by the state or do not recognize the contents of the interpellative exchange because of linguistic and epistemic differences? One only need to think of the consequences for not participating in the hailing processes as seen in the recent New York police assassination of the West African émigré Amadou Diallo for not understanding the officers' English commands. I also think of the countless Spanish-speaking peoples in the United States who are beaten, arrested, deported, killed, and falsely imprisoned because they did not understand the hailing processes of the border patrol and police agents.

Althusser's idea may work well within a continuous language group whose members share similar linguistic and cultural formations; that is, people who share a language and recognize codes in a similar way. However, the processes of European colonialism and Euro-American manifest destiny are marked by the collision and clash of culturally relative generative languages, hermeneutics, ideologies, and epistemologies and a "naturalized" imposition of Western symbols and codes that are constructed as "transcendental" markers of "civilization." In *The Darker Side of the Renaissance* (1995), a compelling and broad-ranging study of the colonial imposition of Spanish literacy in the Americas, Walter Mignolo argues that "one can accept, then, that in the Americas, during the sixteenth and seventeenth centuries, the problem of cultural relativism as confrontations of *incommensurable* conceptual frameworks was indeed the case. It is in such a context that the denial of coevalness is justified" (327).

The way these symbols are processed and understood by indigenous peoples—albeit through violence—speaks to a complicated politics of translation, and ultimately a subversion and reclamation from one epistemological world to another. To illustrate this point, during the conquest of the Indies the Christian cross was violently deployed by Spaniards as the symbol of Christian faith. However, the original meaning of the cross was subverted by the Nahuas and Mayas who understood and reclaimed it as a literal symbol of the four directions that reflect and generate the cosmological patterning of the universe.[18]

The price that tribal peoples paid for trying to negotiate the confrontation between "incommensurable frameworks" is poetically illustrated in Eduardo Galeano's chronicles of the conquest of the Americas, *Memory of Fire: Genesis* (1985). One story that illustrates this process well is "Sacrilege," set in La Concépion, Haiti, in 1496. The story opens with Christopher Columbus's brother, Bartholomew, attending "an incineration of human flesh," which Galeano ironically refers to as the "grand opening of Haiti's incinerator" (51). The six men who are "playing lead" in this theater of terror are being punished for burying the images of the Christ and the Virgin in the soil. Galeano poignantly comments: "No one has asked them why they buried the images. They were hoping that the new gods would fertilize their fields of corn, cassava, boniato, and beans" (51). The question remains: How is ideology translated across linguistic and cultural borders? Perhaps this need to find a way to translate preempted the acts of extreme violence inflicted by the conquistadores on tribal peoples, which, in the case of the Conquest is couched in the mission of religious conversion, civilizing the "natives" by the sword and the cross. In the initial violence of the Conquest, was hailing enacted through branding, dismembering, burning, and disembowling Mexican, Maya, Yaqui, and other tribal peoples of the Americas? I argue that their bodies became the site and text of interpellation.[19] Pain, fear, torture, rape, and mutilation are the language of interpellation.

With this in mind, the inspiring narratives of resistance transcribed in *Memory of Fire: Genesis* needs to be celebrated further. I refer to another well-known story that dramatically reflects the crisis of subjection and resistance at the early stages of the Conquest. Hatuey, a chief of what is now called Haiti, is asked if he wants to convert to Christianity before he is to be executed. Ironically, Hatuey responds, "If there are any Christians in Heaven then I definitely prefer to go to hell" (57). I argue that his response is the final act of resistance to the violence of colonial subjection.

Put simply, in order for the addressee to turn around at the time of hailing, there must be an interpretive signal of significant clarity for the addressee to understand that he or she is being hailed. In the case of torture, it is through the literal branding of symbols on the body that hailing, however brutal, occurs.

Given the implied social conditions of industrial and postindustrial countries, Althusser presumed that there must be a certain degree of mobility allowed to be able to even turn around in the hailing process. How does hailing function in cases of subjects constrained by shackles, as was the case of Ibo peoples in U.S. cotton plantations? Is hailing more direct on those whose bodies are forcibly constrained by colonialist modes of operation or on those manipulated by bodily torture by the colonialist apparatus? These questions are illuminated by examples such as the Chichimecas in the death camps at the mines in Mexico in the sixteenth and seventeenth centuries, the FMLN guerrillas tortured in Salvadoran death-squad camps, and the undocumented Mexican immigrants hog-tied and beaten because they do not understand the English commands of a police officer.

In the case of African slaves in the British and U.S. plantation context, *Scenes of Subjection* (1997) by Saidiya Hartman discusses how the transfer of a regulatory ideology operated through corporeal violence. Hartman convincingly argues that the systemic use of brutal violence on the bodies of African slaves was justified and mediated by discourses that pathologize the black bodies of African peoples as less sensitive to bodily pain: "The black is both insensate and content, indifferent to pain and induced to work by threats of corporeal punishment. These contradictions are partly explained by the ambiguous and precarious status of the black in the "great chain of being"—in short, by the pathologizing of the black body—this abhorrence serves to justify acts of violence that exceed normative standards of the humanely tolerable, though within the limits of the socially tolerable as concerned the black slave" (51).

Kaja Silverman ends her summary of Althusser in *The Subject of Semiotics* by stating that "a speaking subject would always be sharply differentiated from the spoken subject" (49). Her distinction is crucial to understanding the politics of representation in colonial, neocolonial, and postcolonial discourse, and it highlights questions on the location and direction of agency. Now that an unprecedented number of narrative works have been published by people forcibly "otherized" by colonial discourse, the questions remain: first, how does one disrupt how one is spoken of by a dominant or hegemonic discourse? and, second, how does one translate one's subjectivity into narrative terrain guided by rules of language-play that emerge from culturally different epistemologies?

Silverman ends her discussion of Benveniste by pointing out how subjectivity is constructed as a set of relationships in a signifying system, which can open ways to understanding the interplay of the spoken and the speaking: "In other words, subjectivity is not an essence but a set of relationships. Moreover, it can only be induced by discourse, by the activation of a signifying structuralist system which pre-exists the individual, and which determines his or her cultural identity" (52). Although the structuralist notion of a preexisting system that drives many theories of knowledge and representation, anthropology especially may be problematic, the understanding of the relationality of the subject is central to this discussion. Obviously, the notion of the relational disrupts notions of the autonomous, masculinist, rational self as idealized by the French Enlightenment, Immanuel Kant, René Descartes, and as wedded to the "civilizing" imperial project.[20] In "Myth, History, and Identity in Silko and Young Bear" (1993), literary critic David Moore sets out the relationship between the autonomous subject and the imperial project: "When autonomous agency is added to Western individualistic concepts of subjectivity, the imperial self is born, with drastic consequences for native cultures" (372).

The model of relational subjectivity allows understanding of subjectivity in nonessentialist terms, what many poststructural and psychoanalytic theorists have called the "decentered subject." In "Cultural Feminism versus Poststructuralism" (1988), Linda Alcoff summarizes how different methods of understanding the subject deconstruct essentialist notions of the subject: "Lacan uses psychoanalysis, Derrida uses grammar, and Foucault uses the history of discourses all to attack and 'deconstruct' our concept of the subject as having an essential identity and an authentic core that has been repressed by society" (163).

In her famous essay "The System and the Speaking Subject," linguist and philosopher Julia Kristeva intervenes into the discourse of the speaking subject (1986). Kristeva points out that much of linguistics relies on the philosophically grounded assumption that the transmitter of speech is the *transcendental ego*. On close inspection, as certain linguists (from Jakobson to Kuroda) have shown in recent years, this speaking subject turns out in fact to be that transcendental ego which, in Husserl's view, "underlies any and every predicative synthesis" (27). In considering the relationship among the subject, language, and power Kristeva argues that the notion of "Generative Grammar" is based firmly on the masculinist, transcendental subject central to a Western system of knowledge and its authority. This argument contradicts the conceptions of the speech act as a "thetic" or teleologic and determinative function of this grammar, and challenges the field of semiotics to look at its own presuppositions, analytic rigidity, and the collusion with regulatory state apparatuses; that is, to look at the need to systematize, homogenize, and contain social heterogeneity: "And yet semiotics, by its attempts to set itself up as a theory of social practices using language as its model, restricts the value of its discovery to the field of its practices which do no more than subserve the principle of social cohesions, and of the social contract" (26).

Kristeva proclaims that the "theory of meaning now stands at a crossroads" (27). The theory of meaning must either continue "as the act of transcendental ego, cut off from its body, its unconscious, and also its history," or "attune itself to the theory of the speaking subject as a divided subject" (28). For Kristeva the heterogeneity of the *langue poetique* will "fracture the symbolic code" and reorder "the psychic drives" of the transcendental speaking subject and its complicity in patriarchal enunciative dominance, "thus poetic language making free with the language code; music, dancing, painting, reordering the psychic drives and thus renewing their own tradition; and in a different mode experiences with drugs—all seek out and make use of this heterogeneity and the ensuing fracture of a symbolic code which can no longer 'hold' its speaking subjects" (32).

The hinge of Kristeva's argument is that because the subject renews herself or himself by entering into the process of heterogeneous signifying practices, the subject should thus be understood as a "subject-in-process." Kristeva challenges the barrier of objectivity that the trope "pure science" ensures the semiotic critic, which in Kristeva's case was the literati of the Tel Quel Group of Roland Barthes, Michel Foucault, and Gerard Gennette, from which she was expelled: "The subject of the semiotic metalanguage must, however briefly, call himself in question, must emerge from the protective shell of a transcendental ego within a logical system, and so restore his connection with that negativity—drive governed, but also so-cial, political, and historical—which rends and renews the social code" (33). Kristeva calls for a reevaluation of epistemological foundations in tradi-tional system-driven semiotics, proclaiming the death of the transcenden-tal subject and predicting the rise of postmodern and postcolonial theories of subjectivity: "The present mutations of capitalism, the political and eco-nomic reawakening of ancient civilizations (India, China) have thrown into crisis the symbolic systems enclosed in which the Western subject, offi-cially defined as a transcendental subject, has for two thousand years lived out its life span" (31).

In sum, Kristeva's formulation of the subject-in-process, along with Silverman's assessment of subjects formed through relationality in dis-course, combine as useful preconditions to understanding subjectivity as mapped out in the political economy of neocolonial power relations. How-ever, Kristeva's revolutionary critique of recurrent transcendentality in the thought and systems of social analysis must be recognized as such, and at the same time critiqued for its limitations. Kristeva's notion of the subject-in-process was intended to provide an understanding of subjects strug-gling in culturally and racially homogeneous settings, against patriarchy, the state, and postindustrial capitalism. Her circle of reference, like those of other vanguard French theorists (feminist, structuralist, and poststruc-turalist), limited her understanding of social relations to those in indus-trialized and postindustrialized countries as mediated by power relations of capitalist economies and statist governments. Without denying issues of patriarchy and the violent power relations of gender among the privi-leged of industrialized nations, Kristeva's theory of the subject-in-process does not take into account the struggle for identity as mediated by the con-texts of colonialism and neocolonialism, which include such elements as cultural and material imperialism, racism, sexism, and sexual exoticism.[21]

In fact, Kristeva's theorizing on the speaking subject stops at the di-rect consideration of peoples whose subject positions have been created by colonial invasions, displacements, and appropriations on material levels (land, resources, indigenous technologies) and on discursive levels (educa-tion, history, and modes of perception). Hence, we lack a consideration of the questions of agency and voice of subjects who resist the way they have been spoken for in totalizing and inferiorizing terms that justify their ma-terial, corporal, and cultural appropriation by the dominant, imperializing culture. How does the notion of the subject-in-process apply to subjects struggling in the borderlands of colonial subjectification and resistance in sites of social relations both in first world and third world countries — for example, ethnic "minorities" in the United States or African postcolonials working underclass jobs in France? Likewise, how does this notion apply to peoples struggling against neocolonialism and absentee colonialism in third world countries stratified, segmented, and marginalized by the globalizing system of power relations?

Relational Subjects: Postcolonial Feminist Epistemologies

The essay "Cartographies of Struggle" (1991) by Chandra Mohanty directly addresses questions of power relations by providing a way to link the struggles of women of color in the United States with women in third world countries. Mohanty questions the way Western scholars replicate power relations by identifying "third world women" in terms of "what they do not have." Victimization by global relations of power denies agency and resistance to these women, who are dominated by practices of racism, sexism, classicism, and first world ethnocentrism. Mohanty points out that "scholars often locate 'third world women' in terms of underdevelopment, oppressive traditions, high illiteracy, rural and urban poverty, religious fanaticism, and the 'overpopulation' of particular Asian, African, Middle Eastern, and Latin American countries" (6).

Mohanty argues that the "representations of third world women in social scientific knowledge production" freezes these women in "time and space" in the "form of a spectacle," and disavows the "everyday, fluid, fundamentally historical and fundamental nature of the lives of third world women" (6). Moreover, Mohanty critiques the universalizing ethnocentrism involved in Western scholarly practices that are supposedly progressive, liberal, and feminist: "Finally, defining third world women in terms of their 'problems' or their 'achievements' in relation to an imagined free white liberal democracy, effectively removes them (and the 'liberal democracy') from history, freezing them in time and space" (7). Clearly Mohanty's response to ethnocentric and homogenizing tendencies in Western scholarly practice signals how these scholarly practices replicate the larger axioms of power relations that force third world women to struggle against "sexist, racist, and imperialist structures" (7).

Unlike Niranjana's exclusive focus on colonial power relations in India, Mohanty illustrates the links between the struggles of third world women and those of women of color in the United States. Mohanty argues against defining women of color and third world women in biological and sociological terms, and she considers their affiliations as political constituencies. Using Chela Sandoval's notion of oppositional consciousness, Mohanty describes these alliances as follows: "What seems to constitute 'women of color' or 'third world women' as a viable oppositional alliance is a *common context of struggle* rather than color or racial identifications. Similarly, it is third world women's oppositional political relation to sexist, racist, and imperialist structures that constitutes our common potentiality" (7).

Mohanty's work understands the subject as relational — *the subject in process* that responds to specific junctures of power in the political economy. Mohanty breaks the homogenizing tendencies of the Western gaze in even feminist discourse, understanding third world women as relational, resistant, and in process. Fully aware that "the notion of an interdependent relationship between theory, history, and struggle is not new," Mohanty suggests the following mode of analysis that drives the site-specific readings of subjectivities in the subsequent chapters: "I want to suggest that it is possible to retain the idea of multiple, fluid structures of domination which intersect to locate women differently at particular historical conjunctures, while at the same time insisting on the dynamic oppositional of individuals and collectives and their engagement in 'daily life'" (13). What makes Mohanty's work so important to issues of subjectification and resistance as they apply to third world women is the way she discusses the inherent tensions in colonial discourse and the fluidity and multiplicity of resistance in macro and micro sites. In her essay, in the section "Colonialism, Class, and Gender," Mohanty considers how colonial rule needed concrete divisions in ascending hierarchies of privilege according to race and sex, as well as a moral system that "naturalizes" the violence of domination: "The physical and symbolic separation of the races was deemed necessary to maintain social distance and authority over subject peoples. In effect, the physical details (e.g., racial and sexual separation) of colonial settings were transmuted to a moral plane" (17).

Mohanty discusses the tropes that drive the embodiment of the "ideal imperial agent." The white man is "naturally" born to rule, demonstrating the following characteristics: "authority, discipline, fidelity, devotion, fortitude, and self-sacrifice" (13). At the same time, savages, whether the noble children of nature or the fierce cannibals of Satan, were "incapable

of self-government" (13). What is ignored is the complex political organization of social life among the so-called "primitives." In fact, to understand
the extreme hypocrisy that underpinned the colonial enterprise one needs
only to consider how the frame of the Constitution of the United States
is based in large part on ideas of democratic and representational voting
adapted from the Iroquois League of Seven Nations.[22]

Mohanty continues her analysis of colonial discourse by examining the
maintenance of strong "sexual and racial boundaries" between the "legiti-
mate rulers" and the "childlike subjects." These boundaries precluded, for
example, violent sexual unions of white men and native women, which in
the case of plantation slavery was a way of increasing slave stock (Takaki,
1990), at the same time that they enforced social barriers by punishing the
unions of "native" men with "civilized" women.[23] Mohanty argues the importance of understanding that this "racialized, violent masculinity was in
fact the underside of the sanctioned mode of colonial rule" (17). Colonialism operated on principles of rigidity controlled by the naturalized power
of the "rulers"; however, colonial discourse always enforces its contradictions with violence. With regard to the relationship of domination and
resistance, Mohanty states "resistance clearly accompanies all forms of
domination" (38). She considers resistance in ways that are equal to or
more fluid than the deployment of power, whether actual colonial rule
or the rulings of capital by multinationals in third world countries. However, Mohanty intervenes into these spaces, articulating the micropolitics
of power, offering a framework for building oppositional alliances across
differences, and questioning the sociality of political groupings. She considers the fluidity and vitality of resistances as follows: "However, it is not
always identifiable through organized movements; resistance inheres in
the very gaps, fissures, and silences of hegemonic narratives. Resistance is
encoded in the practices of remembering, and of writing. Agency is thus
figured in the minute, day-to-day practices and struggles of third world
women. Coherence of politics and of action comes from a sociality which
itself perhaps needs to be rethought" (38).

The essay "The Theoretical Subject(s) of *This Bridge Called My Back* and
Anglo-American Feminism" (1991) by Chicana theorist Norma Alarcón
analyzes the micropolitics of power, agency, and subjectivity—the plurality
of the self—especially relating to Chicanas. Alarcón compares the Anglo-
American feminist project with radical women of color in the groundbreaking anthology *This Bridge Called My Back* (Anzaldúa and Moraga

1983). Alarcón argues that Anglo-feminism replicates notions of the subject that are similar to Eurocentric and patriarchal notions of the subject, questioning the ethnocentrism that drives their desire for unified subjects: "The subject (and object) of knowledge is now a woman, but the inherited view of consciousness has not been questioned at all. As a result some Anglo-American feminist subjects of consciousness have tended to become a parody of the masculine subject of consciousness, thus revealing their ethnocentric underpinnings" (30).

Regarding the speaking and writing subjects of the *Bridge* anthology, Alarcón distinguishes fundamental differences of position, location, and goals of Anglo-American feminism: "As a speaking subject of an emergent discursive formation, the writer in *Bridge* was aware of the displacement of her subjectivity across a multiplicity of discourses: feminist/lesbian, nationalist, racial, and socioeconomic" (28). Alarcón argues that these speaking/writing subjects enunciate themselves in response to a displacement across a multiplicity of discourses operating in the political economy: "The peculiarity of her [women of color] displacement implied a multiplicity of positions from which she was driven to grasp or understand herself and her relations with the real, in the Althusserian sense of the word" (28). Alarcón also discusses the issue of multiple voices and women of color. Similar to Mohanty, Alarcón comments on the notion of multiple voices, problematizing the desire for a unified subject that occludes and homogenizes difference. For Alarcón, the theoretical subjects of the *Bridge* are also political, presenting models of subjectivity that emerge across many junctures of discourse and power. Even though these radical women of color ally themselves in shared and different subject positions to offer an epistemology of oppositional consciousness that challenges the intersections of racial, gender, class, and sexual hegemonies, Alarcón critiques how the academy fetishizes women of color through widespread consumption of literary, historical, and theoretical texts by women of color in the academy without offering any sustained political commitment to provide placement or support for such women in and outside the academic community, particularly for lesbians who also struggle against even the heterosexism of other women of color.

The essay "Chicana Feminism: In the Tracks of 'the' Native Woman" (1990), by Alarcón considers the tensions of subjectification and resistance, specifically for Chicanas. She charts the Chicana struggle for identity in the flux of postmodernist capitalist relations, the cult of the ideal family, recalcitrant cultural nationalism, and neocolonial social relations in the United States and Mexico. Further, Alarcón surveys the male-dominated "Chicano political class," which in the 1960s and 1970s was eager "to redefine the economic, racial, cultural, and political position of the people" (248). She argues that the crucial involvement of Chicanas in the movement has been historically unrecognized as a result of exclusionary practices of "a patriarchal cultural and political economy" that are congruent with gender practices in Mexico (249). Regarding the 1980s, however, she observes "a re-emergence of Chicana writers and scholars who have not only repositioned the Chicano political class through a feminist register but who have joined forces with an emergent woman-of-color political class that has national and international implications" (249). Alarcón maps the complex issues of Chicana identity across "the multiple migrations and dislocations of women of 'Mexican' descent" (250). The name Chicana is "consciously and critically assumed" to dismantle "historical conjunctions of crisis, confusion, political and ideological conflict" (250). When Alarcón considers the Chicanas' relationship to a precolonial past, she is arguing that the quest for identity embodies the selves multiplied and dislocated by conquest and colonizations.

Decolonization is not a recovery of "a lost 'utopia' nor the true essence of our being" (251). Instead, identity is an interplay of "plural historicized bodies with respect to the multiple racialized constructions of the body since 'the discovery'" (251). Alarcón lists these constructions as "criolla, morisca, loba, . . . china . . . and mulatta" depending on types of mestizaje that occurred (African, Basque, and Tarascan, Filipino, Spanish, Nahua and so on). Mestizaje, however, did not occur only in the context of colonialism. Intermarriage among different tribes was and is common practice. Alarcón confronts the issue of internalized colonialism in Chicanas (and I would add all peoples of Mexican, and Latin American, descent) by considering the politics of subjectivity involved in the act of remembering or invoking indigenous women. She argues that "invoking the 'dark Beast' within and without, which many of us have forced to deny, the cultural and psychic dismemberment that is linked to imperialist racist and sexist practices are brought into focus" (251). Further, Alarcón points out that these practices are still occurring with the same brutal urgency of the initial phases of the conquests, and she mentions the massacres of the Mayas in Guatemala as well as the death squad repression of Central and South America as examples.

Alarcón has intervened in the discourses of the speaking subject and the subject-in-process, and she has questioned the desire or *telos* for unified subjectivity as practiced in Eurocentric exchanges. Using an epistemology of the borderlands—contestatory discursive practices emerging in different historical and cultural signifying practices, such as Hegelian dialectics and mestiza poetics—she negotiates an understanding of the alliance of identity that disrupts Eurocentric notions of the autonomous subject. Skillfully, Alarcón considers the culturally *different/différant* notions of unity and unification for Chicanas, and argues that "the complex effort to unify, however tenuously, Chicanas' consciousness which is too readily viewed as representing 'postmodern' fragmented identities' entails not only Hegel's *Aufhebung* with respect to Chicanas' immediate personal subjectivity as raced and sexed bodies, but also an understanding of all past negations as communitarian subjects in a doubled relation to cultural recollection, and re-memberance, and to our contemporary presence and non/presence in the sociopolitical and cultural milieu" (251).

Alarcón summarizes the complicated processes for decolonization and rememberance in the construction of indigenous mestiza subjectivities across the violent, genocidal, and patriarchal histories of colonial and neocolonial fracturing of women's bodies and subjects framed against the contemporary struggles for survival along multiple practices of racism, sexism, invisibilization, and poverty.

In alliance with Alarcón and Mohanty, Chela Sandoval's book, *Methodology of the Oppressed,* on differential and oppositional consciousness by "U.S. third world feminists of color" bridges the limits of mainstream feminist theory and the limits of ethnic and critical theory. Sandoval resituates analysis, praxis, and epistemology to the liberation of subjugated knowledges and native feminist practices in colonized peoples:

> This methodology is arising from varying locations, through a multiplicity of terminologies and forms, and indomitably from the minds, bodies, and spirits of U.S. feminists of color who demanded the recognition of *la concienca de la mestiza,* indigenous resistance, and identification with the colonized. Only when feminist theory self-consciously recognizes and applies this methodology can feminist politics become fully synonymous with anti-racism; only when cultural, critical, and ethnic theory recognize this methodology can they become synchronous with feminism and each other. (267)

Mohanty, Sandoval, and Alarcón offer a methodological praxis to understand the location of subaltern identity in a coexistence of multiple scripts and operations of colonial, neocolonial, and patriarchal power by grounding the politics of resistance to the social-political and corporeal consequences of living in and on the margins of nation-states, especially the U.S./Mexico border, and the ensuing violence and exclusion on multiple fronts produced by the "borderless" travel of global capitalism. By mapping the model of the subject-in-process to consider the enunciative powers of multiple, hybrid, mestiza, and indigenous mixed-race subjects, the epistemic possibilities of the subject-in-process as an interpretive model can liberate our understanding of subaltern subjectivity and signifying acts of cultural and political productions. This model disrupts totalizing and inferiorizing forces in colonial discourse that attempt to regulate and contain subaltern subjects in static and oppressable modes of production.

By examining the theoretical and political promises of Chicana feminist, U.S. third world feminist, and border studies grounded in anticolonialist and anticapitalist methodologies, in the following chapters I attempt to read the multilayered politics of autoethnographic subaltern speaking-subject decolonizations found in the U.S./Mexico borderlands across a variety of genres including ethnography, literature, autobiography, and film. By de/constructing or de/colonizing our subjectivities as hybrid, mestiza/o, and indigenous peoples, we can resist and disrupt different loci of social power and begin to understand ourselves as bordered and multiple beings who can draw on different reservoirs of signifying practices. Instead of returning to an essentialized, anthropologically imagined place —the lost Eden of Western civilization—we can reclaim a vital heterogeneity that reconfirms our interconnectedness with all of our relations. Speaking and acting as anticolonial, antiracist, and antisexist subjects-in-process is generative, a way to be in the world that speaks against our otherized selves and further situates possibilities and tactics of strategic and spontaneous resistance.

2

When Mexicans Talk,
Who Listens?
The Crisis of Ethnography
in Situating Early Voices
from the U.S./México
Borderlands

We were thrown out of just about everywhere, but what really made me feel bad was when we tried to go into a restaurant or a restroom downtown, and we were told, "No you can't use it." The police would always come and say, "This is a public place, you have to get out, you're not allowed here." — María Elena Lucas, *Forged Under the Sun*

As we download the next millennium, we see an abundance of corporate, media, and Western nation-state-driven simulacrums of a borderless global community of seemingly mutually informed cosmopolitan consumers of technological and ethnically flavored artifacts.[1] These market-driven simulacrums celebrate the transnational movements of capitalist investment and development as the alchemy of globalization at the same time that they mask and ignore the further stratification, disempowerment, hyperexploitation, and increasing abject poverty of subaltern communities, peoples (especially women and children), and bodies who produce, harvest, and assemble goods consumed on the global market.[2] Globalization magnifies the dual and uneven edge of national borders in general, and the U.S./Mexico border in particular. Funds move back and forth in the "borderless" global free-trade market, legalized by such precursors to the World Trade Organization (WTO) as the General Agreement on Trade and Tariffs (GATT) and the North America Free Trade Agreement (NAFTA). Encouraged by privatization, neoliberalism, and investment-seeking by underdeveloped countries, "borderless" capital creates more "maquiladora zones" (assembly plants) on the U.S./Mexico border and a proliferation of sweatshop "zona franco" (free zone) industries in Central America and Southeast Asia.[3]

In contrast to the borderless movements of instant online fund transfers, Lear jets, high-speed Euro trains, and visa-carrying tourists "doing" "cheap" and "exotic" countries, survival movements for subaltern peoples displaced by predatory global capitalism, and military and political pressures are dangerous and restricted by national borders. When Mexicanas/os and Centro Americanas/os move in a south-to-north axiom across multiple borders to the United States because, among other reasons, of economic and political displacements, they must avoid robbery, assaults, and rape by a variety of predatory groups and endure human rights abuses by militarized border patrols. After crossing the U.S./Mexico border, people live in fear of deportation while they confront racial and sexual harassment and face further exploitation.[4]

The cultural-studies challenge of Chicana/o border studies is to analyze the complex relationships among the uneven edges of the U.S./Mexico border, the articulation of racialized, subaltern, feminist, and diasporic identities, and the politics of hybrid and mestiza/o cultural productions.[5] To contribute to the challenges of border studies, in this chapter I seek to analyze stories and *testimonios* of south-to-north border crossers who eloquently testify to the social and historic forces that intersect their physical and psychic survival in the borderlands between the U.S. and Mexican nation-states. This chapter begins with remembered narratives of border crossers whom I have met as well as border crossings that I have experienced. I do this to contextualize my discussion of Mexican immigrant narratives in the earlier part of this century (1910–1930) whose "life stories" found in *The Mexican Immigrant: His Life Story* (1931) by Manuel Gamio speak to the historical forces at play on both sides of the border.

As we shall see, these diasporic *testimonios* echo timelessly to the discrimination, enforced liminality, and anti-Mexicano/Latino state violence dominating the recent political milieu in the United States. By listening to Mexican speaking subjects, whether border crossers at the *fin de siglo* (end of century) or at the *principio de siglo* (beginning of century), their stories and *testimonios* bear witness to and challenge the scripts and practices of racism, sexism, and neo-Fordist predatory capitalism that reduce the historicity and heterogeneity of Mexicanas/os to criminalized and sexualized anonymous bodies straining to meet production quotas and shift dead-lines.

Voices from the Frontier/Voces de la Frontera

A few days after Christmas in the mid-1990s, I take advantage of the long winter break to return to Mexico. I catch a flight to San Diego, and then take the trolley from downtown San Diego to San Ysidro, where I cross into Mexico by foot, pushing the turnstile open ahead of me. Despite the cacophony of human traffic, and cars, trucks, and buses, as soon as the turnstile is behind me the tension in my shoulders drops away, my psychic shield fades, and my breathing slows measurably *Safe again.* In the United States, I feel this kind of security only in the expanses of the mountains, deserts, and oceans and with my wife, close friends, and *familia.*

Whenever I return from Mexico, the opposite occurs. As I reach the U.S. side of the border (whether by foot or by plane) the mere thought of passing immigration and customs makes my stomach tense. I double-check my documents and act out scenarios in my head and rehearse re-sponses to their paranoiac questions. I remember all of the nightmarish Immigration and Naturalization Service (INS) interviews I have had. Ar-rogant INS agents bark, "What is the purpose of your visit?" I respond, "Visit family, friends, and do research at the UNAM." They stare at my U.S. passport, question its authenticity, and yell, "Sign your name here! Again! Again! Do you have another identification, like a social security card? Sign here! Again!"

In my experience, INS agents of Hispanic descent are the most likely to interrogate other Mexicanas/os and Latinas/os. They have the most to prove to their superiors that the enforcement of the juridical nation-state apparatus must transcend any ethnic and cultural affiliations. They stare the longest at my passport. They interrogate my wife in their broken Span-ish to make sure her green card is not false. They are more convinced than Anglo officers that I am smuggling contraband. "Step over there . . . unzip your bags." In their eyes, ceramic mementos and small clay pots all of a sudden become drug paraphernalia and justify more rigorous unpacking of bags, more questions.

But that December day I make my way to the main bus station outside of downtown Tijuana by taking a series of buses that move through areas that few U.S. tourists have seen, and I am dropped off at the line that passes by the main terminal on the way to Mesa Otay. Buses from the main terminal take people to points south of the border, even all the way to the Guatemalan border. I enter the huge bus station. A sea of people carry suitcases bulging with gifts and belongings, along with cardboard boxes tied with thin nylon cords; they buy their tickets and wait for their departures. Returning from el Norte or the maquiladoras they are on their way to be with their familias, villages, and cities, to pass the *Año Nuevo* (New Year) celebrations and show off their children to their parents, grandparents, and extended families.

As I board the Tres Estrellas de Oro (three gold stars; a popular bus line) that will head toward Mazatlán, the sun begins to set. I am going to visit my *tía* (aunt), who left her life in Mexico City to *tirar su fortuna* (seek her fortune) in Mazatlan. She is finding life difficult. Acceptance does not come easy because she is an outsider, a *chilanga* (slang for someone from Mexico City). I have not seen her in years, and I have never met her children.

I sit on the bus, wrap myself in my poncho, and try to relax for the twenty-three-hour bus journey. As the bus is about to pull out, a young man about seventeen years old, looking tired and thin, climbs aboard and sits next to me. We talk. Juan Manuel is returning, defeated and penniless, to his village in the state of Guanajuato, Mexico. I tell him my family is originally from Guanajuato. His eyes light up.

I learn from him that ever since the price of corn dropped, his family's small land tract was not producing enough to support his family members. Because he was the most physically fit, as well as unmarried and without children, his extended family chose him to go to el Norte and find a job. Once he was settled, his plan (like so many others) was to send money back to his family to help them overcome their financial crisis. To pay the *coyote's* (contractors who bring undocumented people over the border) fee of three hundred dollars to lead him across the border to Los Angeles (cheap by current standards) and give him enough money to survive for a week or two, his extended family had a meeting and everyone contributed what they could for his journey.

Juan Manuel then proceeded to recount his border-crossing experience: *la migra* (INS officers) came with their white four-wheel-drive trucks, floodlights, and helicopters to stop the group, and they all started to run. The INS officers began chasing them—batons out, stun guns and rifles ready— yelling in English and broken-accented Spanish. Because the coyote didn't tell them which way to run in case they were pursued by the INS, Juan and everybody in his group panicked and started running in all directions. Juan told me that he decided to follow close to the heels of the coyote, even though the coyote told him to back off.

The coyote grudgingly took him to a duplex in National City, which lies on the U.S. side of the border between Tijuana and San Diego. There the coyote forced him to hide under a bed all night. Frightened, Juan Manuel stayed under the bed until ten o'clock the next day, while the coyote and his girlfriend stayed on top of the bed. Juan could hear them whispering about him, trying to decide his fate—specifically, who would pay the largest commission to buy his labor. Juan waited until they left the room (around noon), and then, nervous and frightened, he sneaked out of the house and caught the trolley back to the border.

After losing his family's savings in a crossing with no results, he had just enough money for a ticket back to his village. I ask when last he ate, and he shows me a pack of chiclets, and asks me if I want one. I invite him for dinner at one of the rest stops, then we got back on the bus. A few miles down the road a man in his late twenties, José Orozco, overhears us talking about la migra and el Norte and asks me if I know how to read English. He wants me to translate the detention notice issued to him when he was arrested by the INS. The notice is a citation that reads something on the order of "illegal aliens have no legal right to enter the sovereign territory of the United States of America. Pursuant to Congressional Code 1263, aliens are subject to immediate deportation upon inability to prove their residency and citizenship status." Innocently, he asks me if the notice will give him a better chance of getting a tourist visa at the U.S. embassy in Tijuana. He wants to go to his uncle's wedding in Los Angeles. Before he decided to take his chances and cross, he had tried to get a tourist visa in Tijuana, standing in lines starting at five o'clock in the morning. Even though his family, work, and home is in Sonora, Mexico, he did not earn enough money to prove sufficient economic ties to Mexico, and he was denied a visa.

He tells me how he was returned to Tijuana that morning at Mesa Otay. He had tried to cross earlier that week and was detained and arrested by la migra. He had not been able to outrun them. He tells us about spending the night in an overcrowded detention center where the toilet was clogged and everybody had to piss and shit in full public view. However, what made him most angry was the unwillingness of any INS official to listen to his reasons, his stories, and his humanity: "I just want to go to my uncle's wedding. I have work in Mexico."

Then, he exclaims, "they treated us like dogs. . . . They don't explain anything to us. . . . They only jostled us with their *pinche* [damn] batons, ready to draw their weapons at any time." But, he adds, "at the same time they kept calling us *amigo* and *pancho.*" Juan and I listen quietly, letting him say what he needs to say. He keeps repeating: "Why are the gringos so damn arrogant with us? Why do they treat us like children? Like liars? Like dogs?"

I nod in agreement with him, saying "you're right . . . you're right." Feeling powerless, angry, and sad, I think of the trajectory of historical forces and their narratives that have created this particular disjuncture of power: the Conquest, colonialism, U.S./Mexico relations, the rise of multinationals, and the rapid and vicious plays of market politics framed against a resurgence of American nativism. Also, I begin to measure my experiences felt since childhood of otherization as a Chicano in the United States, coming from Mexico City as a child, poverty, racism, police harassment, and invisibility against the incontrovertible privilege that a passport offers. The only advice that I am able to offer to Juan and José is that if they are to cross again they should ask around their communities for a *coyote de confianza,* someone whom a family trusts and has worked with on several occasions (a tenable solution to a situation that is truly absurd, if you think about it). I also tell them that even though the rents in San Francisco are very high, San Francisco, unlike San Diego and Los Angeles, is a declared "sanctuary zone," where in theory the INS has to seek a subpoena to deport Latinos.[6]

I also think about young Juan Manuel and José Orozco when I think about the contradictions of border crossings where multinational corporations are given privileged passage across the border to buy property, resources, and contract Mexican workers at substandard wages, taking advantage of extreme inequities in global pay scales displaced by market depreciations of agricultural goods. At the same time there is congressional spending for more border patrol agents and more development of "alien" detection technologies such as ground sensors, night goggles, and laser trip beams (these have a "trip" sensor that allows the INS to locate and track crossers), coupled with nativist citizen groups who "light up the border" and practice vigilante war games such as "shoot the wetback."

Border Frenzy and the Representation of Mexican Immigrants

Indeed, much of the rhetoric about immigrants presently being heard in government and in the media is virtually identical to the anti-immigrant pronouncements
that were commonly heard in the 1890's, the 1920's, the 1950's, and again in the
1970's. — David G. Gutiérrez, *Walls and Mirrors* (1995)

Mirroring the political and media focus on Mexican and Latino immigrants, the publishing industry entered into the "border hysteria" surrounding immigration and the U.S./Mexico border. The 1980s and 1990s
witnessed a high volume of sales of anthropological and journalistic accounts that claim to capture the "authentic" voice and experience of the
"south of the border Other" for a Euro-American audience. Apart from
assimilated Hispanic American Richard Rodriguez's encounter with the
poor and marginalized communities of Tijuana, Mexico, these texts represent Euro-American encounters with the Other: namely Mexicanas/os and
other Latinas/os who travel through what I term the "razored porosity" of
the U.S./Mexico border.[7]

The stated and implied intent of these accounts is to "humanize" the
"aliens" and draw sympathy from the dominant culture. However, I argue that these captivity narratives of the 1980s and 1990s fulfill the Euro-
American desire, production, and consumption of the Other. In many
cases, they confirm fears of the dominant culture of being overrun by
hordes of "illegals."[8] Cover copy and art, titles, and other marketing devices shout out to the reader: "Read and experience the exotic and violent
life on the other side," and, patronizingly, "Sympathize with the plight of
the poor illegals." Consider the semiotic charge in the title of Ted Conover's
account of his "brave" encounter with the other *Coyotes: A Journey Through
the Secret World of American Illegal Aliens* (1987); the *Hard-Copy*-like cover
on Debbie Nathan's *Women and Other Aliens* (1991), which dramatically
depicts a Latina being carried across the Río Grande on the shoulders of
a shirtless Latino; or *Mexican Voices/American Dreams* (1990) by Marilyn
Davis, who argues that her "robust" and "affectionate" Mexicans come to
seek the American dream just like anyone else. In more literary realms,
The Tortilla Curtain by T. Coraghessan Boyle (1995), with its dramatic cover
of a cactus, is an award-winning novel of an *ilegales* couple who forage for
survival in modern-day Topanga Canyon in Los Angeles. In the case of the

latest novel by famed Japanese writer Haruki Murakami, *South of the Border: West of the Sun* (1999), the term "south of the border" metaphorizes the underground sex economy of Tokyo.

However, there is a history of ethnographic studies and collected testimonies that attempt to represent the diverse experiences of Mexican immigrants in the United States, starting in 1931 with *The Mexican Immigrant: His Life Story* by Manuel Gamio. It was followed by *Five Families* (1959) and *The Children of Sanchez* (1961) by Oscar Lewis; *Two-Cultures: The Life of a Mexican American* (1973) by John Poggie, and so on to the present.

This chapter analyzes the groundbreaking transcription of diasporic Mexicana/o voices in the United States found in *The Mexican Immigrant: His Life Story* (1931) by Dr. Manuel Gamio. *The Mexican Immigrant* is an ethnographic transcription, interestingly categorized as "life histories," by renowned Mexican anthropologist Manuel Gamio. Gamio's "life histories" pioneered a major attempt to represent the voices and experiences of a wide range of Mexicanas/os who crossed the relatively newly formed border between 1900 and 1930 to work.[9] This transcription of Mexican voices was funded to serve as a companion to Gamio's more "scientifically" rigorous study *Mexican Immigration to the United States* (1930). Both volumes were produced for an English-speaking audience under the guidance of Robert Redfield and were funded by the prestigious Social Science Research Council in 1926.

The Mexican Immigrant is foundational to U.S./Mexican border studies, Chicana/o Studies, and ethnography studies. The testimonies not only give historical insight into the politics of immigration at the turn and beginning of this century (1900–1930), but also echo timelessly the discrimination, enforced liminality, and anti-Mexicano/Latino violence that dominates the current political milieu in the United States. My purpose here is to analyze the autobiographic voices in *The Mexican Immigrant* and discuss the politics of representation in the text. In doing so, my analysis will determine whether this ethnographic transcription provides the reader with Mexican voices that are autobiographically liberating, eloquent testaments of the social turbulence of their time.

The period surveyed by Gamio was one of great upheaval, with the United States involved in World War I and Mexico in the middle of the Revolution of 1910. Both countries were struggling to develop and enforce their nationhood. The émigrés were literally caught in a liminal position between these two nation-states: the borderlands. In a sense, *The Mexi-*

can Immigrant is converged by the dual edge of the U.S. and Mexican border. How is Gamio's ethnographic apparatus intersected by the chains of discourse and power circulating in the cultural economies of the United States and Mexico? How does this text illuminate the relationship between nationhood, citizenship, race, class, and gender?

At first glance, *The Mexican Immigrant* seems to provide the reader with a rich and varied constellation of Mexican immigrant voices that testify to historical conditions. However, my interest here is to discuss the politics of representation in *The Mexican Immigrant* by unraveling the relationship between its ethnographic apparatus and the discourses that essentialize and marginalize subjects according to race, class, and ethnicity. In doing so, I question the complicity of the ethnographic project with the racialist discourses of marginality circulating on both sides of the border. I ask these questions: How much does the ethnographic apparatus limit, border, or annul the self-representation of Mexican border émigrés? What is the relationship between autobiographical impulse and the monologic constitution of informants common in ethnographic representations? How are these tensions reflected in the text? In sum, do these immigrants form themselves in this text, or are they formed by Gamio and his editors? Does the reader take a cue from Robert Redfield's totalizing comments in his introduction to *The Mexican Immigrant*? He writes: "Because there are so many of them, and because in many ways they are alike, through them to some degree we come to know not a particular Mexican immigrant but a sort of generalized Mexican immigrant" (viii). Finally, is *The Mexican Immigrant* an extension of the ways Mexicans have been constructed in colonialist ideologies: inferior, primitive, and animalistic peoples who, due to their "Indian" blood (Hanke 1959), will mongrelize the imagined purity of the nation (De León 1983)?

Put simply, do these Mexicans talk, or are they constructed to confirm public sentiment around the "scary" growth of immigration of Mexican nationals and thus satiate their fears? Does Gamio allow the Mexicans to speak in their own terms? If so, what do these people say?

To begin to answer these questions, let us briefly consider Manuel Gamio (1883–1960), the primary investigator in charge of this study. Gamio was one of Mexico's most celebrated anthropologists, and his archeological and ethnographic work and policy initiatives, especially regarding indigenous peoples, played a crucial role in post-revolution Mexican society. Franz Boas trained Gamio in anthropology, linguistics, and philosophy at Columbia University, where Gamio received an M.A. in 1911 and a Ph.D. with highest distinction, in 1921. According to "Nationals and Foreigners in the History of Mexican Anthropology" (1992) by Guillermo de la Peña, in 1917 "Gamio was appointed Director of Anthropology in the Ministry of Agriculture and Development, a post created especially for him" (290). And by 1924, "the Directorate of Anthropology was transferred to the Secretary of Public Education, and Gamio was promoted to the rank of Undersecretary." He was also a prominent member of such U.S. scholarly societies as the American Anthropological Association and the American Antiquarian Society.[10]

The *Diccionario porrúa de historia, biografía y geografía de México* refers to Gamio as "the true pioneer of modern indigenismo in Mexico and the continent" (my translation) (1143). In fact, Gamio served as the Director del Instituto Indigenista Interamericano from 1942 to 1960. In *Indigenistas de México* (1968), Isidoro Castillo praises Gamio's plan to integrate anthropology with plans of social action (135–41). Even before he became director of the institute, Gamio initiated a series of campaigns to provide education to indigenous peoples, increase the production of agriculture, and introduce soy beans to indigenous agriculture. His treatise on the challenges of unifying the Mexican nation, *Forjando patria* (1916), which later I analyze in more detail, had a significant influence on the major revolutionary intellectuals. Further, it predates the influential treatise on Mexican racial-national formation *La raza cósmica* (1925) by José Vasconcelos. In *México Profundo* (1996), Guillermo Bonfil Batalla rightly states that *Forjando patria* "spell[ed] out the fundamental direction of indigenismo" and laid the philosophical and political blueprint for indigenous policy in the Americas until the 1970s (115–16).

The Frontier Zone of Ethnography: A Metaphysics of Indian Hating

Ostensibly, Gamio tried to humanize the Mexican immigrants in consideration of his Euro-American audience. But starting with the title *The Mexican Immigrant: His Life Story* and moving forward, Gamio, in collusion with Robert Redfield, makes an effort to create the representative immigrant experience, and in doing so stays true to the traditional sociological impulse of reducing the heterogeneity of human subjectivity into universalized, and in this case, a racialized male essence.

However, what makes Manuel Gamio atypical in the "self-Other" binary found in most ethnographic projects is that Gamio is Mexican, and was commissioned to study other Mexicans. One could expect that Gamio's subject-position and his political commitment toward the indigenous peoples of Mexico would produce a less colonialist construction of his informants. However, I argue that Gamio's subject-position vis-à-vis his "Indian" and "Mestizo" informants reflects power relations in Mexico, illustrating real differences between race, class, and ethnicity.

In *For Those Who Come After* (1985) Arnold Krupat examines the ethnographic encounters between European and Euro-American anthropologists and Native American informants at the turn of the century. He provides a framework that partially explains Gamio's ethnographic project. Krupat understands American ethnographic practice as follows: "[Ethnographies] function to affirm the central authority of the American progressivist ideology, offering testimony of 'savagery' by 'civilization' " (47). The logic of this viewpoint is that the author, a member of the dominant mainstream, "a man of culture," formally constructs himself through the perpetuation of the object's position as a "child of nature." Because this colonialist relationship is set, Krupat argues that "the signifier's complex composition is the result of a historically specifiable mode of production—the result, not only of the confrontation of the individuals, but equally in Fredric Jameson's terms, 'the confrontation of two distinct social forms or modes of production, a collective, as well as an individual encounter,' i.e., 'power relations' " (9).

Krupat understands the transcription as a "bicultural composite composition," a borderland or frontier between two cultural subjects and nations with distinctly different modes of production and unequal power relations framed in the contexts of colonial domination and resistance.

How does this analysis apply to Gamio's relation to the immigrant "subjects"? Gamio himself is caught in a type of borderland. As a *traductor* (translator or "converter" of cultures [my translation]), Gamio has to cross many borders to convey the stories of the immigrants to his North American audience.[11] He has to translate the stories into English to make them marketable to an American audience. Audience specificity, and Gamio's need to appear "civilized," "objective," and "authoritative," coupled with his nascent positivist beliefs, circumscribed Gamio's limits as a traductor of culture.

Gamio is the study's principal investigator and hence the ultimate authority on how the studies were conducted and then produced as a textual commodity. But it is also worth wondering how much the printed version of Gamio's text was the process of Robert Redfield's editing and thus questioning the apparatus of power relations further between Gamio and the subjects, and Gamio and the general editor.

The frontier created by Gamio's transcription of the Indian "voice" is a "bicultural composite composition" that reflects the relationship between race, class, and ethnicity and race in a newly forming Mexican nation. Gamio, the principal investigator, is a *criollo* (a Spaniard born in Mexico). His representation of the informants mirrors the caste system in colonial Mexico that supposedly was abolished after Mexico attained its independence.[12] Gamio borders the subjects according to their appearance. He privileges the "white" informants and denigrates those who appear Indian. He places the "white" informants as the most sophisticated and the "Indian" subjects as most ignorant, unreliable, and emotional. Gamio uses typological references before each testimony: "Francisco Gomez is *white*, 54 years old" (71). "Jesus Garza, *mestizo*, markedly *Indian*, twenty-four years of age" (14). This imposed typology reduces the heterogeneity of human subjectivity to a racial commodity type that predicates a certain type of response and credibility.

Although Gamio is Mexican, he reproduces colonial and neocolonial scripts of subjection on his Mexican immigrant subjects, thus drawing into question the relationships between cultural representation, ethnographic practices, and nation-state formation. Perhaps the question that Tejaswini Niranjana asks in *Siting Translation* (1992) is appropriate here: "Is there something in the very nature of the problems posed and the kind of solutions adopted in translation studies and ethnography that lends itself, borrows from, authorizes the discourse of colonization that underwrites the project of imperialism?" (65).

If all ethnographies are an extension of imperialism, then what is the role of the critic? How do we intervene into the ethnographic site to illuminate discourses and ideologies of power, while at the same recover voices subaltern in the political economy and made insignificant by the ethnographic apparatus? *The Predicament of Culture* (1988) by James Clifford challenges critics to read "against the grain of the text's dominant voice, seeking out other half-hidden authorities" (53).

In contradiction to these typological acts, Mexicans (as with most people) refer to themselves as coming from one region, city, barrio, or even street, drawing in relief tensions between a monologic constitution of the Other and localized autobiographic self-formations. Whenever I meet Mexicans and Chicanos, whether in the United States or Mexico, the first question we ask each other is where in Mexico or the States are we from — for example: *"Yo soy de Tepito, D.F.,"* or "I came up on Bryant Street, *La Misión,* San Francisco." For Mexicans and Chicanos, these regional, even barrio, differences are key to understanding each other.

In fact, almost every individual in Gamio's narratives states at the out- set what region they are from: "I am a native of Culiacan, Sinaloa," (104); "I was born on an estate near Zamora, Michoacán" (87); "I am a native of Saltillo, Coahuila" (66). The fact that the people interviewed clearly state where they are from shows Gamio's editorial "violation" of these subjects' self-narration processes by reducing them to a racial type. A need to iden- tify oneself by one's region of origin may be seen as a continuation of tribal consciousness wherein one's self-identification rested on one's tribal and clan designations. But this possibly "romantic" speculation of the precolo- nial past needs to be mediated by the understanding of regionalism as formed in resistive response to nation-state building. The relationship be- tween individual, region, and nation is precisely what was at stake directly prior to, during, and after the Mexican Revolution of 1910.[13]

Gamio's use of racial types forges heterogeneous cultural identities into homogeneous commodity types. Gamio systematically privileges the "white" informants. Similar to Krupat's analysis of the ethnographic en- counter, Renato Rosaldo in *Culture and Truth* (1989) argues that the "ethnographic gaze" structures the informants closest to the ethnographer as "civilized," "rational," and interestingly "culturally invisible," and there- fore more "objective" and "realistic" (198–99). In the section "The Leader and the Intellectual" Gamio explicitly states: "The following section as- sembles the accounts of immigrants with greater *sophistication* and educa- tion. These persons are in most cases, of *white blood.* It is not surprising to find them giving fuller expression to their race consciousness and . . . to hear from them a fairly *objective* and *realistic* statement as to ethnic dif- ferences and as to race relations" (emphasis added) (183). The bias is made clear by Gamio's equation of the quantity of "white blood" with the terms "sophistication," "objective," and "realistic." The implication then is that "Indians" or "mestizos" are too "subjective," "irrational," and "ignorant" to offer any "scientific insight" into the processes of identity formation after crossing the border. This inference inadvertently denies authority to the voices categorized as "Indian."

In fact, in the section titled "The Village Indian" (42–43) Gamio sets up the reader by characterizing the Indians and their relationship to the United States as follows: "The three men whose accounts follow are un-educated, and were brought up in villages or small rural communities" (42). Already, Gamio uses a Eurocentric and universalist model of educa-tion and culture. Meaning that because they did not attend formal school-ing in Mexico, whether due to the lack of schools in their villages or because of the need to work to help out their family, they are labeled "uneducated." However, who is to know how "educated" they are in their tribal histo-ries, language, customs, medicine, and healing practices? In a patroniz-ing fashion, Gamio is almost surprised at his informants' ability to adapt to the demands of U.S. society: "When such persons come to the United States, the differences in custom and in modes of social control must be especially great. Yet these men have managed to get along well enough, partly because their relations with the American world remain exterior, confined largely to selling their labor and buying their food and recreation" (42). Taking Gamio's commentary literally, a reader may expect that these "village Indians" will only speak about where they worked and how much they earned. However, these testimonies (42–45), especially that of Isi-dorio Osorio, reveal a consciousness of their exploitation that goes well beyond the superficiality of labor exchange that Gamio describes. Osorio, "an Indian native of Penjamo, Guanajuato," ironically compares his exploi-tation as a subaltern in Mexico and in the United States: "Over there in Mexico or here, it is about the same for us ignoramuses because we always have to work. The only thing is that here one has to work harder and wear ourselves out twice as fast as there" (42). Osorio continues in a tone comi-cal in its ironic characterization of his exploitation in the United States: "The Americans only say 'puri gud man' when they see one working so hard that one almost coughs up one's lungs, but later when they don't need one or see one is old they give us our time" (45). Osorio also comments on the role of Catholic religion in maintaining people in a state of passivity and acceptance of their social condition. Osorio critiques the complicity of religious ideology and the exploitation in tones reminiscent of ideas of lib-eration theology: "You know that they say that a leaf of a tree doesn't dry up without the will of God and the priests say that one should suffer here with patience the laws of Calles rather than want to rise up in arms? No sect convinces me, for they all say that one should suffer here now and that one will be happy in the other world and in the meantime one wears out one's lungs with working so hard" (44).

Pedro Nazas, another "village Indian" from Zapotlan, Jalisco, who lives in Los Angeles, California, provides a commentary on social conditions on both sides of the border that contrasts with Osorio's. For Nazas, the United States offers a greater sense of freedom from racial discrimination and his earning potential. Nazas states: "You can go into any restaurant or any theater and seat yourself by the side of the rich. It isn't like in Mexico where some feel themselves to be aristocrats and they feel themselves humiliated if some poor man seats down besides them. No Sir!" (48). Nazas commentary raises many questions about why he feels less discriminated against in the United States: Is he just lucky? Is he in denial of his exploitation and racism? Does he think the interviewer is a U.S. agent? (This issue comes up in professed socialist Guillermo Salorio's testimony [128–30]). However, Nazas makes a terse point about his treatment as a "village Indian" in Mexico: in the pyramid of race and class instituted by the caste system, people of European blood are *gente de razón* (people of reason), with all the social privileges and legal rights in their favor. The Indians at the bottom of the pyramid are numerically larger, yet are exploitable outcasts in their own lands.

Gamio's editorial violations racialize his informants in ways consistent with colonially embedded eugenic attitudes in both U.S. and Mexican bourgeois cultures that position whites as civilized, scientific, and harbingers of modernity and characterize Indians as inferior, immoral, and locked in prehistory. These editorial violations are consistent with Gamio's views on race, ethnicity, and nation-building as expounded on in his *Forjando patria*, as well as in the *Aspects of Mexican Civilization* (1926) lectures he delivered at the University of Chicago with José Vasconcelos. In both of these texts, as in *The Mexican Immigrant*, Gamio divides the ethnic composition of Mexico into White, Mestizo, and Indian, conveniently denying the African presence in Mexico as seen in the Afro-mestizo coastal communities of Veracruz and Guerrero.[14]

Even though Gamio champions his own lack of racial prejudice, the chapter "Nuestra cultura intelectual" (93–107) in *Forjando patria* belies a positivist vision of nation-building that calls for a plan of cultural assimilation using scientific principles. For Gamio the diverse indigenous communities in Mexico are living "con un retraso de 400 años" (in a backward state of 400 years) and their cultural manifestations are "anacrónicas e in-apropiadas, poco prácticas" (anachronistic and innappropriate, and of little practical use). He continues by arguing how indigenous leaders who know the movement of sun and moon would seem "ridículos si les instala en el Observatorio Astronómico" (95) (ridiculous if you installed them in the Astronomical Observatory) (my translations).

In *Aspects of Mexican Civilization,* Gamio clarifies further the differ-ences in intelligence between white minorities and Indian majorities: "The Indian, because of his cultural inferiority, has the right to expect the white to understand his particular ways of thinking since he cannot be expected to ascend mentally, rapidly, miraculously, to the plane of diffi-cult ideological and material mechanism which characterizes the modern civilization of white minorities" (126). For Gamio, the key for Mexico's entry into modernity is to lift the diverse indigenous communities out of prehistory by forcibly assimilating them into a scientifically driven and ho-mogenous mimicry of Western civilization at the expense of indigenous self-determination.

Even though some writers, such as José Limón in his *American Encoun-ters* (1996), refuse to consider the racial positivism present in Gamio's early work as anything other than a "miscalculation," other scholars, including Guillermo Bonfil Batalla in *Mexico Profundo* (1996), argue how Gamio's indigenismo lays the nationalist blueprints (1916–1970) for the cultural ethnocide of the diverse indigenous communities in Mexico: "Indige-nismo did not contradict in any way the national plan that the triumphant Revolution had been crystallizing: to incorporate the Indian, that is, de-Indianize him, to make him lose his cultural and historical uniqueness. The question was how to do it more effectively" (116).

At first, Gamio's colonialist views of indigenous peoples seem contra-dicted by the fact that he spearheaded the excavation and restoration of Teotihuacán, the major metropolis of Mesoamerican civilization of im-mense architectural and artistic sophistication that flourished between 200 and 700 A.D. However, Batalla lucidly comments on the intersections of indigenismo and the nationalist imaginary that glorify the Mesoameri-can past of Mexico: "The Indian presence as depicted in murals, museums, sculptures, and archeological sites, all open to the public, is treated essen-tially as a dead world" (55). At the same time, living indigenous peoples are "viewed through the lens of an easy prejudice: the lazy Indian, primitive, ignorant, perhaps picturesque, but always the dead weight that keeps us from being the country we should have been" (19). Efforts at cultural, linguistic, and political self-determination must be thwarted by the nationalist and neoliberalist agendas: "What exists is an asymmetrical relationship of domination and subjugation in which the majority Indian population is not conceded the right to conserve and carry out its own civilizational development" (58).

Clearly, the way Gamio privileges his informants indicates his own indoctrination into a subject construction of the Indian or *Indio* that predicates his own position as *criollo,* whose race and class caste privilege is directly related to the historical subordination of tribal peoples in Mexico.[15] Unfortunately, these power relations are still very much at play today. Consider, for example, the Zapatista rebellion in Chiapas. The mainly Mayan Zapatistas, in alliance with other indigenous (rural and urban), student, and labor and human rights groups, are holding the neoliberalist policies of the Mexican government accountable for its continued denigration of indigenous peoples, for governmental corruption, for ladino and multinational control of native-owned land and resources, and for repression inflicted by the police and army (Clarke and Clifton 1994).

Historical Context: "Push-Pull" Factors, U.S. Race and Immigration Debates (1916–1930), and the Mexican Revolution of 1910

Mexican discourses of Indian devalorization (an internalized colonialism) travel across the border; however, Indian hating in the United States also becomes Mexican hating.[16] To begin discussing the historical context that shapes the milieu of these social actors on the U.S. side of the border, I would like to highlight Policarpo Castro's testimony found in Gamio's work. Castro is a mestizo and a native of Guadalajara, Jalisco. In Mexico, Castro worked as mason where he learned "everything from how to use the shovel to constructing a house." However, once in the United States Castro faces the limits imposed on him by the U.S. overculture: "When I got to (El Paso) the first thing I did was sign up to work on the railroad because there was *not anything else* and one always needs money and one has to take whatever work one can find or else starve to death, especially in this country where they don't know what kindness is and where we Mexicans have no protection" (emphasis added) (97).

When Castro seeks admittance into the mason union, he is rejected because he is Mexican. By dint of his racial features and ethnic and national designation, Castro is fixed into certain positions of work. He is locked into a labor situation where he has little choice in occupation or salary: "Then bad times came and I have gone from one place to another working as a laborer for I haven't found anything else because the mason union don't want to admit Mexicans" (96).

Clearly, Castro locates his own historicity and speaks to his exploitation and racial victimization as a worker in the United States. His story illustrates how the border once crossed becomes a barrier that is elastic for Mexicans; the border travels with Mexicans wherever they go in the United States, making them invisible noncitizens prey to hyperexploitation and violence with impunity.

When Gonzalo Galvin describes his experiences, he uses a metaphor that is key to understanding Castro's and countless other immigrants' experiences: "I like it here in the United States because I live here, but this is only *a jail in disguise*. One's life is a real struggle for what can one do but endure these bolillos who do whatever they want to with one" (emphasis added) (25).

Gonzalo Galvin's metaphor of "the jail in disguise" is a poetic description of what Mario Barrera in *Race and Class in the Southwest* (1979) describes as "internal colonies." Barrera argues that Mexicans were "pulled up" from Mexico between 1916 and 1930 as a "separate but not equal" laborforce designated to meet the increased demands for industrial and agricultural activity. Likewise, in *Mexican Emigration to the United States* (1980) Lawrence Cardoso argues that one of the main reasons that *braceros* (physical laborers) were pulled up to meet the labor needs of U.S. agriculture and industry was the fact that over one hundred thousand U.S. citizens were conscripted into the armed services, leaving a huge labor void in the United States (45). Furthermore, Barrera demonstrates that the laborers were locked into exploitative conditions with set wages systematically less than the wages earned by the Euro-American workers (65), a pattern that can be seen with workers of Asian descent and other historically disenfranchised ethnic groups.

Although Barrera does not give much attention to the Mexican Revolution of 1910 as a causal factor of emigration, he does present a lucid analysis of how the United States pulled the labor force displaced by war up from the northern region of Mexico, El Norte, to meet the labor shortage in the United States and the needs of the employers in what is now called the U.S. Southwest: "During the First World War, congress bowed to employer pressure and allowed the secretary of labor to exempt Mexicans from the head tax, the literacy tax and contract labor provision. Under this exemption, a considerable amount of workers were brought in between 1917 and 1921" (73).

President Wilson waived for the Mexican workers in 1917 the head and literacy taxes levied against European immigrants as a way of curbing their immigration. Apart from the obvious reason of World War I, why did the United States give this apparent preference to the Mexican workers and not the Europeans? A large part of the answer lies in the need for cheap, exploitable, and expendable labor. And race was central to the decision.

The main employers vying for the *braceros* were the railroad and the mining and agricultural industries, especially the sugar beet field owners. These industries required strenuous work that was easy to exploit. Barrera asserts that the growth of American industry and agriculture was a direct result of this labor influx: "The Mexican laborers, by accepting these undesirable tasks, enabled agriculture and industry to flourish, thereby creating attractive opportunities for American workers in higher job levels" (79). Americans wanted to restrict competition from Europeans with whom they were at war, and to do that they needed to create a pool of workers to do the arduous work, at substandard wages, that Americans did not want to do. Once the Mexican laborers were exempted from these restrictions, U.S. industry owners sent agents to cross the border and sign Mexican workers onto work crews, actually pulling the Mexican laborers across the border. The immigration numbers are clear testament to the conditions set by the "push-pull" factors: before 1910, 21,732 Mexicans immigrated, by 1924 this number had increased more than tenfold to 249,248 people (8).

The "pulling" of increasing numbers of Mexican laborers into North America did not go without significant debate in Congress and among other major public figures in the United States. As discussed in David Guitiérrez's *Walls and Mirrors* (1995), xenophobia and eugenicist fears of miscegenation dominated the debates on Mexican immigration (45–69). For example, consider how Texas congressman John C. Box's rationale for opposing Mexican immigration is based on protecting the "American racial stock from further degradation or change through mongrelization" with already "mongrel" Mexican peons. His statements echo Samuel Holmes eugenic fears of race mixing. "The great majority of the white persons of the United States are not of the Mediterranean, but of Nordic and Alpine races or their crossings. More race mixture would result from crosses with

Latin Americans and this is to be regarded with disfavor" (Holmes, qtd. in Lipschultz 1962: 57). Likewise, in a 1924 congressional debate Ralph Taylor attributes Mexico's industrial instability to the following factors: "Prodigality, love of gambling, fondness for intoxicants and improvidence, doubtless account for much of the Mexicans' industrial instability" (43).

These views resonate with those of the prominent American eugenicist Madison Grant. Grant's *Race Determinism* (1916) views race-crossing of Aryans with non-Aryans as a "retrograde step." In terms somewhat more extreme than Gamio's models of racial evolutionism, Grant directly equates race and blood quantums with social behaviors. In a type of pre-Nazi rhetoric Grant calls for a further "restriction" of non-Aryan races immigrating into the United States: "When the unemployed and unemployable human residuum has been eliminated together with the great mass of crime, poverty, alcoholism and feeblemindedness associated therewith it would be easier to consider the advisability of further restricting the perpetuation of the least remaining valuable types" (45). Grant compares the greatness of the United States with the instability of the Mexican nation and equates race and blood with the capacity for government stability. He argues: "The greatness of the U.S. is a reflection of the immigration of the Nordic races of Northern and Western Europe. The more prolific Mexican Indian with his bad blood had bred out of existence the "good" white blood of the Spaniards. The resultant hybrid mestizo inherited only the bad traits of parent groups; he was mentally and morally crippled and had no capacity for self-government" (45).

With reference to the politics of conquest, Grant argues that: "no ethnic conquest can be complete unless the natives are exterminated and the invaders bring their own women with them" (46). The extent of Grant's popularity, as evidenced by the brisk sales of his pamphlets and the high demand for his appearance in lecture circuits and reading groups, is frightening (King 1981).

Despite a general consensus in the view that Mexicans and other Latinos were of an inferior race, the reason for allowing Mexican immigration and not actively engaging in their direct annihilation was their potential contribution to American economic growth. The most telling point was P. G. Beck's argument to except Mexican immigrants from the restrictions imposed on other ethnic groups at the time: "It is true that stoop labor is arduous work. However, the major reason for employing Texas Mexicans is that they will represent a docile, illiterate and inchoate group of people who are more readily available than local workers to accept the unattractive working conditions of sugar beets" (Beck, qtd. in Lipschultz 1962: 67). The obvious implication of Beck's assertion is that Mexicans would be granted a limited discursive and material entrance into the United States that locks them into a secondary economic status, a pattern that clearly exists today.

Beck's view was the prevalent one. However, Elias Garza's eloquent testimony in *The Mexican Immigrant* provides another view. Garza, interestingly typologized as "white," was driven to despair by the endless exploitation and dehumanization of the people around him. Garza rails against his subjectification as "docile and inchoate." In fact, the conditions of exploitation are what make him docile: "My life is a real story, especially here in the United States where they drive one crazy from working so much. They squeeze one here until one is left useless and then one has to go back to Mexico to be a burden to one's countrymen" (149).

Garza outlines specific historical, colonial, and economic processes that were at play before and during his migration north: "It is a favor that we owe Don Porfirio [President Porfirio Díaz] that we were left so ignorant and so low minded that we have only been fit for rough work." His anger is made more effective by his ironic use of the phrase "it is a favor."

Many historical processes at play prior to and at the time of Gamio's transcriptions caused the Mexican immigrants to be "pushed" up from Mexico. Put simply, the Mexican Revolution of 1910 ignited itself in direct reaction to Díaz's regime of feudal-like haciendas, which kept the workers in a state of peonage. Friedrich Katz's study "Labor Conditions on Haciendas in Porfirian Mexico" (1974) provides a good survey and analysis of the violence of the Díaz regime and the effects of that regime on Mexican laborers. His analysis of the hacienda system makes clear the relation between North American capital growth and the expropriation of Mexican industrial control: "The number of laborers available to central Mexican haciendas greatly increased from 1876 to 1910 as the massive expropriation of the period created a new landless proletariat which the limited industry in most parts of Central Mexico could not absorb" (45).

Likewise, *A History of Mexico* (1970) by Henry Parkes examines how much of industry in Mexico is owned and controlled by American interests. Parkes comments that "American interests—the Hearsts, Guggenheims, United States Steel, the Anaconda—owned three quarters of the minerals and more than half of the oil fields" (309). North American industrial interests undermined the resources of Mexico during Díaz' reign. In addition, *Revolutionary Mexico* by John Mason Hart (1987) argues that by 1910 over 100 million acres of Mexican land were under American control, resulting in mass displacements of indigenous campesinas/os communities and families: "The American Smelting and Refining Company, Phelps Dodge, William Greene, Edwin Marshall, American Railroads, Los Angeles Times Company, The Corralitos Company, William R. Hearst, Cargill, Edward Doheny, and the Texas Oil Company joined other U.S. interests and benefited in the acquisition of cheap lands totaling over 100 million acres" (47). The elite hacienda owners, in consort with Díaz, profited from the vulnerability and desperation of the landless and jobless peasants, who had nothing else on which to fall. When Madero, a *criollo* bourgeois elite, declared the Revolution in 1910 to overthrow Díaz and the hacienda system, this mass of "unskilled" workers became available to be pulled up north, only to continue in a state of peonage labor once across the border, as well as the newly educated technical workers. Although the Revolution of 1910 had lofty aims, Cardoso argues in *Mexican Emigration* that "the revolution initiated a ten year period of instability and violence. The resultant inflation, starvation, unemployment and lack of personal security forced upwards [to the United States] 10% of Mexico's population" (40).

Resistance in the Ethnographic Encounter

Many postcolonial critics have pointed out that colonial discourse—the formation of the colonial subject—contrary to its own narcissism is never complete and never absolute.[17] I would like to devote this section to a consideration of how these Mexican immigrant postcolonial voices resist, escape, and cross the borders intended for their containment. Their self-sentience rasps the grain of the ethnographic apparatus and its complicity with Eurocentric racial ideologies, dignifying the articulation of subjectivity.

Recent critical examinations of the process of cultural translation in anthropological and ethnographic writing—the process by which subjects are formed in narrative—have begun to open the hermetic seal that protected the anthropologist, ethnographer, and the cultural field worker.[18] By interrogating agency, these interventions elucidate how cultural translation has functioned not only within the context of colonial discourse and practice, but also as an extension of the global colonial paradigm and its practice. Central to Marxist, poststructural, and feminist critiques of "writing culture" is the attempt to dismantle the authority that supposed objectivity offers the anthropologist. By dismantling the colonially embedded ideologies that drive the slippery ruse of "objective" authority in cultural anthropology, the process of "writing culture" in narrative can be evaluated.

In addition to offering more liberating ways of constructing ethnographies, this confluence of postcolonial and poststructural interrogations of authority and textual production can be used to reevaluate earlier works of cultural transcription and can help to understand the complicated process of how subjects are formed. The imperative to understand texts written in the past by asking new questions can have dual results: first, this type of critical project can unveil the power apparatuses involved in the invention and simulation of the peoples formed through their encounter in narrative; and, second, critics can reexamine texts to uncover resistances, voices, and impulses that have been buried by the monologic forces of the time.[19]

However, this leaves the discussion open to many questions: How do we as scholars perceive these acts of resistance? How do we recognize and celebrate moments of resistive agency in the ethnographic site? The adjectives "transitory" or even "elusive" characterize my understanding of this ethnic autobiographic moment or "site."[20] This moment is not a fixed, stable entity, but a "centrifugal" force created through literal slippages in the ethnographic encounter—especially slippages created by humor or those in codes not understood by the ethnographer because of his/her cultural restraints.[21] In *The Dialogic Imagination* (1981) Mikhail Bahktin defines the centripetal force of discourse in opposition to the centrifugal: "These are respectively the centralizing and decentralizing (or decentering) forces in any language or culture. The rulers and the high poetic genres of an era exercise a centripetal—a homogenizing and hierarchicizing—influence; the centrifugal (decrowning, dispersing) forces of the clown, mimic, and rogue create alternative 'degraded' genres down below" (425).

Without denying the rich traditions of trickster play among tribal peoples of the Americas, Bahktin's ascription of centrifugal forces to only "clown, mimic and rogue" is an unsettling understanding how informants can decenter the ethnographic encounter. I say this while aware of the importance of humor, irony, and satire as forms of resistance. These terms become dangerous when they are out of the control of the informant/speaker and can act as a further typology traceable to colonial modes of representation both by the popular culture and its "scientists" of the colonizing community; that is, the stereotypes that Mexicans are poor because they drink too much or have too many parties.

Nevertheless, the centrifugal concept is useful in understanding how an interviewee can disrupt the centripetal authority, what anthropologist Renato Rosaldo in *Culture and Truth* (1989) sardonically calls "the lone ethnographer's mask of innocence" (31). Rosaldo explains this mask further as the "detached impartiality" of the ethnographer, who "barely concealed his ideological role in perpetuating the colonial control of 'distant' peoples and places" (31). Such disruption allows speakers to "seize" the process of translation and cross the border of this encounter, to inscribe their subjectivity in their own terms, sometimes unbeknownst to the cultural translator.

Border Crossings: Resistance and Subversion

Gamio's *The Mexican Immigrant* provides scholars ways to understand the processes used by immigrants to negotiate identity and livelihood in the United States; that is, voices of real people negotiating real lives. By reading these distinct and varied stories of experience, we can begin to somatize the effects that historical forces, not to mention the forces of discrimination and racism, had on these immigrants. These autobiographical narratives offer priceless insight and testimony to these historical moments. However, in Gamio's study *Mexican Immigration to the United States* (1930) he declares that the value of "autobiographies" is "generally slight and relative . . . of doubtful veracity" (xii).

In contrast, I view these autobiographic narratives as "concrete utterances" belonging to speakers whose voices reflect their social and historical consciousness. In *The Dialogic Imagination* Mikhail Bahktin characterizes the voice as "the speaking personality, the speaking consciousness" (434). For Bahktin, the voice "always has a will or desire behind it, its own timbre and overtones" (434). These autobiographic narratives are a polyphony of voices that challenge not only the monologizing impulses of Gamio's ethnographic apparatus, but also the hegemonic forces at play on both sides of the border.

The section "The United States as a Base for Revolutionary Activity" (*Mexican Immigration,* 29–36) offers important perspectives on the role of the U.S./Mexico border in the Mexican Revolution. Señora Flores de Andrade, one of the few women interviewed in Gamio's ethnography, tells a story of rich historical importance. In fact, most of the men interviewed are dismayed at the "liberties and rights" that women have in the United States. La Señora Andrade played an integral part in the revolutionary activities of the time, and she used the apparent "sanctuary" of the border towns on the U.S. side to help the battle against the Díaz regime.

To appreciate the significance of this narrative, it is important to consider how la Señora Andrade is positioned along axes of race, class, and gender. In "The Theoretical Subject(s) of *This Bridge Called My Back* and Anglo-American Feminism" (1991) Chicana theorist Norma Alarcón provides a way to understand the multiplicity of oppression and the significance of radically challenging discourses and institutions of power: "As a speaking subject of an emergent discursive formation, the writer in *Bridge* was aware of the displacement of her subjectivity across a multiplicity of discourses: feminist/lesbian, nationalist, racial, and socioeconomic. The peculiarity of her displacement implied a multiplicity of positions from which she was driven to grasp or understand herself and her relations with the real, in the Althusserian sense of the word" (Althusser 1971: 28–39).

Andrade's subject position is located on multiple sites of class, gender, ethnicity, and race. She provides a voice marginalized by the universalizing and patriarchicalizing tendencies in both social science and mainstream historical practice, as well as by the social relations operating at the time. Most histories of the Mexican Revolution are dedicated to male hero worship, exclusively focusing on the roles, activities, and psychology of male leaders.[22] Andrade's testimony, however, powerfully connects with the catalytic processes of the revolutionary movement and adds to the richness of our understanding of the Mexican Revolution itself.

La Señora Andrade's story is one of conscientization, par excellence, to the social and political forces at play. Despite great peril to herself, Andrade, a speaking/acting subject, confronts the hegemonic structures of power emerging from the Mexican ruling-class circles. Rather than basking in the safety of the class privilege of her birth, Andrade becomes a subversive agent in the Revolution through her alliance with and support of Mexican anarchist Flores Magón.

Born a member of the ruling class in Mexico, La Señora Andrade states: "I was born in Chihuahua, and spent my infancy and youth on an estate in Coahuila which belonged to my grandparents who adored me" (29).

After she inherits her family's hacienda, Andrade contradicts the exploitive practices of her class: "The first thing that I did in spite of the fact that my sister and my aunt advised me against it was to give absolute liberty on my lands to all the peons" (29). Andrade declared people free of debts, and she divided the lands and capital "in equal parts" with the workers—an act of socialist equality that mirrored to varying degrees the ideals of revolutionary change. Her family's ensuing outrage impelled Andrade to become even more politicized in her efforts toward defeating the colonial rule of Díaz.

Interestingly, as Andrade became more politicized in her critique of Mexican ruling-class violence, she became poorer in material wealth. As she says, she became a widow with six children and "passed four bitter years in Chihuahua." Poverty drove her to El Paso, Texas, in 1906. There she became even more militant in her organizing, first with Flores Magón, the exiled revolutionary anarchist and editor of *Regeneración,* and then with General Madero, who catapulted himself into power by orchestrating the downfall of Porfirio Díaz's regime to which Andrade's family presumably was connected. Andrade took charge of "collecting money, clothes, medicines, and even ammunition and arms to prepare for the revolutionary movement" (32). She even housed and hid Madero and helped him return across the border. After the Revolution broke into the fights between Villa and Carranza, Andrade withdrew from political life.

Andrade's narrative has an incredible energy of resistance and subversion. The fact that she crossed the border to escape Mexican hegemony and to fight for the social cause of the people can shift the way we understand the border and its discourse of inferiorization and can highlight its porosity. Why did Gamio devote a section of the narratives to such a phenomenon? Perhaps he wanted to alert his American audience to the "dangers of the border." Andrade's narrative shows how the border—a barrier and zone of violence and a producer of elastic and arguably infinite liminality for the Mexicans moving up—becomes a safe zone for activists, "a den of revolutionary activity" before and during the Mexican Revolution.

Before the atrocities committed by the U.S. border patrol reached levels of widespread attack on all Mexicans entering without documentation, Mexicans could temporarily enter a zone made safe by their anonymity and by the lack of infrastructure on the part of the Mexican judicial system. In this zone, they could organize for political action in Mexico. However, even during temporary visits, it is doubtful that Mexicans were immune from feeling their otherness and subalternity. Marginalization was and is produced by second-class treatment in stores and proclaimed by signs such as "No Dogs, Mexicans, Indians Allowed," still on display in tourist-attraction saloons in Arizona and in tourist-trap mining towns in the Sierra foothills, such as Placerville, which in Spanish means "town of pleasure."

Pascual Tejeda, a bilingual university graduate, speaks directly to the racist ideologies circulating in the Euro-American cultural and political economy. He speaks directly to discrimination against Mexican immigrants and argues that these racist attitudes are "due to a lack of culture" on the part of Anglos: "Judging the problem of Mexican immigration into this country in general, I should say that the humiliations, the prejudice and the lack of esteem which are shown toward the Mexican race here are also due to the lack of culture of the American people" (*The Mexican Immigrant*, 185).

Another informant, Wenceslao Iglesias, typologized as "white," speaks even more directly to the impunity with which Euro-Americans act violently toward Mexicans (176). Iglesias describes his own experience in the railroad camps in Amarillo, Texas, a borderland town: "Some Mexicans who were around there without work and looking for it serve as playthings for them. The *botudos* [cowboys] get to shooting bullets at them. Of course since they are sure-shots, they only shoot holes in their hats and make the bullets whistle around them. But if by mistake they do kill one they leave him there and no one finds out why they killed that poor Mexican" (176).

Iglesias' narrative gives insight into the many edges of the U.S./Mexico border—an elastic barrier and zone of violence that has infinite repercussions. His narrative clearly shows how the *bordered* inferiorization of Mexican immigrants leads to linguistic and physical violence probably enacted with zeal by the dominant culture: "Ah hell, they are just bunch of Messicans anyway." The inferiorization or animalization of the Other, in this case Mexicans, benefits the dominant culture in not only obvious ways, but also it creates an ellipsis of denial in acts of violence. Members of a dominant culture can commit "unchecked" atrocities without moral conscience or, even more frightening, with the "moral" imperative of racial betterment, a patriotism of doing one's share for the country. The actor/violator is momentarily transported to a space that resembles a void: a moral ellipsis that is repetitive and temporarily transcendent. This "negative" space endorses the mechanical metonymy of literally pulling a trigger without any real body sensation: an act that is subconsciously and overtly patriotic.[23]

Assimilation and Cultural Resistance

In addition to the brutal acts of racially motivated violence, more subtle and dispersed borders and barriers convey to Mexicans in the United States the message that they are not wanted and that they will always be given second-class status. For example, consider how Jesus Mendizabal laments over the "Americanization" of his children: "They are being American-ized here in the American school. They speak almost more English than Spanish. I have taught them what little Spanish I know so that they will always remember their country, but it seems that they will be American citizens since they were born here and don't know anything about Mexico" (132). Material, linguistic, and cultural colonization involves an active era-sure of cultural memory and a reforging of consciousness to mimic Euro-American subjectivities.

A somewhat parallel study of the complex nexus of linguistic, discur-sive, and material processes of Americanization for non-European immi-grants is Ronald Takaki's *Strangers from a Different Shore* (1989), in which he describes in detail the transformation of Asian immigrants once they come to the United States "to build a new life with untried materials" (4).[24] However, I am cautious about drawing direct parallels to the pro-cesses of Americanization for both immigrant groups, namely because the land of origin for Mexicans is separated by a *line* that was arbitrarily constructed by historical agreement—most of the territory that the immi-grants are "locked" into is originally Mexican.[25] This does not deny, how-ever, that Asian immigrants did not have to fight similar processes of sub-jectification that limited their labor mobility, such as the exclusion laws that barred Chinese immigration in 1917 and 1924. One needs only to look at the Chinese railroad workers of 1850 to see how because of their racial formation they were locked into very specific occupations and low wage scales.

Lorenzo Cantú, a bilingual Baptist minister educated in American uni-versities, comments on this process of Americanization: "I think that in general the Americans treat the Mexicans very well, but they are very ego-tistical and only let one get to a certain place and then wish to close the way for them so as to always have control over them" (1931: 203). His comment echoes Galvin's metaphor of a jail in disguise: Borders travel infinitely with Mexicans no matter the level of education or number of generations of residence in the country. Cantú connects the racial otherization of Mexican immigrants with imperialism in Latin America and calls for a pan-Latino unity: "I think that Latin America is one of the prizes they (Americans) are after, and for that reason all the Spanish Americans, who make up a single race, should join together to defend themselves" (203).[26]

Americanization (assimilation, acculturation, and citizenship) is not willingly embraced by most of the immigrants Gamio interviewed, especially by the first generation. Many of the immigrants interviewed maintain a fierce alliance to Mexico. A striking example of this is Carlos Ibáñez's strongly nationalistic narrative. Ibáñez is typologized as "*mestizo*, markedly Indian" and even though he has been in the United States for more than "twenty-five consecutive years," he states, "I would rather cut my throat before changing my Mexican nationality. I prefer to lose with Mexico than to win with the United States" (46). He asserts a cultural strength that defies Americanization. Although Ibáñez is physically in U.S. national territory, he remains loyal to his Mexican nationality. His desire is to return to Mexico "when there is absolute peace. . . . I haven't lost the hope of spending my last days in my own country" (46). Ibáñez is in a diasporic and liminal condition, echoed in such more recent narratives as Ramón Pérez's *Diary of an Undocumented Immigrant* (1991).

Nationalism is even more strongly embraced by Vicente Gaumer, whom Gamio includes in his section " 'Spanish' Mexicans" (176–83). Gaumer is light-skinned with "blue eyes and brown hair," and he is mistaken "very often for an American." These mistakes of identity makes him "very angry, for here and wherever I am, I am a Mexican and I won't change my citizenship." Because of his phenotypic characteristics, this man can "pass" the racial-discursive and material borders imposed on most Mexicans. However, Gaumer's nationalism contradicts the ethnocentric assumption that everybody wants to become American if given a chance. In fact, Gaumer hates "gringos" and their egotism: "I can't understand the gringos and I hate them because of their ways. They aren't like we are who have no interest in money. They don't care about anything as long as they have money" (181). These testimonies illustrate how the U.S./Mexico border acts as a line of demarcation that translates ethnic differences into scales of hierarchically defined Others. This line produces an infinite state of marginality, liminality, and invisibility for Mexicans, Chicanas/os, and other Latinos living in the United States.[27]

Oppression, Nationalism, and Gender

Most of the male narrators presented in Gamio's transcriptions had no problem discussing their racial and class victimization. At the same time, however, several of the narrators are appalled at the "freedom" that women have in the United States. Almost all of the narrators invariably stated that they would prefer to be married to Mexican women. However, the reasons for their nationalistic choices for spouses reveal disturbing attitudes toward gender.[28]

For example, there is Wenceslao Orozco, a "mestizo of distinctly Indian type" from Durango, Mexico. Even though he is "a carpenter and repairer of furniture and doors," he is not able to get into the carpenters' union that guarantees "work at ten dollars a day" because he "doesn't speak English and is very dark" (51). However, the testimony ends by him discussing the reasons he wants his son to live in Mexico. Orozco's testimony is given in third person: "[Orozco] still keeps his view that the man is the one to decide things and that the woman ought to obey; so that he wants to take his son to Mexico because here the old women want to run things and a poor man has to wash the dishes while the wife goes to the 'show' and for that reason not even 'for fun would he get hitched to a gringa'" (53).

Likewise, interviewee Carlos Ibáñez, the interviewee who stated he "would rather cut my throat before changing my Mexican nationality" does not want to get married in the United States because he does "not like the system of women here." Ibáñez' reasons are as follows: "They are very unrestrained. They are the ones who control their husband and I nor any other Mexican won't stand for that" (46). Furthermore, Ibáñez is frustrated by his inability to beat or cheat on his wife (I presume), without legal consequences: "We are rebels and our blood is very hot, and in this country a man who opposes his wife may lose her and even his wages if he isn't careful, for the laws and authorities are on the side of the woman" (46). Ibáñez laments that these laws of tolerance and protection influence Mexican women. He states: "Now the Mexican women who come here also take advantage of the laws and want to be like the American women. That is why I have thought it better not to marry; and if I do get married some day it will be in Mexico" (46). Ibáñez ends the testimony by stating that "I think that he who lets himself be bossed by a woman isn't a man" (47).

As a contradistinction, la Señora Ponce's testimony describes the oppressive conditions generated by attitudes of dominion over women such as those described above, underscoring the intersections of race, gender, and class. Ponce's testimony is found in the section Gamio called "Mestizo and Middle Class" (49–69), where even the title essentializes the relationship between race and class. Are all mestizos middle class? Are all *criollos* upper class? Are all *indios* lower class? The testimony begins by affirming that even though la Señora Ponce is middle class, her way of being lingers from her working-class origins: "Sra. Ponce is originally from a humble class. Her outward appearance and speech have not altered" (53). Ponce, originally from Puebla, Mexico, is a small-restaurant owner and importer of Mexican products in San Antonio, Texas. She recounts the reasons she came to the United States: "Just imagine, I was about nineteen when I was married and my husband was sixty-six. I respected him but I didn't love him. His two former wives had died. My husband didn't know what was the matter with me and he gave me a card so that I would go to a priest and confess myself" (54). But all did not go well with Ponce's experience in confession: "The poor fool [the priest] went and told my husband [that I didn't love him] the next day and he got angry. We then came to the United States" (540). Ponce describes the oppressive conditions of her life once in the United States, conditions that came not from her exploitation by U.S. industries, but from the patriarchal power structure in her own home: "My husband was very jealous and didn't want me out on the street, so that in the fourteen years that I was here I only went out twice, until a short time ago, when he died at an age of more than eighty" (54). Unfortunately, analyses of race and class oppression in Chicano labor history rarely consider issues of gender in not only the workplace of a given industry, but also the domestic sphere.[29] Testimonies like those of la Señora Ponce can help to redefine the understanding of work to consider the relations of power in domestic situations, prolaterianizing "housewives," and illustrating patriarchal modes of control.

The Great Return: Temporary Diasporas

As a final point of bringing the entire text back into its actual historical context, Gamio's interview transcriptions were published in 1931 at the height of the Great Depression. In *Mexican Emigration to the United States* (1980), Lawrence Cardoso examines how Mexican immigrants who were "pushed and pulled" up to the United States returned or were actively deported back to Mexico during the Depression: "Emigration ended soon

after the onset of the Great Depression in October 1929. Industrial and
agricultural production slumped and their by-product of high unemployment caused very harsh conditions for Braceros" (47). Cardoso points to
the fact that 1931 witnessed the greatest return of Mexicans to Mexico:
"The largest number of Mexicans, over 124,000, crossed back into Mexico
in the year 1931 and by 1935 about five hundred thousand Braceros had
gone back" (148).

The economic downturn, beginning with the crash of 1929, was the im-
petus for much hostility toward Mexican immigrants. Not unlike today,
Mexicans were the scapegoats for U.S. economic problems. In *Border: The
US/Mexico Line* (1989), Leon Metz shows how Anglo workers who had previously refused menial jobs now came to the fields and railroad yards out of
economic desperation: "The Stock Market crashed and people blamed immigrants for a large share of the unemployment. Business leaders worked
in kitchens, and farmers, mine owners and railroad magnets dismissed
their Mexican help and hired Americans who now accepted the menial
jobs. The Mexican had no place to go except home, back to Mexico" (383).

In *Mexican Workers and American Dreams* (1994), Camille Guerin-
Gonzales addresses the politics of Mexicans returning to Mexico during
the Great Depression. Guerin-Gonzales demonstrates how policies aimed
at deporting Mexican immigrant families who were receiving work-relief
aid in Los Angeles were actually aimed at the Mexican population as whole,
from long-term multigenerational residents and property holders to recently arrived immigrants (even those legally contracted by U.S. companies).

Guerin-Gonzales argues that this was the first time the federal government "sponsored and supported the mass expulsion of immigrants,"
specifically Mexicans (78). In the chapter "Mexicans Go Home" she argues that: "Because federal, state, and local authorities refused to recognize that Mexican immigrants were permanent members of U.S. society,
people of Mexican descent were especially vulnerable to governmental
programs to deport and repatriate foreigners as a panacea for economic
depression" (76).

Throughout the study, Guerin-Gonzales considers the ideological underpinnings that drove the deportation of Mexicans, many of whom were
fifth-generation residents or original inhabitants of territories ceded by the
Treaty of Guadalupe Hidalgo (1848). She summarizes the mind-set that
drove U.S. Secretary of Labor William N. Doak to order the Bureau of Im-

migration to locate and deport all illegal aliens in 1931, especially those involved in strikes and other labor disputes: "The US secretary of labor, William N. Doak, had a simplistic explanation for the Depression and an equally simple solution: the country was in economic trouble because US workers were unemployed; workers were unemployed because aliens had taken their jobs; therefore, once aliens were expelled from the country, US workers would find employment, and the depression would end" (79).

However, Guerin-Gonzales argues that local citizen campaigns and police were more effective in intimidating Mexicans to accept passage on the trains and ships contracted for their deportation. Many of these people who were long-term residents and property holders had to gather their most valued belongings (not to exceed the maximum allowed by the trains and boats, 150 pounds per person) and return to a similar economic crisis in Mexico (92). *From Out of the Shadows* (1998) by prominent historian Vicki Ruiz characterizes the brutality of these scare tactics as follows: "The methods of departure varied. A historian of Los Angeles, Douglas Monroy, recounts how la migra trolled the barrio in a 'dog catcher's wagon.' In one instance, immigration agents tore a Los Angeles woman from her home in the early morning hours, threw her in the wagon, and left her toddler screaming on the front porch. Even if such scenes were few and far between, they certainly invoked fear among Mexicanos, many of whom decided to take the county up on its offer of free train fare" (29).

Active deportation continued until 1933 when the admittance procedures became much more strict in an attempt to regulate completely all border entry by 1940. After 1940, the Mexican immigrants became susceptible to the laws of American demand. Like commodities with no fixed value, they were pulled up to meet labor demands under the new Bracero Program in 1942. Fortunately, this program offered somewhat more protection for the worker than did the previous era, but not much.[30]

I end this chapter by leaving readers with some unsettling questions. In terms of *The Mexican Immigrant* I ask: To what degree were the Mexicanas/os interviewed conscious of what was ahead of them in terms of the deportation campaign and the "scareheading" tactics? Were they deported, and what happened to them? How does the reader or critic mediate this strange sense of dramatic prescience then—and now?

Imagine that a family member who runs to the corner store to buy milk does not return, only to discover that he or she was caught in an INS sweep. In fact, when nationwide ins raids invade worksites, homes, and school parking lots from Oakland, CA, to Atlanta, Georgia, Mexicanas/os, Chicanas/os, and Centroamericanas/os are afraid to leave their homes. As witnessed in the July 1997 citywide police and ins deportation raids in Chandler, Arizona, subjects fitting the description of "illegals" were pulled over, beaten, interrogated in their homes without search warrants, handcuffed in stores, made to kneel on sidewalks in the 107 degree heat, and falsely deported. Those who were able show that their citizenship and residency papers were in order—such papers were assumed to be false.

PART II

Narrative Disruptions:

Decolonization, Dangerous Bodies,

and the Politics of Space

3

Counting Coup:
Narrative Acts of
(Re)Claiming Identity
in *Ceremony* by Leslie
Marmon Silko

The people he mistakenly and unrepentantly called "Indians" have indeed "learned to speak," appropriating the master discourse—including the utterance "Indian"—abrogating its authority, making the invaders' language our language, english with a lower-case *e*, and turning it against the center. —Louis Owens, *Mixblood Messages*

In Mexican popular culture, when one Mexicana/o wants to put another Mexicana/o in her or his "place" in everyday social interactions there is a saying that attempts to mark hierarchic differences along class, racial, skin color, and gender lines: "Oyé, la Revolución no nos hizo iguales!" (Hey, the Revolution [of 1910] did not make us all equals). As discussed in the previous chapter, Manuel Gamio, one of the intellectual architects of the post-1910 revolutionary Mexican national culture and its promises of social and legal equality, determined the "apparent worth" of informants based on their perceived racial makeup. The ethnographic apparatus in *The Mexican Immigrant* positions the "white" informants closer to Gamio's own subject-position as a *criollo* and hence "reasonable" and "educated." The subjects described as "Indian" and "mestizo" and "markedly Indian" are characterized as "simple" and "ignorant," and their testimonies are understood as scientifically "worthless." In doing this *The Mexican Immigrant* (re)produces the racial stratification of colonial Mexico and echoes the race and class inequities of the caste system[1] where, like Anglo-Americans in the United States, *criollos* of white Spanish descent are given more privileges than mestizas/os, who in turn have more privileges than the Indians and Africans.[2]

This chapter examines how *Ceremony* (1977) by Leslie Marmon Silko, a mestiza of Laguna, Mexican, and Euro-American descent, provides alternate epistemologies of subject-formation that shift the crucial issues of identity for contemporary indigenous peoples in the United States and the Americas out of the terrains defined by colonial and neocolonial ethnographic apparatuses and juridical practices that essentialize the relationship between blood quantum and identity. More specifically, by examining how *Ceremony* complicates the relationships between "fullblood" and "mixblood" Amerindian characters, I consider how Silko challenges the colonially imposed parameters that determine "Indian" authenticity by physiognomic characteristics (that is, he/she "looks" Indian) and the policy-driven blood quantum inventions of "real" Indians.[3] Silko critiques rigid and causal relationships between blood quantum, ethnicity, authenticity, and identity and challenges how the colonialist trope of racial essentialism has been internalized in the identity politics of many Native American peoples.

To counter this trope Silko presents a model of decolonization that reaffirms the power of precolonial matrifocal Laguna Pueblo stories to generate identities and (re)claim time, space, and language. She regenerates the tradition of the novel, ingeniously hybridizing it and subverting it to the communal power of her oral tradition. Silko's work does not depend on platonic notions of pure origins and essences. She refutes linear understandings of history dependent on notions of a past that is lost, colonialist tropes that freeze and sterilize the heterogeneous play and vitality of ethnicity and culture. Silko, along with other Native American writers, locates the struggle for identity in the collective enunciative power of her ancestors and in the changing nature of stories that generate meaning and create universes.

This chapter attempts to understand how Silko deconstructs and reclaims the politics and poetics of identity in a decolonial "writing" practice that emerges from the conflicted ethnic terrains of what is now called the American Southwest: Puebloan, Mexican, and Anglo. Her writing travels in and across the borders of time, space, and cultural differences and emerges from and returns to "Ts'its'tsi'nako, Thought-Woman," an originary feminine matrix of generative power that never syncretized with the imposition of the Roman Catholic system of religious colonization of the Americas. *Ceremony* begins with the following:

Thought-Woman, the spider,
 named things and
 as she named them
  they appeared.

She is sitting in her room
 thinking of a story now

I'm telling you the story
 she is thinking.

  .   .   .   .   .   .

   What She Said:

The only cure
I know
is a good ceremony,
that's what she said. (1–3)

Reclaiming "Writing" from Logos

In order to appreciate how Silko subverts the (e)nglish language and novel genre to inscribe a polyvocal consciousness that decolonizes the federal imposition of linguistic, legal, religious, and epistemic authority, let us remember that the materiality of writing with a phonetic alphabet is considered one of the prime indicators of Europe's status as the holder of "culture" and "civilization." The ethnocentric belief present in the initial colonial conquests of the sixteenth century reasserts itself in the continued use of literacy in Eurocentric models of knowledge as the universal measure of intelligence in the neocolonial educational systems of the early twenty-first century.[4] On the other side of colonialist dialectic, the so-called savage cultures are considered to be at primitive stages whose simple expressions of the oral traditions affirm and reaffirm their bonds with nature.

In colonialist evolutionary mindsets, tribal cultures, as the lost Eden of Western man, are at a stage of prewriting and precivilization.[5] These cultural evolutionist tropes driven in tangent to systemic material and territorial dispossession by post-Renaissance colonial regimes disenfranchise complex acts of literary and cultural significations that preexist and co-exist with the imposition of logocentrism and (re)produce colonialist hier-archies from which false and often violent racial judgments are made.

To understand how Silko's polyvocal narrative terrain decenters the colonial imposition of logocentric hierarchies, I consider how Derrida's model of *écriture* provides an important metacondition to begin unravel-ing literary production across the borders of colonial difference. In *After the New Criticism* (1980), Frank Lentricchia credits Jacques Derrida with initiating a series of philosophical interventions that challenge the meta-physical authority of "fixed origin" and "immutable center" in such lit-erary, philosophical, and anthropological schools as New Criticism, neo-Kantianism, and structuralism in the "human" sciences (158–62). For the purposes of this chapter, my interest in Derrida is limited to how several essays in *Of Grammatology* (1976) can lend themselves to the critique of epistemological authority in colonial discourse, deconstructing relation-ships between language, culture, and power. These essays repatriate the concept of writing in cultures considered too primitive to practice writing and contribute to the growing body of postcolonial cultural studies that (re)empower subaltern cultural production.[6]

In general, *Of Grammatology* loosens the stranglehold of structuralist methods on such "human" sciences as linguistics, philosophy, and cul-tural anthropology. *Of Grammatology* critiques the relationship between transcendentality, logocentrism, and ethnocentrism. When categories of being are monumentalized, meaning becomes fixed and the "play of signi-fying references" (signs) are repressed (7). Derrida, however, argues that all categories of thought, meaning, language, and epistemologies guid-ing metaphysical authority (including all a priori assumptions) are ines-capable from the play of signs. Therefore, narcissism and ethnocentrism guide Western man's obsession with the signs of his own transcenden-tality.

In a foundational essay that challenges colonialist discourse, "The Vio-lence of the Letter," (*Of Grammatology*: 101–18), Derrida deconstructs eth-nocentric conceptualizations of writing. Derrida critiques ethnocentric tropes that understand writing only in the "narrow sense of linear and pho-netic notation" (109). Derrida states that "all societies capable of produc-ing, that is to say, of obliterating their proper names, and of bringing clas-sificatory difference into play, practice writing in general" (109). Derrida attacks structuralist anthropology, especially Claude Lévi-Strauss, arguing that the assumptions that drive Lévi-Strauss's project are dependent on Rousseau's opposition between nature and culture. For Lévi-Strauss, writing in the limited sense of "phonetic notation" is *the* activity that drives the transformation of society from primitive (nature) to cultured (civilization). Derrida states: "No reality or concept would therefore correspond to the expression 'society without writing.' This expression is dependent on ethnocentric onerism, upon the vulgar, that is to say ethnocentric, misconception of writing" (109).

In general, Derrida considers writing to be the play of significations across a field of meaning. Derrida rightly bases his argument on the arbitrariness of the sign as an interplay of signifier/signified relations as the basis of all linguistic activity. Derrida argues that the institutional designation of phonetic writing as the evidence for the transcendentality of culture is a form of ethnocentric violence: "Actually the peoples said to be without writing lack only a certain type of writing. To refuse the name of writing to this or that technique of consignment is the ethnocentrism that best defines the prescientific vision of man" (83).

In another important essay, "Of Grammatology as a Positive Science," Derrida continues his critique of the ethnocentrism that drives the exclusionary postures that consider phonetic writing as the only writing. Derrida considers the "writing" that emerges from differing cultural systems: Aztecan, Mayan, and Chinese (88–93). Regarding Aztec codices and the Mayan glyphs (and note that the terms "codices" and "glyphs" are imposed categories of understanding because they do not emerge from the cultures in question), Derrida argues that the picture-puzzle, a representation of the thing, signifies itself "to a thing and to a sound" (90). The thing exists in "a chain of differences 'in space.'" The sound is "also inscribed within a chain" (90). Derrida argues that "we are dealing then with a script apparently pictographic and in fact phonetico-analytical in the same way as the alphabet" (90).

Derrida does not regard the ideogrammatic and algebraic scripts of the Japanese and the Chinese as precursors to phonetic writing. He challenges the attitudes that understand these forms of writing as "normal outcome, as an historical telos" of an "unfulfilled alphabet" that attempt to justify Western writing systems as the ethnocentric summit of all world civilizations (91). He argues that nonphonetic writing should be understood as different without hierarchical judgements: "We thus have testimony

of a powerful movement of civilization developing outside of all logocentrism" (90).

In terms specific to the material relationship between linguistic and
territorial colonization in sixteenth-century Mexico and the Americas, *The
Darker Side of the Renaissance* by Walter Mignolo (1995) argues that Spain's
attempt to colonize Amerindian language, space, and time depended on
the imposition of what I term a "self-reflexive" epistemological authority
that monumentalizes European letters as the evolutionary nadir of civilization and Christianity. As Mignolo points out, even when Spanish colonial
elite were faced with such ample "evidence" of literacy as the *amoxtli* of the
Mexica and the *vuh* of the Maya, the process of colonialism is based on a
systemic *denial of coevalness* (71–79).[7] The denial of coevalness caused the
first auto-da-fe's of the "new world," where the sacred and scientific texts
of the Mexica and the Maya were tossed in fires as heretic "works of the
devil," evidencing how, in my mind, the inquisitorial practices of Spain col-
luded with the linguistic, religious, and territorial colonization of Mexico
and the Americas (71).

Mignolo challenges critics and scholars committed to theorizing decolonial consciousness in postcolonial subaltern "writing" practices to engage in what he terms the "denial of the denial of coevalness": "Thus while
the denial of coevalness emerged as one of the main conceptual consequences of the growing privilege of time over space in the organization
and ranking of cultures and societies in the early modern . . . period, the
denial of the denial of coevalness is one of the major tasks of postcolonial
theorizing" (xii).

Mignolo's challenge to deny "the denial of coevalness," in conjunction
with Derrida's discussion of écriture provides important epistemic cues
to begin to understand culturally different writing and literary practices
on their own terms. These epistemic and political interventions can aid
critics to challenge the colonialist and ethnocentric attitudes that inferiorize culturally different writing practices. Specifically, they help us map
how multiethnic writers such as Silko, whose work emerges in the fissures
of colonialism and neocolonialism, hybridize and subvert diverse "writing
practices" and (re)claim enunciatory spaces.

In the case of contemporary U.S. multiethnic and postcolonial novelists,
writers reclaim and subvert the novel genre, a genre that *The Colonial Rise
of the Novel* (1993) by Firdous Azim reminds us was born in a specific set of
social conditions in Europe: the rapid growth of industrialism, global im-

perialism, the rise of the bourgeois family, and the cult of the autonomous subject.[8] Entering what Bahktin in *The Dialogic Imagination* (1981) categorizes as the "openended discourse" of the novel to engage in a richness of chronotopes and heteroglossia displaced by colonialism, multiethnic writers hybridize that genre with signifying practices that emerge from other cultural systems of "writing" that continue to operate despite the sustained onslaught of colonial logocentrism: Ibo, Maori, Laguna storytelling, and Nahuatl *disfrasismo* in Chicana/o speech acts (Arteaga 1997), to name a few.[9] For example, consider how notions of the individual are reconceptualized and African proverbs and popular culture are translated in *Things Fall Apart* (1959) by Chinua Achebe; how the mestizaje of the Philippines (Spanish, Chinese, United States, and Pinoy) is translated or reflected in *The Dogeaters* (1990) by Jessica Hagedorn; how Confucian stories are reinscribed in San Francisco in *The Woman Warrior* (1976) by Maxine Hong Kingston; and how Anglo and Maori identity is negotiated in *The Bone People* by crossblood Maori writer Keri Hulme.

In the case of contemporary Native American novelists, we can understand the novel as a hybridization of literary or writing practices combining, for example, communal storytelling with certain aspects of the realistic novel tradition of Europe. By illustrating how the "novel is a system of languages that mutually and ideologically interanimate each other" (Bahktin 1981; 130) these writers create new imaginations by reclaiming signifying practices previously and currently denigrated by colonialist thought and practice. They create crosscultural literary genres that emerge from differing cultural sites and put into practice a dialogics of hybrid or bordered subjectivities.[10] The clash and confluence of cultural trajectories create zones of the hybrid that liberate the "spoken" subject to speak in emergent terms of decolonization. The liberated subject in narrative provides counterhegemonic and reclamatory enunciatory spaces that reconceptualize notions of the individual and challenge the complicity between Western ontological discourse and the proliferation of imperial subjects.

Contemporary Native American novelists create epistemic time-space zones of the hybrid that are more complex than the hierarchical classifications of "myth" versus "realism" and oral versus written. In *All My Sins Are Relatives* (1995), Nez Perce crossblood novelist and critic W. S. Penn attributes the empowerment of Native American writing to foundations in the oral tradition and argues that Native American writing exists in the gap between Western written traditions and oral tradition. However, Penn gives agency to orality for subverting Western literary traditions: "What I am trying to suggest is that it is in the conflict of the Western written tradition with the Native American oral tradition that the gap was created; and it is because of the continuing conflict that what is surely proof of the flexible animatedness of American Indian storytelling—its ability to absorb and adapt—that mixblood writing remains postmodern" (153). Furthermore, I argue that oral performance narratives are communal speech acts that are not only dialogic with their audiences, but also reflective of originary speech acts and utterances that are intrinsically dialogic, heteroglossic, and heterogeneous. Through language, these tribal stories speak in multiple voices of multiple worlds that overlap and reflect one another.

In *All My Relatives* (1993), a comparative study of multiethnic writers in the United States, Bonnie TuSmith argues that most African American, Native American, Asian American, and Chicana/o and Latina/o writers share a sense of community characterized as the "dynamic interdependence of all life forms rather than the stagnant, conformist vision" (vii).[11] For TuSmith most multiethnic writers share the need to inscribe the "individual" in terms of the communal, thus breaking from the "ideology of the individualism," which views itself as "existing in a vacuum," and "self-interest as the ultimate value" (vii). With this premise, TuSmith argues that the communal and relational are ways that subjects are formed in differing narrative sites such as those developed by Maxine Hong Kingston, John Edgar Wideman, or Sandra Cisneros.

In the section of *All My Relatives* titled "Storytelling as Communal Survival," TuSmith observes that *Ceremony*, much like N. Scott Momaday's *House Made of Dawn*, "had not been midwifed or mediated by a white editor/co-author" (119). For ethnic writers in general, and Native American writers specifically, the power relations between editors and writers influence how texts are transformed to fit prescribed models to make them more marketable to Euro-American audiences.[12] In reference to *Ceremony*, TuSmith points out the effects on the reader of layering or splicing tribal stories with the story of Tayo's return to Laguna: "This splicing technique simulates the atmosphere of storytelling—as if the reader were actually listening to and watching an oral performance. It effectively disabuses us of arbitrary separations such as the past versus the present, dream versus reality, and the animate versus the inanimate" (122).

Likewise, in *Other Destinies* (1992) literary critic and novelist Louis Owens challenges the Westernizing force of individualism as it applies to

Native American novelists. Owens enters full-force into the contemporary cultural studies debates concerning identity, authenticity, and representation. Specifically, Owens discusses the conflicts between producing a text with an "authorial" signature, an object or commodity to be sold in the literary marketplace, and stepping "back into the collective anonymity of the tribal story teller" (11). Owens describes the cultural tensions that drive American Indian novelistic practice by Native Americans: "Yet through the inscription of an authorial signature, the Indian writer places him- or herself in immediate tension with this communal, authorless, and identity conferring source, at once highlighting the very questions of identity and authenticity the new literature attempts to resolve: 'Who really spoke? Is it really he and not someone else? With what authenticity or originality?' " (11).

To apply these questions to *Ceremony*, the opening of the novel invokes "Thought-Woman," a feminine creator in Laguna understandings of the universe and her creation.[13] Thought-Woman's names, thoughts, and stories literally generate the universe and all its worlds. *Ceremony* is a web of many stories generated by Thought-Woman and told through the narrator:

> Thought-Woman, the spider,
>   named things and
>   as she named them
>   they appeared.
>
> She is sitting in her room
>   thinking of a story now
>
> I'm telling you the story
>   she is thinking. (1)

From its opening, *Ceremony* draws into play the tensions described by Penn and Owens. We are reading a book called *Ceremony* written by Silko; however, from page one Silko decenters readers invested in linearity, causality, and the possessive space of the "I," thereby making the reader question what he or she is reading and who is telling the story. Silko negotiates her individual signature by displacing Western notions of individualism. She tells stories through a narrator: the "I" of the text mediates and transmits Thought-Woman and Thought-Woman is the ultimate agency that transmits the stories into the text.[14]

Mixbloods, Identity, and Decolonization

As a writing subject, Silko inscribes a type of consciousness within narrative that liberates the understanding of contemporary crossblood and mestiza/o identities. Her writing disrupts, heals, and transforms; it is a narrative of decolonization and reappropriation. *Ceremony* creates an open-ended and polyvocal narrative zone that disrupts colonially driven expectations of identity. Identity is inscribed through a simultaneous process of deconstruction and remembering, giving ultimate agency to the generative power of tribal stories and storytelling. To deconstruct the way one is invented by the dominant culture implies remembering modes of being in a world denigrated by colonialist discourse. Memory is central to decolonization. Memory—remembering a way of doing things that has been forgotten in neocolonial culture—is at the center of Silko's work. However, in my understanding memory is not the process where one travels back in time along a line of history to reconstruct an invented and static conception of a cultural reality that existed long ago but now is lost by the march of progress and industry.

Ceremony counterwrites the ways in which "Indians" and crossblood peoples have been invented and marginalized in colonial and neocolonial consciousness. *Ceremony* presents an array of crossblood and mestiza/o characters, especially that of Tayo, which challenge the ways in which peoples of mixed racial descent in the United States are constructed as "tragic," "impure," mongrels and are made "invisible," as discussed in the volume *Racially Mixed People* (1992) edited by Maria Root. Like Momaday's *House Made of Dawn*, the unifying narrative in *Ceremony* is about a person of mixed racial descent (Laguna Pueblo, Euro-American, and Mexican). This character, Tayo, is a veteran of World War II who returns to the Laguna community in a state of posttraumatic shock.[15] The novel charts Tayo's moves from a fractured psychic or psychological condition of disjuncture to decolonial integration within community and universe via storytelling and ceremony.[16] The return is structured within the context of stories that have existed and continue to exist before the imposition of a phonetic alphabet.

Undergoing profound decolonial transformations, Tayo journeys "home" to a feminine heterogeneous universe. I place the term "home" in quotes in order to avoid the social-science tendency to idealize an edenic or prelapsarian past within tribal cultures. This tendency perpetuates the view that real Indians are no longer alive, having lived only in the absolute past (the real ones have vanished!)—a view that denies the survival, complexity, and vitality of contemporary tribal peoples and their literary and cultural production.

In addition, the interpretation of "journey" must not be understood as the Western *telos* of self-fulfillment, as seen in such classic journeys as the *Iliad* by Homer. Even less appropriate are the archetypal models of stasis, crisis, and resolution, such as the Freytag's Triangle model, that chart the development of a protagonist in terms that are linear and causal.[17] The essay "Standin' in the Middle of the Road" (1992) by Patricia Riley distinguishes *Ceremony* from classical Western models of a protagonist's fulfillment: "Euroamerican culture's demand for individuality in the extreme, dictates that the protagonist must leave home in order to experience full self-realization. Tayo, Silko's tribal protagonist, must do the opposite. Haunted by his experiences and alienated by his 'halfbreed' status in tribal society that places a great deal on the value on 'pure' blood lines, the road to healing lies in Tayo's ability to find his way back to his community and his traditions" (9).

Tayo's seemingly individual journey "home" is a decolonizing (re)awakening that is imaginatively constructed as a continuation of stories and journeys that have been followed by the Western Pueblos, specifically the Lagunas, for thousands of years. Escaping the brutal violence of World War II, and with his alienation as a crossblood rejected on all sides, Tayo is reclaimed by the Mother Iytakiu (the feminine goddess of the Pueblo). He returns to a moving state of balance between the masculine and feminine principles of the universe, and in the human, animal, and spirit communities. As Louis Owens (1998) states, Tayo becomes an "animate transcultural space and a rich resource for his Indian community. Descending into the sacred kiva at the heart of the pueblo community in order to tell his story, Tayo is able to articulate, to make whole and heal, his split self, community, and world" (35).

By choosing Tayo rather than a fullblood to articulate the "road to healing" Silko undermines the relationship between blood quantum and identity. The issue of verifying identity is of crucial importance for tribal peoples today. For example, it can mean access to land, health care, counseling, and scholarships for higher education. In "Blood Quantum" (1992) Terry Wilson points to the federally imposed divisions between mixed and fullbloods: "Indian identity with its mixed-blood and full-blood connotations stems from attitudes and ideas fostered by the majority white culture and government. Before the white man's coming there was intermarriage and interbreeding across group lines, and no one marked the offspring as mixed-blood nor kept an accounting of blood quantums to determine tribal membership or degree of culture or acculturation" (116).

I argue that through her narrative choices Silko, a crossblood herself, is in direct agreement with this critique of internalized government-defined identity and membership practices.[18] In an interview about her own identity, Silko states: "The white men who came to the Laguna Pueblo Reservation and married Laguna women were the beginning of the half-breed Laguna people like my family, the Marmon family. I suppose at the core of my writing is the attempt to identify what it is to be a half-breed or mixed-blooded person; what it is to grow up neither white nor fully traditional Indian" (quoted in Owens 1992: 167).

As a point of textual interrelatedness with the politics of identity in the "real" world, *Ceremony* was published around the time of the landmark case of *Santa Clara Pueblo et al. v. Julia Martinez et al.* The hearings began in 1975, two years before the publication of the novel. The legal precedent dealt specifically with issues of tribal membership and entitlement to cultural and economic tribal privileges. Julia Martinez from the Santa Clara Pueblo married a Navajo man and was denied benefits for her children. The act reads as follows: "Action was brought by female member of the Indian tribe for declaratory and injunctive relief against enforcement of tribal ordinance denying membership in tribe to children of female members who married outside of the tribe while extending membership to children of male members who married outside the tribe" (436 U.S. 49, 98 S. CT. 1670).

According to the history of the case, the appeal for Julia Martinez was granted and then reversed. The reversal decision seems to be justified by the need to uphold the matrilineality of most Western Pueblos, and it is indicative of strict membership, even in intertribal unions. Used as a contextual referent, the case can help explain why Tayo was marginalized as a result of his mother's sexual union with a non-Laguna man. The case frames the importance of identity in the legal politics of the "real" world and illustrates how crossblood subjects are marginalized by juridic practices that legally define membership and exclusion.

Silko chooses Tayo as the narrative figure who is healed from the alienation of capitalism, colonialism, and militarization and is returned to a self-consciousness of interconnectedness within the universe. In choosing Tayo instead of a fullblood (the characters Rocky or Emo), Silko celebrates the power of tribal literary consciousness. And, doing so, she articulates a subject that is positioned in what I term an "other's Other." In "Blood Quantum" (1992) Terry Wilson describes the marginalization of light-skinned Indians by dark-skinned Indians. The light-skinned Indians (crossbloods) are seen as "second class" or of "other Indian status" by dark-skinned Indians (fullbloods) (121). Crossbloods occupy a space of ambivalence, what Homi Bhabha in *The Location of Culture* (1994) calls "the ambivalent world of the 'not quite/not white'" (85–92). However, in the case of Tayo the ambivalence is "not quite/not Indian enough."

Silko's narrative choice challenges the tropes of racial purity (blood quantum) as the sole determinants in identity formation and entitlement. She provides an alternate narrative that challenges tribes to break free from federally defined juridic practices of determining who is and who is not "Indian" based solely on proving their "blood quantum" and ensuring that their baptized family name is on Bureau of Indian Affairs (BIA) tribal rolls. Silko challenges those invested in the politics of indigenous survival and sovereignity to remember the ancestral stories of creation, change, and struggle and to (re)locate the processes of identity and place in the inclusiveness of tribal literary practice.

The tension that is at the center of my reading of Silko is the one between fullblood and crossblood characters. The question that drives my reading as a Chicano crossblood is how Silko plays with the colonially inflected expectations of behavior in her characters. She constructs some fullbloods as assimilationist, and some crossbloods as more Indian, thereby lifting the issues of Indian/non-Indian identity out of the sludge of racial essentialism.

To analyze these tensions, I ask: Why did the narrator in Silko create a crossblood, Tayo, as the protagonist? Why did the narrator construct a rich array of transformational crossblood characters such as Betonie, the Navajo and Mexican shaman; Night Swan, the Mexican Flamenco dancer; and T'seh, the Mount Taylor spirit woman, to aid Tayo in his journey? Why did the narrator construct some Laguna fullbloods who resist the Mother Iytakiu and who actively try to assimilate into the dominant overculture?

The desire for assimilation is a symptom of internalized colonialism or cultural schizophrenia in the Fanonian sense.[19] Silko calls internalized colonialism "witchery." The witchery of internalized colonialism affects such fullbloods as Rocky, Tayo's auntie (his principal caregiver), and Emo. Rocky deliberately avoids "the old-time ways" (51), has faith in the omniscience of "books and scientific knowledge" (76), and enlists to fight in World War II to prove his patriotism. Rocky's mother (Tayo's aunt) is a "devout Christian and not immoral or pagan like the rest of the family" (77). In the case of Emo, the character becomes so mesmerized by the erotics of cannibalistic violence produced by the U.S. military war machine that he becomes the key agent in the "the witchery of the destroyers": "Tayo could hear it in his voice when he talked about the killing—how Emo grew from each killing. Emo fed off each man he killed, and the higher the rank of the dead man, the higher it made Emo" (61). Emo acts out his victimization by what Jack Forbes in *Columbus and Other Cannibals* (1992) terms the *Wétiko* psychosis. Forbes defines the colonially imported psychosis as cannibalism based on the "consuming of another's life for one's own private purpose or profit" (34).

In *Ceremony,* old Grandma, Josiah, and other village traditionalists are constructed in direct resistance to this cannibalizing witchery, making the fullblood and crossblood issue much more complicated than simple binary reversals. The narrative tension catalyzes the exploration of representational issues and what literary critic Tey Diana Rebolledo calls the "politics of poetics" (1991). As narrative figures, crossbloods disrupt imported constructs of essential, pure, and homogeneous racial subjects: S/he is Indian, therefore . . . s/he is white, therefore. . . . These racial constructs have had their authority colonially institutionalized by scientific traditions of biologic and genetic determinism.[20]

Tayo finds himself situated or "located," to use Lata Mani's term (1990), in an intense place of racial and cultural marginalization (38). He is alienated by both the Laguna and the dominant Euro-American culture. Tayo negotiates a liminal bordered space between worlds. Painfully, he lives in the interstices of contradictory discursive and material forces—in a state of internalized colonialism or cultural schizophrenia. To use Gloria Anzaldúa's analysis of mestiza identity in *Borderlands/La Frontera* (1987) Tayo is "in a constant state of mental nepantilism, an Aztec word meaning torn between ways" (78). This state of "mental nepantilism" positions Tayo in a cultural-psychic zone characterized by "the coming together of two self-consistent but habitually incompatible frames of reference, [which] causes *un choque* or cultural collision" (78). In fact, the name Tayo, which also sounds like *taya,* the Mexican word for snake, could come from the Spanish verb *tallar*, which means to rub together or to engrave.[21] Tayo, the verb's first-person present tense, translates to "I rub." In the third-person past tense, *tayó* means "he, she, or you rubbed."

Tayo's fullblood aunt is a Christian assimilationist. According to Terry Wilson's (1992) analysis where "Blood Quanta are putatively tied to questions of culture and degrees of acculturation and assimilation" (109), Auntie is a contradiction in terms. In arguments of racialist essentialism, Auntie should be more "Indian" than the crossbloods; it should be crossbloods who embrace Christianity as a symbol of their assimilation into the overculture.

Throughout the story, the aunt continually marginalizes Tayo: "She wanted him close enough to feel excluded, to be aware of the distance between them" (67). Auntie treats Rocky, her fullblooded son, differently: "She gave Rocky little pieces of dough to play with: while she darned socks, she gave him scraps" (67). In addition, because the novel is set in the 1950s, racist attitudes of the dominant culture permeate the narrative world in which Tayo lives—attitudes that construct the products of any race-crossing with non-European racial groups as "mongrels, diluted, invisible" (Nakashima 1992: 171).

Once Tayo's mother disappeared, the aunt took over the responsibility of raising him. The commentary in the text that describes the experience of boarding school traces some of the root causes of why Tayo's mother ran away. As a young teenager, Tayo's mother struggles to maintain her cultural identity and assume her identity as a woman. Silko describes the denigration of her cultural identity and simultaneous sexualization as follows: "Shamed by what they taught her in school about the deplorable ways of the Indian people; holy missionary white people who wanted only good for the Indians, white people who dedicated their lives to helping the Indians, these people urged her to break away from her home. She was excited to see that despite the fact she was an Indian, the white men smiled at her from their cars as she walked from the bus stop in Albuquerque back to the Indian school" (68). For a young teen-age girl, this is a violent message of racial inferiority coupled with an "exoticization" of her sexuality.[22] Historically, her sexualization by the patriarchy of the Euro-American dominant cultures echoes with early colonialist attitudes toward native or tribal women and their "sensual, enticing and indulgent" nature that piqued the "carnal interest" of English men (Smits 1987: 161).

As narrative commentary, the text implicates the federal boarding

schools in fostering and perpetuating colonially "signed" sexual relationships between white men and tribal women. By such lowering of their cultural self-esteem, girls seek out affirmations through relationships with
men who are supposedly "civilized" and "superior." As evidenced by Tayo's
mother's own experience, this "conditioning" is false: "But after she had
been with them, she could feel the truth in their fists and their greedy
feeble love-making" (69).

Perhaps akin to the Métis women of Canada, Tayo's mother pays a price
that is simultaneously ostracism and colonial exoticism, made intense by
the implied and real racial and sexual violence of the dominant culture.[23]
When she leaves the Pueblo, the mother is literally and metaphorically
"naked except for her high heel shoes/under that big cottonwood tree"
(68). Auntie was the last to see her go.

Mental nepantilism has become the clash that gives birth to Tayo. As
Gretchen Ronnow states in the essay "Tayo, Death, and Desire," (1989),
Tayo inherits "a triple dose of shame . . . the 'texts' and memories of
his mother's shame" (74). The inheritance is reinforced by the actions of
Auntie, which purposefully alienate and marginalize Tayo. Auntie holds
Tayo accountable for circumstances he had no control over, which, in the
implied and real context of discursive and material colonial violence, are
understandable. As a narrative figure, Tayo is situated in multiple sites
of disenfranchisement and is victimized through replicating marginaliza-
tions enforced through Auntie, whose actions and attitudes constitute a
terse declaration of internalized colonialism.

Attempts at a Context: Origins and Cultural Heterogeneity

To understand further the politics of cultural identity, especially as they
relate to questions of multiple marginalization, I will attempt to place or
intertextualize *Ceremony* with the social, linguistic, and historical forces at
play in the U.S. Southwest. Because I was not raised on or near the Laguna
Pueblo, I consulted principal anthropological and ethnohistorical studies
of traditional Laguna culture to inform a reconstruction of the novel's implied knowledge concerning Tayo's upbringing, or lack thereof. However, I
do this conscious of how the history of anthropological practice has served
as an extension and justification of colonial practice: it is imbricated in
the invention and cultural consumption of the savage Other as a primitive
and subhuman subject. Inspired by recent interventions into the politics

of writing culture by such anthropologists as James Clifford (1997) and Renato Rosaldo (1989) to name a few, the following analysis will contribute to a mosaic of understanding regarding the historical importance of *Ceremony* as a tribally centered counternarrative that challenges the sterilizing and homogenizing impulses in ethnohistorical and anthropological writing.

Available information on traditional Laguna childrearing patterns and the importance of mothers—both physical and the all-encompassing "Ts'its'tsi'nako, Thought-Woman"—indicate that young children were born into a clan and initiated into a religious society that taught the child about his or her relationship to his or her family, culture, and universe. The child was then given the teachings of the proper attitudes, ceremonies, and rituals that would ensure the continuation of the harmonious relationship and the perpetuation of the Pueblo on the mother earth (Ellis 1950; Eggan 1950; Ortiz 1972; Swann 1988; Allen 1987; Parsons 1920).

Many studies point to the importance of clear boundaries between what is accepted and tolerated in the Western Pueblo world and what is not (Ortiz 1972; Eggan 1950; Ellis 1950; Hawley 1950). However, commentary made on how the Pueblo region served as a zone of interaction and trade both among the Pueblos and with the cities and villages in the valley of Mexico is also significant. Trade continued with the Spaniards and the Europeans (Eggan 1972; Parmentier 1979; Spicer 1962). In fact, according to many historical sources, the settlement of Laguna occurred as an aftermath of the Pueblo Revolt of 1678, wherein eastern and western peoples united to evict and hold the Spanish accountable for their barbarous acts of violence on the Puebloan peoples. Bands of Keresan peoples seeking refuge in Acoma migrated to what is now called Old Laguna (Eggan 1950; Ellis 1959), or so goes the "official" representation of history. With regard to what actually happened, I would feel more comfortable talking to a tribal elder at his or her choosing about the origins of the Laguna Pueblo.

However, the Laguna Pueblo do not have the same claim to longevity of location "being in the same Mesa for thousands of years," as do the Hopi and the Acoma peoples. With this in mind, Laguna are of a mixed background sharing many other Puebloan principles and ceremonies while retaining their own unique identity and language systems. Being hybrid and geographically more expansive than just one Mesa—not to mention having a history of intermarriage among different tribal cultures before the onslaught of European colonialism—does problematize the concept of a "pure" origin and make more emphatic the narrative tension of the fullbloods and crossbloods.

Silko may be evoking the issue of multiple origins through her imaginative references to "the Mexican cattle who are released to go back towards Mexico," as well as through the importance of her crossblood Mexican characters Betonie, Night Swan, and T'seh Montano. These references to Mexico echo chronotopes of ancient times that speak of the significant interconnection between the Valley of Mexico (Anahuac) and the multiple cultures of the Southwest.[24] Also, they reflect ethnic tensions among Hispanas/os and Puebloans in New Mexico. These issues are raised in the important literary works *Albuquerque* (1992) by Chicano writer Rudolfo Anaya and in *So Far From God* by Ana Castillo (1994). One of Anaya's protagonists is Chicano and Puebloan; the other is Chicano and Anglo, a *coyote* in the Hispano popular culture of New Mexico. As narrative acts, these chronotopes resist linearity and deny power to borders imposed by nation-state formations that crisscross the diverse indigenous lands of the Americas.

The Mexican people, mestizas/os with their "hazel green eyes" (T'seh, Betonie, and Night Swan), serve as role models and healing catalysts for Tayo.[25] Their own self-acceptance provides and reflects a psychic space/ place that allows a polyphony of cultural confluence, and this is part of what heals and regenerates Tayo, who struggles to reconcile the multiplicity by remembering the ways of the ancestors: " 'This is the only way,' she [the Mexican woman] told him. 'It cannot be done alone. We must have power from everywhere. Even the power we can get from the whites' " (150).

In *Cycle of Conquests* (1962), Edward Spicer comments on how the languages of the Pueblos changed over time, influenced by the presence of other languages, first Spanish and then English: "All observers agree that some 350 years later not more than 5 percent of Spanish words were included in the vocabulary of the three languages mentioned" (450). This incredible testament to the agency of the Pueblo peoples demonstrates their ability to resist the violent forces of imperialism (material and linguistic). With specific reference to the Laguna, Spicer comments that the Keres (Pueblos) "did not make new words after the manner of Tewa speakers, but rather extended new meanings to old words" (451). In contrast to Eastern Pueblos, "the Tewa and Tiwa, rather than borrowing words for new items brought by the Spanish (bread, coffin, hammer), made their own words"

(451). Continuing his analysis of linguistic resistance, Spicer states (1962): "Words for doing and acting—verbal expressions—were not borrowed, nor were other kinds of words, so that the main fabric was not at all affected by contact with Spain and Spanish speakers" (451).

Furthermore, regarding the impact of English on the Pueblos' language in the 1950s, Spicer notes: "In this situation, individuals lived double lives to some extent as they became proficient in English and were attracted to the cultural world which it designated and expressed" (458). Perhaps these linguistic strategies help us understand how Silko elides the multiple narratives in her text without losing the Pueblo center. Maybe Silko extends new "meanings to old words" and creates "new words." In the "Dialogic of Storyteller" (1989) Arnold Krupat comments on the tension surrounding narrative authority in the work of Silko: "For all the polyvocal openness of Silko's work, there is always the unabashed commitment to Pueblo ways as a reference point. This may be modified, updated, playfully construed; but its authority is always to be reckoned with" (65).

Dancing Away the Disease of the "White"

If the commentaries above bear on *Ceremony*'s implied knowledge, they bring us back to questions of representation and authenticity. As mentioned before, these questions are crucial for readings of tribal literatures and histories. The consequences of viewing both the production and criticism of Native American literature as creative and intellectual acts of imaginative pursuit without direct ethnic entitlement are seen in the types of literary poaching and colonial simulations committed by "white" writers trying to write "Indian poem cycles." In the name of literary freedom, some writers achieved fame on their self-pronounced ability to enunciate, articulate, and present in a more "accurate" fashion the supposed "shamanic" rhythm principles of the Native American ethno-oral tradition. As evidenced by the sales, popularity, and inscription into the canon of contemporary American poetry, these poets, including Gary Snyder, Jerome Rothenburg, and Jamake Highwater, have been well received by the general American audience, especially in the 1970s. In the essay titled "The Rise of the White Shaman as a New Version of Cultural Imperialism" (1979), Geary Hobson comments: "Writing from what they generally assume to be an Indian point of view, calling their poems 'shaman's songs,' posturing as 'shamans' and pontificating about their roles as remakers of the world through the power of the words, they seem to have no particular qualms about appropriating the transliterated forms of American Indian songs and then passing off their own poems based on those transliterations" (102).

Paula Gunn Allen, a Laguna crossblood critic, poet, and novelist who has published many works, illuminates another pole of criticism surrounding the issues of agency and representation in *Ceremony*. In her essay "Special Problems in Teaching Leslie Marmon Silko's *Ceremony*" (1990), Allen sees Silko as so close to the cultural truth of Laguna ceremonies that she accuses her of revealing a clan story. Allen admonishes Silko by stating that "the story she lays alongside it is a clan story and is not to be told outside of the clan" (383).

However, in an interview with Jane Ketz (1980), Leslie Marmon Silko clarifies that her goals in writing *Ceremony* were to "go beyond any specific kind of Laguna witchery or Navajo witchery, and to begin to see witchery as a metaphor for the destroyers, or the counterforce, that force which counters vitality and birth." Clearly, *Ceremony* is a literary product of decolonial imaginative force that articulates witchery as a metaphor that speaks both to localized identity issues and to such global concerns as the destructive and life-giving aspects within all peoples, the crises of mass starvation, resource depletion, biosphere destruction, and the threat of nuclear annihilation. The power of Silko's narrative is the space of simultaneity between Tayo and his journey toward decolonization and the global concerns of militarization and predatory capitalism.

Tayo is on the "border of time" (Bahktin 1981). As a narrative figure, he resists the witchery brought through the white people; a witchery produced by imbalances in tribal narratives; a witchery that according to Betonie taught "people to despise themselves" (132). Before Betonie draws the sand painting that accelerates Tayo's healing process, he counsels Tayo: "But white people are only tools that the witchery manipulates; and I tell you, we can deal with white people, with their machines and their beliefs. We can because we invented white people; it was Indian witchery that made white people in the first place" (132). This comment testifies to the power of "Indian" narrative practice, repatriating "writing" as a generative force and shattering the dichotomies produced by colonial discourse: white/indian, savage/civilized, literary/oral, and Christian/pagan.

Returning to the question of why Silko chose Tayo, a mixblood, to undergo the journey, I argue that Tayo has the necessary "shamanic" potential to transform the "sickness" of colonialism, violence, and enforced poverty. That is, because Tayo is part white he can fool the sickness to center on him—the sickness is in him—and he can transform it through a type of shamanic deception, and then he can purge it.

To use a term that came up in my interviews with Northwest Coast master shaman Johnny Moses regarding traditional healing practices, Tayo is a "wounded healer." Tayo's wounds, the sicknesses of white culture— colonialism, alienation, and internal colonialism—and the scars he develops, prepare him. He understands the sickness. His enunciative power is stronger than the "story of the witch's magic." Tayo's "hazel green" eyes may well be a mask to tease the sickness out of the wounded. His dance with the disease of colonialism—external, internal, and the cultural schizophrenia it produces—will transform the psychic and political stasis and entropy.

Furthermore, Silko's choice to focus on the role of crossbloods in *Ceremony* gives respect to the Mother Creator. Silko does not depend on blood quantums to determine the validity of a story; she does not state that the Mother Creator's power stops at the fullbloods. The generative power of Thought-Woman is invoked. Her power is both omniscient and infinite:

> Ts'its'tsi'nako, Thought-Woman,
>   is sitting in her room
> and whatever she thinks about
>   appears.
>
>   She thought of her sisters
>   Nau'ts'ity'i and I'tcts'ity'i,
> and together they created the Universe
>   this world
>   and the four worlds below. (1)

In the final scenes, which take place in an abandoned uranium mine, Emo, along with Pinkie and Leroy, brutalize Tayo's drinking-friend Harley in order to taunt Tayo out from the boulders. Pinkie pounds on the car trunk with Harley inside; the rythmic pounding puts Tayo on edge. The pounding announces the final test that Tayo must confront in the ceremony: "The sound set his teeth on edge and angered him in a way he had not felt since the day he had stabbed Emo. It was the sound of witchery:

smashing through the night, shrill and cold as black metal. It was the empty sound of his nightmares; even the voices he recognized" (250).

Harley, who is inside the trunk, is accused of letting Tayo go and getting "all that had been intended for Tayo" (251). Emo, Pinkie, and Leroy beat and stab Harley, then remove pieces of his flesh, light him on fire, and hang him up in the barbed wire. Emo cuts the whorl off of Harley's big toe, telling him to "'Scream!' . . . 'scream loud so he can hear you'" (251). Then, before grinding a bottle into Harley's mouth, Emo holds a bag of cut flesh and screams at Tayo: "Look at this, you half-breed! White son of a bitch! You can't hide from this! Look! Your buddy, Harley" (252). All of this is meant to provoke Tayo to enter the sickness of the destroyers and challenge them. The suspense that the narration generates is made acute by the detail of the observations: "He [Tayo] visualized the contours of Emo's skull; the GI haircut exposed thin bone at the temples, bone that would flex slightly before it gave way under the thrust of the steel edge" (252).

However, when Tayo chooses not to drive the screwdriver in the skull of Emo, it is a refusal to engage with their violence. In doing so, Tayo shifts the direction of events: "The witchery had almost ended the story according to its own plan; Tayo had almost jammed the screwdriver into Emo's skull the way the witchery had wanted, savoring the yielding bone and membrane as the steel ruptured the brain" (253).

By restraining himself, Tayo did not complete the "deadly ritual for the autumn solstice." The consequences of the stories change: Leroy is killed by Pinkie and Emo, and Pinkie is killed by Emo. Emo is told to leave Laguna, and he goes to California. The witchery neutralizes itself:

> Whirling darkness
> started its journey
> with its witchey
>   and
>   its witchery
> has returned upon it.
>
> Its witchery
> has returned
> into its belly.
>
>   .   .   .   .   .
>   It has stiffened
> with the effects of its own witchery. (261)

Silko is very clear in indicating that the witchery is not terminated, but only frozen or "stiffened." The passage is made ominous by the final refrain, repeated as a chant:

It is dead for now.
It is dead for now.
It is dead for now.
It is dead for now.

The ceremony is complete. *Ceremony* ends by returning to the beginning, Sunrise, reaffirming a time and space that is cyclical and connected to the rhythms of the earth and the universe. In the beginning of the novel, the narrator set up the story as follows:

The only cure
I know
is a good ceremony,
that's what she said.

Sunrise. (3–4)

The final page, as if all the events in the novel took place in one full cycle of day and night, states:

Sunrise,
accept this offering,
Sunrise. (262)

Blood, Identity, and the Witchery of Colonization

As discussed earlier, the crossblood shaman Betonie answers Tayo's concern about the hegemony of white culture, "their wars, their bombs, their lies," by saying that the belief that "all evil resides with white people" is a "trickery" of "witchcraft" (132). Betonie tells Tayo that "we can deal with white people, with their machines and their beliefs. We can because we invented white people; it was Indian witchery that made white people in the first place" (132). Then Betonie tells the story of how white people were created by a witch, whose story "set in motion" the invasion of the Americas.

In *Ceremony*, the witch was nameless and "no one ever knew where this witch came from/which tribe" (134). However, in a later novel, *Almanac of the Dead,* Silko names many witches and forms of witchery through the character of Yoeme, which in Yaqui is the sacred name of "the people," starting with 1533 Spanish conquistador and slave raider Diego de Gúzman, the famed Yaqui butcher. *Almanac* makes the witchery specific to militarized violence in the Americas, U.S.-backed death squads, trafficking in human organs, serial killings, bestiality, neonazism, brutal sexual violence, the destruction of ecosystems for corporate and real estate gain, and the insidious processes of internalized colonialism in peoples whose ancestry is tied to the struggles against colonial and neocolonial appropriations of land, culture, and memory. In both novels, Silko subverts official practices of history that understand colonialism and cultural domination as linear materialist movements of manifest destiny from east (Europe/New England) to west (Americas/California), and north (Alaska) to south (Argentina). Silko's interpretation of the invasion of the Americas relocates the ultimate agency to the tribal peoples and the generative power of stories and ceremonies: they create and counterbalance witchery. In doing so, she disrupts paternalistic views of native peoples as passive victims. The subversion of historical understanding and method places Western civilization—and its notions of cultural superiority—literally on its head. For Silko, the Western empire is a puppet of witchery and blood sorcery.

Silko's understanding of colonialism challenges those commited to the multilevel tasks of decolonizing from imperial and patriarchal forces of subjection to ask and consider some of the most complicated and profound questions in subaltern cultural studies of the Americas. Without denying the colonially embedded privilege of "whiteness," I ask: If white people were created by Indian witchery, are they not somehow Indian, too? Are mixed bloods contaminated by the witchery of white blood? Are all white people agents of witchery? If so, why does Silko have characters such as Emo, a Laguna fullblood who thrives on death and violence (in *Ceremony*), or Menardo, who denigrates his identity as a Mexican Indian (Zapotecan) and whose "universal insurance" guarantees the smooth operation of right-wing terrorism and ladino and foreign business interests in Mexico and Central America (in *Almanac*)? Perhaps Silko is forcing us to think less about who we are racially and our relative percentages of Indian, Anglo, or Spanish blood quantums, to name a few, and to think more about where we stand in relation to the witchery of the destroyers (the wetíko psychosis) whose worship of blood transcends blood quantums.

4

Toward a Hermeneutics
of Decolonization:
Reading Radical Subjectivities
in *Borderlands/La Frontera:*
The New Mestiza by
Gloria Anzaldúa

Third space feminism allows a look to the past through the present always already marked by the coming of that which is still left unsaid, unthought. Moreover, it is in the maneuvering through time to retool and remake subjectivities neglected and ignored that third space feminism claims new histories, Chicana feminist histories that may one day—finally—"forget the Alamo."—Emma Pérez, *The Decolonial Imaginary*

When subaltern subjects in the U.S./Mexico borderlands perform what Mary Louise Pratt (1992) calls "autoethnographic expression" to contest how they have been simulated and disciplined by racialized and sexualized master-narratives of savagization, infantilization, and criminalization, they engage in decolonial processes that (re)claim and enunciate bodies of knowledge that are subjugated, silenced, and outlawed by colonialist and patriarchal apparatuses of power and representation.[1] As the previous chapter suggests, Leslie Marmon Silko, through the enunciatory figure of *Ceremony*'s mestizo character Tayo, inscribes a model of decolonization that challenges the internalization of federally imposed norms that equate "blood quantum" with "true" Indian identity. In doing so, she returns the epistemology of subject-formation to matrifocal tribal stories of change, creation, and transformation that predate the arrival of the European colonial empire in the Americas. Post(?)colonial hybridized narrative forms that mix, overlap, and conjoin genres, languages, and cultural epistemologies subvert the taxonomy of genres whose hierarchic demarcations evidence the disciplinatory apparatus of modernity.[2]

Gloria Anzaldúa, a Chicana from the south valley Texas/Mexico border region and one of the most important writers, feminists, and cultural activists to emerge in the 1980s and 1990s, prescribes an "unruly" (Fraser 1989) enunciatory practice that converges radical autobiographic, historiographic, *testimonio,* and theoretical modalities of self-representations that she calls *autohistoriateoría* (autohistorytheory; my translation).[3] This chapter is dedicated to understanding how the pluri-genre *Borderlands/La Frontera: The New Mestiza* (1987) by Gloria Anzaldúa (reprinted in 1999 with a scholarly introduction by Sonia Saldívar-Hull) puts into practice a radical hermeneutics of antisexist decolonial *autohistoriateoría. Borderlands* negotiates the "real" and the discursive in ways that chronicle and challenge the multiplicity of oppression that impinges on Chicana/o and Mexicana/o communities along the U.S./Mexico border. The essay "Anzaldúa's *Frontera*" (1996) by Norma Alarcón describes these geopolitics of power in the U.S./Mexico borderlands as follows: "These borderlands are spaces where, as a result of expansionary wars, colonization, juridico-immigratory policing, coyote exploitation of émigrés and group vigilantes, formations of violence are continuously in the making" (44). At the same time, *Borderlands* charts how oppression travels across the registers of race, class, gender, and sexuality and provides models of political and epistemological resistance that put into practice multilayered and rebellious enunciations that ground U.S. third world feminist oppositional subjectivities to the specific U.S./Mexico borderlands geopolitics of power.

This chapter is divided into several interrelated sections. First, I contextualize the heteroglossic poetic terrains of *Borderlands* to frame how feminist, Latin American *testimonio,* and Chicana critiques of the bourgeois, Eurocentric, and male-dominated field of autobiography and autobiographical studies aid our understanding of autohistoricization in the pluri-genre *Borderlands*. Then, I consider how *Borderlands* challenges the internalization of colonially imposed viewpoints and value systems that denigrate Chicana/o and Mexicana/o and indigenous peoples—specifically women. *Borderlands* offers strategies of decolonization that engage the genealogical range of mestiza/o identities (Indigenous, African, and European) by (re)centering gender, sexuality, and desire in the vocabulary and practice of cultural resistance. "On the Social Construction of Whiteness within Selected Chicana/o Discourses" (1997) by Chicana theorist Angie

Chabram-Dernersesian characterizes the pluri-topic diacritics of Anzaldúa's decolonial project: "She does this in many ways, taking us light years ahead of patriarchal nationalist narratives that plot Chicano histories of expropriation along a unidimensional racial line and a collective epic legacy full of traditional cultural bliss, compulsory heterosexuality, and singularly racial traumas" (124).

Anzaldúa conceptualizes or (re)conceptualizes Chicana/o identity to embrace the Mesoamerican past as a living cultural and psychic force that informs and sustains the present. *Borderlands* bridges the separation between Chicana/o and Native American autobiographic, literary, and historical expression, articulating a consciousness of the Americas that challenges the hegemonic orders of Euro-American, Spanish, and Mexican nation-states at the same time that it confronts sexism and homophobia in the Anglo, Chicano, and Mexican communities. Walter Mignolo (1995) describes the enunciatory space of transcultural oppositional aesthetics in Anzaldúa's project as follows: "Gloria Anzaldúa, for instance, has articulated a powerful alternative aesthetic and political hermeneutic by placing herself at the crossroads of three traditions (Spanish-American, Nahuatl, and Anglo-American) and carving a locus of enunciation whose different ways of knowing and of individual and collective expressions meet" (13).

Through the agency of writing, Anzaldúa enunciates herself as a speaking subject that resists both genre boundaries and national boundaries, challenging the racist, sexist, and heterosexist operations of disciplining power in the Anglo-dominated political economy in general and the patriarchal and homophobic regulation of power in Mexican and Chicano cultural economies in particular. Anzaldúa articulates how Chicanas/os, especially working-class Chicana lesbians, are positioned along axes of multiple marginalization, and she posits models of resistance, opposition, and transformation. With respect to sexuality and gender in *Borderlands,* Chabram argues that this "is the other narrative; it features another kind of wounding and exile, exposes and contests gender relations and the patriarchal traditions of Mexican culture, and imagines a socially nuanced lesbian identity" (125).

Anzaldúa's exploration of identity is also driven by incisive critiques of material economies of exploitation, marginalization, and dependency of Mexican labor in the U.S. economy. In *The Dialectics of Our America* (1991), José David Saldívar captures the intensity of Anzaldúa's multilevel critique of Chicana/o identity, framed against racially coded conditions of material subalternity imposed by late global capitalism: "At the heart of her dissent from racialist purity and patriarchal postmodernity is her deep hostility to the process of late capitalism. For Anzaldúa, multinational capital and agribusiness have an impact on the physical world of the Borderlands that is just as devastating as their effects on Chicano workers and landowners" (83).

Borderlands is comprised of two major parts that mirror each other in several important ways. The first part, *"Atravesando Fronteras/* Crossing Borders," is comprised of seven essays; the second, *"Un agitado viento/ Ehécatl,* the Wind," is divided into six sections of poetry. Both the essays and the poetry chart the coming into being of mestiza consciousness as patterns of movements that shift from violent ruptures and dislocations to transgressions and to (re)constitutions of generative epistemic space. "Gloria Anzaldúa's *Borderlands/La Frontera"* (1991) by Chicana theorist Yvonne Yarbro-Bejarano aptly summarizes the enunciatory movements of mestiza consciousness that wind through the essays of *Borderlands:* "The first six essays of the book inscribe a serpentine movement through different kinds of mestizaje that produce a third thing that is neither this nor that but something else: the blending of Spanish, Indian, and African to produce the mestiza, of Spanish and English to produce Chicano language, of male and female to produce the queer, of mind and body to produce the animal soul, the writing that 'makes face' " (17). The essay section of *Borderlands* ends, as the title of the seventh essay suggests, by articulating *"La conciencia de la mestiza:* Towards a New Consciousness." This final essay celebrates the enunciation of mestiza consciousness that operates by dislocating the conditions of multiple marginalization into emergent terrains of generative epistemic space: "In attempting to work out a synthesis, the self has added a third element which is greater than the sum of its severed parts. That third element is a new consciousness—a mestiza consciousness—and through it is a source of intense pain, its energy comes from continual creative motion that keeps breaking down the unitary aspect of each new paradigm" (80).

In addition to the epistemic shifts in differential consciousness described above, the final part of the seventh essay, *"El retorno,"* returns the reader to the regenerative and life-giving forces of the earth, Tonanztin, to reaffirm cyclical understandings of "growth, death, decay, birth. The soil prepared again and again, impregnated, worked on. A constant changing of forms, *renacimientos de la tierra madre"* (113). As a reflection of the "El retorno" section of the final essay, in the final grouping of the poetry of the book, also titled "*El Retorno* (The Return)," Anzaldúa warns the younger generation of Chicanas not to give into the forces of cultural and material marginalization and sexism, and she tells them to honor their ancestral lineages of identity in the Americas:

> Don't give in *mi prietita*
> tighten your belt, endure
> Your lineage is ancient,
> firmly planted, digging underground
> toward the current, the soul of *tierra madre*—
> your origin. (202)

The referencing of the earth recuperates a Mesoamerican understanding of the cyclical nature of time, change, and growth and speaks to the importance of the land that was stolen, swindled, and appropriated by Spanish and Mexican *criollo* colonial regimes and the U.S. government in its imperial expansion. For Anzaldúa, the earth is not a site that is parceled, sold, and exploited for natural resources or turned into a growing area of monocrops whose grain, fruit, and vegetable yields are sold to the highest bidder. In an illuminating interview with Karen Ilkas, Anzaldúa discusses how her experience as a migrant laborer and then a teacher of migrant children formed her and also gave her first-hand respect for the struggles of migrant campesinos: "So I had learned the hardships of working in the fields and of being a migrant laborer myself, and that experience formed me. I have a very deep respect for all the migrant laborers, the so-called *campesinos*" (1999: 227).

Land is a source of revitalization, renewal, and sustenance that was in the stewardship of campesinos and indigenous communities before the creation of the slave-like Spanish and Mexican criollo hacienda systems, the bloody acquisition as U.S. territory, and the control by U.S. multinational agribusiness. As Anzaldúa states in the description of "*La crisis*": "*Los gringos* had not stopped at the border. By the end of the nineteenth century, powerful landowners in Mexico, in partnership with U.S. colonizing companies, had dispossessed millions of Indians of their land" (*Borderlands:* 10). In my reading of *Borderlands,* then, the enunciation of mestiza subjectivity operates simultaneously as the innovative forging of ethnic, linguistic, and sexual mestizaje, the affirmation of the old—even ancient— ancestral lineages to the Americas, the (re)clamation of stolen land and the repatriation of sovereignty, and a recognition of the cyclical processes of Tonanztin.

The Poetics of Heterotopic Space: Disrupting Genres

Like the radical mestiza subject articulated by Anzaldúa, *Borderlands* resists attempts to classify its form and structure into a preset taxonomy of narrative practice. In fact, *Borderlands* challenges the epistemological drives that form taxonomic classifications, blurring and traversing boundaries and borders between genres and between different modes of narrative practice and representation. *Borderlands* operates in the modes of autobiography, historiography, and testimony to articulate what Michel Foucault in "Of Other Spaces" (1986) calls "heterotopia." However, *Borderlands*'s heterotopic spaces of heterogeneous cultural practices are grounded to the geopolitical specifics of the U.S./Mexico borderlands. Here, the disciplinary mechanisms of the U.S. nation-state (INS, corrections, media, schools) attempt to protect the monologic and monolingual "utopias" of a whites-only and English-only America founded on principles of democracy and equality.

Critical Terrains (1991) by Lisa Lowe reterritorializes Foucault's notion of heterotopia and employs the term "heterotopicality" to understand the multiplicity of discursive sites that inform and contest the colonialist practices of orientalism. Lowe argues that "on discursive terrains, such as the one in which orientalism is one formation, articulations and rearticulations emerge from a variety of positions and sites, as well as from other sets of representational relations, including those that figure race, class, nation, gender, and sexuality" (15). In terms specific to the heterotopicality of *Borderlands*, "Feminism on the Border" (1991) by Sonia Saldívar-Hull considers the unclassifiable nature of the heterotopic *Borderlands* as a postmodern act of resistance to Anglo-centric modes of interpretive regulation that mirror the societal regulation, disciplining, and marginalization of Chicana/o and Mexicana/o peoples: "Anzaldúa's text is itself a *mestizaje*, a postmodernist mixture of autobiography, historical document, and poetry collection. Like the people whose life it chronicles, *Borderlands* resists genre boundaries as well as geopolitical borders" (211).

In even the title of the first chapter, "The Homeland, Aztlán/*El otro Mexico*," the reader is taken into the multilingual world (Spanish, Nahuatl, and English) with referential codes that mark this text as emerging in a living and heterogeneous matrix of living Chicana/o historical, cultural, and gender consciousness. Walter Mignolo (1995) characterizes this matrix of border consciousness as follows: "Instead, Anzaldúa displaces the accent from the delimitation of geographical spaces to their borders, locations in which languages (Spanish, English, Nahuatl) and gender (male, female, homosexual, heterosexual) are the conditions of possibility for the creation of spaces-in-between as a different way of thinking" (xiii).

The chapter begins with two important excerpts that immediately catapult the reader into the paradoxical, conflicted, and heteroglossic cultural spatiality of the *frontera*. The first is from the *corrido* (folk ballads) titled "El otro México" by the famous *conjunto Norteño* "Los Tigres del Norte" from their album *Ven,* (Fonovisa, 1985). This corrido reflects the diasporic and repressive conditions of Mexican immigrant workers and adds to the Los Tigres del Norte's extensive repertoire of corridos that express the desires and the materialist socialcultural forces that Mexican immigrant workers unwittingly negotiate in the United States.

El otro México que acá hemos construido
el espacio es lo que ha sido
territorio nacional.
Esté el esfuerzo de todos nuestros hermanos
y latinoamericanos que han sabido
progressar.

(The other Mexico which we have made here,
this space was once part
of our national territory.
Here are the efforts of all our compatriots
and Latin Americans who have known
how to advance.) (my translation)

The *corrido* celebrates how the lost territories of Mexico are gradually being repatriated and reclaimed by Mexicans and Latin Americans who (re)introduce and (re)vitalize Chicana/o and Latina/o cultural practices. The song conveys a feeling of agency, movement, and accomplishment, marked by the past perfect tense use of the second-person plural of the verb *construir* (to construct): "El otro México que acá hemos construido" (The other Mexico which we have made here; my translation) denoting concrete gains. The final part of the lyric, "que han sabido progresar," pays homage to the diasporic struggles of all Latin Americans to (re)constitute home and community in the United States and to advance collectively "out of the shadows" of social and cultural marginalization (Ruiz 1998).

The second excerpt in the first essay of *Borderlands* is taken from *Aztecas del Norte* (1973) by Jack Forbes, a politically important cultural history of Chicanas/os from pre-Cortesian times to the present. Forbes, a Powhátan-Renate historian of indigenous peoples in the United States, Mexico, and the Caribbean, argues that Chicanos are detribalized indigenous peoples who compose "the largest single tribe or nation of Anishinabeg (Indians) found in the United States today." The placement of the excerpt by Los Tigres in conjunction with the one by Forbes juxtaposes two important aspects of Chicano/Mexicano identity: first, the diasporic movements of Mexican workers—an imposed liminality; and, second, the historical root-edness of Chicana/o and Mexicana/o peoples in Aztlán, or what was once northern Mexico and what is now called the U.S. Southwest (California, Texas, Arizona, Colorado, Nevada, Oklahoma, and New Mexico).

The poetry of El otro Mexico evokes the borderzone between Mexico and the United States, marked by allusions to wind, earth, water, and blood: "I stand at the edge where earth touches ocean/where two overlap/a gentle coming together/at other times a violent clash" (1). The poetic intro-duction makes continuous reference to the ocean, waves, and water. Even the way that the stanzas are structured is reminiscent of the waves as they rhythmically expand and recede:

> *Miro al mar atacar*
> > *la cerca en* Border Field Park
> > > *con sus buchones de agua.*
> > an Easter Sunday resurrection
> > of the brown blood in my veins.

At first, these images created a dissonance in my thinking about the geog-raphy of the U.S./Mexico borderlands because, apart from an entry point along the Pacific coast in a San Diego state park and the relatively narrow Rio Grande river, the borderlands terrain is so hot and arid that countless Mexican border crossers have died from dehydration and overexposure. However, the poetic narrator draws on images of the ocean and water to imply a constant cyclical movement of migration of peoples and transfor-mative cultural forces from Mexico to the United States, thereby illustrat-ing the porosity of the U.S./Mexico border:

But the skin of the earth is seamless.
                The sea cannot be fenced,
       el mar does not stop at borders.
    To show the white man what she thought of his arrogance,
         Yemaya blew that wire fence down.[4]

These images, which connote a fluidity of movement, are juxtaposed to the fences and barbed wire of the U.S./Mexico border, ironically called the "tortilla curtain." In the logic of the poetic introduction, the speaking subject—the "I" that is both singular and collective—bleeds through the holes in the fence, causing the wire to rust and weaken by the constant flow of water, people, and culture that began juridically with the Treaty of Guadalupe Hidalgo in 1848. The poetic "I" charts movements from south to north and north to south as a constant resilience and flow of cultural (re)migration marked by the violent conceptualization of the border as a wound on the body of the earth:

1, 950 mile long open wound
      dividing a pueblo, a culture,
      running down the length of my body,
         staking fence rods in my flesh,
            splits me splits me
              me raja me raja

In these stanzas the poetic subject shifts from singular to collective to becoming the body that the border violates, splits, and wounds. The mestiza subject, then, is positioned at the literal crossroads of this wound with such profound multilingual exclamations as "this is my home this thin edge of barbwire," repeated in working-class Spanish, "Yo soy un puente tendido/del mundo gabacho al del mojado" (I am a bridge stretched between the world of the *gabacho* [Anglo] and *mojado* [Mexican immigrant]; my translation).

In these dramatic terms, Anzaldúa articulates the multiple and intersected conditions of Chicana/o subjectivity as violently situated in the interstices of cultures and nation-states. Clearly, Anzaldúa's poetry puts into practice what Rafael Pérez-Torres in *Movements in Chicano Poetry* (1995) considers the primacy of Chicana/o culture—the interstitial flow of heteroglossic discourse: "Chicano culture—particularly poetry—moves both through the gaps and across the bridges between numerous cultural sites: the United States, Mexico, Texas, California, the rural, the folkloric, the postmodern, the popular, the elite, the traditional, and the tendentious, the avant-garde" (3).

However, *Chicano Poetics* (1997) by theorist and poet Alfred Arteaga reminds us how these complex markers of ancestral rootedness and the resistive flow of heteroglossic cultural discourse that shape the diverse articulations of Mexicana/o, Chicana/o, and indigenous identity are disavowed in the nativist imaginary of the U.S. nation-state: "The Chicano is not equated with the Indian because to do so would ascribe to the Chicano the status of native. Because of the border and Mexico, the Chicano can be envisioned as foreigner, so that after rhetorical gymnastics, the Anglo immigrant can write the self as the undisputed original civilized human occupant. Therefore, the Chicano is not indigenous . . . the Chicano is the pest, is the bracero who had the audacity to stay and have children in gangs and on welfare" (88).

By the time we finish reading the first section of Anzaldúa's first essay, *El otro México,* we have come across a *corrido,* revisionary history and poetry transmitted by a speaking subject whose articulations of physical and psychic bodies are both singular and collective, poetic and prosaic, social, global, regional, and intensely personal. So, I ask: What kind of text are we dealing with here? How do we describe the text in terms of its genre? What is the relationship between genre and subjectivity? How does this text challenge preexisting categories of genre definitions, literary analysis, and modes of representation in its desire to enunciate and evoke mestiza subaltern subjectivity?

The essay "Resisting Autobiography" (1992) by feminist theorist Caren Kaplan questions the relationship between genre, subjectivity, and the practice of autobiography. Kaplan asks these important questions: Is autobiography "recoverable as a feminist writing strategy"? Is "Western autobiography criticism itself a form of colonial discourse"? Does "Western feminist autobiography continue postcolonial forms of cultural domination"? (116).

To trace the tradition of Western autobiography, a predominantly male activity of social privilege, Kaplan analyzes the "Conditions and Limits of Autobiography" (1980) by Georges Gusdorf, a foundational essay in contemporary Western autobiographic studies.[5] Kaplan argues that Gusdorf links the autobiographic genre to the formation of national patriarchal subjects whose will to consciousness allegorizes the development, maintenance, and dominance of nation-states. In the life story of a prominent citizen such as Benjamin Franklin, the "I" becomes "a sort of national allegory" (118).

In the words of Gusdorf, autobiography "expresses a concern peculiar to Western man; a concern that has been of good use in his systematic conquest of the universe and that he has communicated to men of the other cultures" (28). For Gusdorf, autobiographic practice is wholly Eurocentric, an unabashedly imperialist and patriarchal project maintaining and enforcing notions of colonially produced civility. Ideologies that underlie traditional autobiographies are also those that drive nation-states and their hegemonic apparatuses of social privilege.

To understand autobiographical practices that are not in the exclusive domain of bourgeois men articulating the ideal citizen and nation-state self, Kaplan examines autobiographic activity that exists at the margins of traditional autobiographic limit or law. Subsequently, these limits of genre are also the limits and margins of nation-states: the laws circumscribe the limits of tolerable behavior, enforcing the authority of states and their hegemonies. Kaplan argues that autobiographic practice at the margins of genre and society should be considered "as counterlaw, or *out-law*." Following Derridian deconstructive logic, Kaplan argues that out-law genres "break the rules of the genre" and deconstruct the "master genres," revealing "the power dynamics embedded in literary production, distribution, and reception" (119).[6] For Kaplan, autobiographic criticism should attune itself to an investigation of both the sociopolitical context and the micropolitics of power in specific autobiographic sites. Echoing Mohanty, Alarcón, and other feminist scholars, Kaplan argues that "instead of a discourse of individual authorship, we find a discourse of situation; a politics of location" (119). Kaplan's mode of analysis provides important insights to how feminist autobiographic practices can disrupt the "Law of the Father" whose symbolic logic regulates the reproduction of imperializing "Men of Reason."

However, the term "out-law" as such has connotations that are problematic when applied to the autoethnographic practices of Chicanas/os and other postcolonial peoples (Filipinos, Yoeme, Maoris, Roma, and Senegalese, to name a few). The term "out-law" perpetuates ways in which non-Western peoples, women, gays, and lesbians have been and are inferiorized, sexualized, and criminalized by patronymic and heteronymic juridic apparatuses of colonial nation-states in general, and the U.S. nation-state in particular.[7] Resonating with the frontier history of the United States — the genocide and forced removal of original inhabitants during Westward expansion — the designation "out-law" furthers colonialist views of peoples living on the supposed frontiers of "civilization": the fierce and noble "savages." In this way the term sanctifies the use of disciplinatory and lethal violence on Native and Mexicana/o peoples because they are deemed wild and "lawless," people who need to be subdued into abject docile bodies and/or erased from the march of Westward expansion. To recap the crude logic of manifest destiny, the U.S. cavalry and the Texas Rangers are sent to "lawless" territories to impose or restore "law and order" and facilitate colonization by invading Euro-Western cultures, thus negating the brutality of racial and sexual murder, extermination, and forced removal.[8]

To illustrate how these processes of legalized racial and sexual violence in the colonial history of the U.S./Mexico borderlands translate into literal desecrations of the abjected other, one needs only to examine the consequences of figures who were perceived as threats to the racial- and gender-coded social order of the United States. This is seen, for example, in the case of the renowned social bandit of the 1850 California gold rush, Joaquín Murieta, who, after being persecuted, ambushed, and executed, was decapitated and his head was pickled and put on traveling display; or the case of the shrunken head of Mexican Revolutionary leader Pancho Villa, a prized collectors' item among prominent Western capitalists. Consider the reprint of a poster advertising the traveling exhibition of the "the head of the renowned bandit! Joaquin!" shown in Figure 2.

According to *The Life and Adventures of Joaquin Murieta, The Celebrated California Bandit* (1854) by Yellow Bird (John Rollin Ridge), a Cherokee-Anglo crossblood, the commissioned California Ranger Captain Love who captured Joaquín Murieta was paid not only the "sum of one thousand dollars," the reward money posted by the governor of California for the capture of the "bandit, dead or alive," but according to Yellow Bird's account: "And subsequently, on the fifteenth day of May 1854, the Legislature of California, considering that his truly valuable services in ridding the country of so great a terror — were not sufficiently rewarded, passed an act granting him an additional sum of five thousand dollars" (158).

Perhaps the starkest example of legalized vigilante violence during the California gold rush years aimed at the Mexicana/o community in general, and women in particular, is the barbaric lynching of Josefa Vasquez, a pregnant woman from Sonora, Mexico. In 1851, Josefa, popularly known as

Fig 2

Juanita de Downieville, in an attempt to defend herself against vile verbal abuse and rape in her own home, stabs and kills Fred Cannon, a well liked Anglo-American miner. At four o'clock that afternoon, when a Kangaroo trial "proved" that Juanita was an "antisocial prostitute" and Cannon was a "peaceful" and "honest" man, Josefa was lynched. *Occupied America* (1988) by Rodolfo Acuña, a Chicano historian, evokes this tragic and brutal moment as follows: "Senator John B. Weller was in town but he did nothing to stop the hanging. Weller was an ambitious politician who was later to become governor, and one voteless Mexican made no difference. Over 2,000 men lined the river to watch Josefa hang at the bridge. After this, lynching became commonplace and Mexicans came to know Anglo-American democracy as '*Linchocracia*'" (119).

Nevertheless, movies and other expressions of popular mainstream U.S. culture reflect a fascination with certain types of antiheroes who supposedly live outside the law: Clint Eastwood in *The Good, the Bad, and the Ugly*, Peter Fonda in *Born to be Wild*, and James Dean in *Rebel Without a Cause*. Meanwhile, for Chicanas/os, African Americans, and people of color in general, the conditions of cultural and material marginality are such that they are subjected by the disciplinatory apparatus of the law whether they choose to or not. In cultures of dominance, criminality is "naturalized" to the other: deviance and sexual violence are essentialized to race, ethnicity, sexuality and class, justifying police violence, repression, and containment.[9] Racialized bodies, women's bodies, and nonheterosexual bodies are sites converged by juridic-legal discourses marking them as Others and transgressors of laws of natural order and therefore dangerous to society. In the disciplinary apparatus of the colonialist nation-state, to live outside the law is to be a criminal; to live outside the law means that you live fully "subjected" by the law with intersecting consequences of police and *migra* harassment, imprisonment, and death. For criminalized bodies, survival and resistance operate against what *Discipline and Punish* by Michel Foucault (1979) terms the power relations of the "body politic" that subjugate human bodies into docile objects: "But the body is also directly involved in a political field; power relations have an immediate hold upon it; they invest it; mark it; train it; torture it; force it to carry out tasks, to carry out ceremonies, to emit signs" (25).

In fact, Anzaldúa's "out-law" text articulates specifically how the U.S./ Mexico border criminalizes peoples of Mexican, Indian, and Latin American descent, as well as those living both at the margins of the nation-state and the edge of the juridic-legal apparatuses that regulate their legislative functioning. Anzaldúa addresses the material appropriation of Mexican and Indian land by the Anglo-American empire after the U.S./Mexico war. She cites William H. Wharton's eugenicist rhetoric taken from Arnoldo de León's dramatic history of manifest destiny in Texas *They Called Them Greasers* (1983):

> The justice and benevolence of God
> will forbid that . . . Texas should again
> become a howling wilderness
> trod only by savages, or . . . benighted
> by the ignorance and superstition,
> the anarchy and rapine of Mexican misrule. (7)

Anzaldúa, then, juxtaposes this proclamation of Anglo-American racial superiority that will "enlighten," "improve," and "redeem" the "wilderness of Texas" with a description of what happened to the Mexican and Indian peoples once Anglo-Americans settled in Texas: "The Gringo locked into the fiction of white superiority seized complete political power, stripping Indians and Mexicans of their land while their feet were still rooted in it. *Con el destierro y el exilio fuimos desuñados, destroncados, destripados*—we were jerked out by the roots, truncated, disemboweled, dispossessed, and separated from our identity and our history" (7). The graphic evocation of the brutal violations of physical bodies, psychic space, and dispossession and forced exile of Mexican and Indian peoples echoes timelessly with the desecration of Mexica and Maya peoples in the 1521 Conquest of Mexico discussed in chapter 1.

Anzaldúa continues telling counterhistory by arguing how Mexicans and Indians had no legal recourse because the new legal system protected the authority of the Anglo-American empire and did not honor the Treaty of Guadalupe Hidalgo (1848) and individual land claims: "But as the courts, law enforcement officials, and government officials not only ignored their pleas but penalized them for their efforts, *tejanos* had no other recourse but armed retaliation" (8). Anzaldúa then moves to a voice that is more personal, autobiographic, and testimonial, comparing how these forces of manifest destiny bore on her family's history: "My grandmother lost all her cattle, they stole her land" (8).

What Is Latent in the Manifesto?

Like Kaplan's essay, Sidonie Smith's *Subjectivity, Identity, and the Body* (1993) provides an interpretive model to further understand the relationship of genre and subjectivity in *Borderlands*. Smith shares Kaplan's argument that normative or hegemonic autobiographic practice and criticism promote imperial and patriarchal dominance. Smith brilliantly argues that after the "dawn of the Renaissance" the notion of a fixed and extra-linguistic universal human subject moved to the vanguard of philosophical thought: "Subsequently pressed through the mills of eighteenth century enlightenment, early nineteenth century romanticism, expanding bourgeois capitalism, and Victorian optimism, the individual came by the mid nineteenth century to be conceptualized as a 'fixed, extra linguistic' entity consciously pursuing its unique destiny" (5). Smith argues that the universal subject is synonymous with the metaphysical and the autonomous: stable, knowable, and circumscribed by a "certitude of rationality." Smith clarifies how the universal subject is conceived, "All I's are ontologically identical rational beings—but all I's are also unique. This is the stuff of myth, imperious and contradictory" (8). However, hierarchies are also implicit in the universal subject: "Founded on exclusionary practices, this democratic self positions on its border all that is termed the 'colorful,' that is, 'other, exotic, unruly, irrational' or 'unnatural' " (9). Hence, like the civilizing subject discussed in chapter 1, the universal subject constitutes itself through the disavowal of the Other: the civilized and savage, the moral and the transgressor, and the good citizen and the criminal. These binary pairs are the dialectics that drive imperial overcultures.

Smith argues that the project of the universal self is dependent on the abjection and subordination of the "female subject," as well as on those subjects who are positioned "peripherally to the dominant group": "The history of the universal subject thereby underwrites a history of the female subject, for the architecture of the universal subject rests upon and supports the founding identifications of those that are nonuniversal, the colorful, among whom is woman" (11).

The final chapter, "Autobiographical Manifestos" analyzes autobiographical expressions that claim a politics of emancipation for subjects in the margins. As a term, "manifesto" usually refers to public proclamations that designate an ideological position. In leftist and cultural nationalist politics, manifestos challenge the status quo and call people to engage in direct social change. Examples include the Black Panther "Ten Point Plan for Liberation," the Chicano "Plan de Santa Barbara," and, of course, "The Communist Manifesto" by Marx and Engels (1848).[10]

Smith further argues that the autobiographical manifesto "contests the old inscriptions, the old histories, the old politics," offering "an arena in which the revolutionary subject can insist on identity in service to emancipatory politics" (157): "Intent on bringing culturally marginalized experiences out from under the shadow of an undifferentiated otherness, the autobiographical manifesto anchors its narrative itinerary on the specificities and locales of time and space, the discursive surround, the material ground, the provenance of histories" (158).

However, when Smith considers *Borderlands,* she provides little to help develop an understanding of the specific historical junctures that inform Anzaldúa's writing project. Anzaldúa "brings to light" a subjectivity that has resisted and resists victimization on multiple fronts even before the European invasion of Mexico in 1521: the indigenous woman, campesina, and Chicana. Anzaldúa writes from the perpsective of an indigena, Mexicana, and Chicana subjectivity marginalized by gender, race, class, and sexuality in each nation-state: Aztec, Spanish, Mexican, and the U.S.[11] For example, in the essay called, *"La herencia de Coatlicue/*The Coatlicue State" Anzaldúa addresses the negotiation of identity across layers of imposed shame and inferiority: "No, it isn't enough that she is female—a second class member of a conquered people who are taught to believe that they are inferior because of their indigenous blood, believe in the supernatural, and speak a deficient language. Now, she beats herself over her head for her 'inactivity,' a stage that is as necessary as breathing. But that means being Mexican. All her life she's been told that Mexicans are lazy. She has had to work twice as hard as others to meet the standards of the dominant culture which have, in part, become her standards" (49).

However, for Smith, *Borderlands* does not promote "a rhetoric of revolutionary explosiveness" but one that "persistently evokes geography." Because of this, Smith mistakenly argues that Anzaldúa writes within a pastoral tradition. Smith locates *Borderlands* in a literary movement that responds to specific historical conditions in Europe: the growth of industrialization and the flourishing of the metropolis. Pastorals such as *Far from the Madding Crowd* by Thomas Hardy romanticize life in the countryside, its values and its simple, good-hearted peasants. Pastorals, however, idealize a way of life that was in itself severe and seldom experienced first-hand by the aristocratic or bourgeois interlocutors.[12]

Like the noble farmer living outside the march of "industry" and "progress," Jean Jacques Rousseau in *The Confessions* and *Discourse on Inequality* (1928) sees native peoples as noble savages, "les enfants de Nature," living pastoral lives unconflicted by "culture."[13] In fact, indigenous peoples are a kind of pastoral in the master-narrative of Western civilization. For Anzaldúa, the U.S./Mexico borderland is not a countryside full of moral goodness and simple life-affirming values, as she states explicitly in her preface: "I have been straddling the Texas-Mexican border, and others, all my life. It's not a comfortable territory to live in, this place of contradictions. Hatred, anger and exploitation are the prominent features of this landscape" (i).

For Smith, Anzaldúa writes within a pastoral tradition; however, the geography that Anzaldúa invokes, according to Smith, is not so much a concrete geopolitical and juridic space of racial, linguistic, and gendered violence on the edge of militarized nation-states as it is a "psychological, physical, metaphysical and spiritual" space. Smith lifts the text out of a "real" geopolitical site—the U.S./Mexico border—and deracinates the text from concrete social and political realities. *Borderlands* resists such appropriations. The preface to *Borderlands* clarifies the border that Anzaldúa writes about: "The actual physical borderland that I'm dealing with in this book is the Texas–U.S. Southwest/Mexican border" (i); that is, the

U.S./Mexico border as an open wound regenerated by a constant flow of blood: "The U.S.–Mexican border *es una herida abierta* where the Third World grates against the first and bleeds. And before a scab forms it hemorrhages again, the lifeblood of two worlds merging to form a third country—a border culture" (3). The question is: Whose blood flows, and under what terms? In answering this question *Chicano Poetics* (1997) by Alfred Arteaga reads how the "genesis of the hybrid subject is in violence to the body, in a wound, and its reproduction transpires in a rupture, in the continual reopening of that wound" (34). Anzaldúa describes the inhabitants who emerge in these bloody ruptures as the "prohibited and forbidden: *Los atravesados* live here; the squint-eyed, the perverse, the queer, the troublesome, the mongrel, the mulatto, the half-breed, the half dead" (3). When people cross into the United States, the "Gringo" treats them as "transgressors" and as "aliens" with or without "documents." Anzaldúa warns Indians, Blacks, and Chicanos not to enter the border zone: "Do not enter, trespassers will be raped, maimed, strangled, gassed, shot" (3).

Recentering the Margins of the *Testimonio*

Although testimonials are conceived as autochthonous to marginal subjects in the "third world," especially in Latin America, I argue that the *testimonio* discourse is useful to understand subaltern practices of autorepresentation in the United States. "The Margin at the Center" (1992) by Latin Americanist John Beverley describes the testimonio as "a novella-length narrative" that is told in "first person" by the protagonist "or witness of the events he or she recounts, and whose unit of narration is usually a 'life' or a significant life experience" (93). The testimonio is "by nature a protean and demotic form" that includes the following categories and genres, among others: "Autobiography, autobiographical novel, oral history, memoir, confession, diary, interview, eyewitness report, life history," and the "all-encompassing form 'documentary fiction'" (93). The testimonio emerges from subjects marginalized in a given social and political economy, and it serves as a means of self-representation: "Those subjects—the 'child,' the 'native,' the woman, the insane, the criminal, the proletarian—excluded from authorized representation when it was a question of speaking and writing for themselves rather than being spoken for" (93). Beverley argues that political urgency drives the testimonio: "The situation of observation in testimonio has to involve an urgency to communicate, a problem of repression, poverty, subalternity, imprisonment, struggle for survival, implicated in the act of narration itself" (94).

Unlike the egocentric "I" of privilege in traditional autobiographic expression, "the narrator in *testimonio* on the other hand, speaks for, or in the name of a community or group." For example, consider the opening of *"Si me permiten hablar . . ." Testimonio de Domitila, una mujer de las minas de Bolivia* (1977) by Domitila Barrios de Chungara:

> La historia que voy a relatar, no quiero en ningun momento que la interpreten solamente como un problema personal. Porque pienso que mi vida está relacionada con mi pueblo. Lo que me pasó a mi, le puede haber pasado a cientos de personas en mi país. Esto quiero esclarecer, porque reconozco que ha habido seres que han hecho mucho más que yo por el pueblo, pero que han muerto o no han tenido la oportunidad de ser conocidos. (13)

> (The history that I am about to tell should not for any minute be considered as only a personal problem. Because I think that my life is interrelated with my people. What happened to me could have happened to hundreds of people in my country. I want to clarify this from the outset, because I realize there have been people who have done much more for the community, but they are either dead or have not had the opportunity to be recognized). (my translation)

Clearly, Domitila breaks the personal into the collective and thereby reaffirms her commitment to the collective *communitas* of Andean miners negotiating their survival in conditions of abject poverty, repression, alcoholism, and workplace and domestic violence.

Domitila wants the testament of the struggle of her experiences to serve the *nueva generacíon,* the new generation of working-class peoples and their struggles, especially indigenous and subaltern women. The testimony culminates in her work in the "International Tribunal for the Woman" in Mexico City in 1975, where she was the only indigenous working-class woman involved. Under these terms, Domitila is willing to have her story published and circulated, transformed from spoken words to written text. Domitila does not care what type of paper it is printed on, "pero si quiero que sirva para la clase trabajadora y no solamente para gentes intelectuales o para personas que nomás negocian con estas cosas" (but I do want this to serve the working class and not just intellectuals and others who work these things; my translation). As "Beyond Testimonial Discourse" (1996) by Javier Sanjines reminds us: "As an act of communication, Domitila's text also touches the corporeal, the human body, in the political struggle for survival. . . . It is an oral narrative that inaugurates a true popular communication, free from the ideological distortions that are inherent in military dictatorships or to bureaucratic authoritarianism" (255–56).

As I read and analyze Beverley's important essay, I pay attention to the people he mentions as practicing testimonio. He highlights important figures in the various social protest movements of South and Central America, such as Che Guevara and Domitila Chungara, and he analyzes Rigoberta Menchú's testimony *I, Rigoberta Menchú* (1993) in depth. However, even in his *Against Literature* (1993) Beverley only briefly concedes that the testimonio activity occurs in the United States. It is almost as if the specific historical conditions that inspire people to testify only happen in Latin America and the third world, denying the militarized racial and sexual violence in the U.S./Mexico borderlands, prisons, urban containment zones (Davis, 1992), reservations, sweatshops in New York and Los Angeles, meatpacking plants in Iowa, and migrant worker communities. The important model of the testimonio merits further expansion to include minority or subaltern subjects in the United States; immediately, one can think of Malcolm X, Angela Davis, Luis Rodriguez, bell hooks, Mary Brave Bird Olguín, Mumia Abu-Jamal, María Elena Lucas, Leonard Peltier, and of course, Gloria Anzaldúa, to name a few.

In fact, because of the way people of color, especially women, are multiply marginalized in the United States, all autoethnographic expression includes elements of the testimonio. For example, consider *Feminist Theory from Margin to Center* (1984) by bell hooks, an African American revolutionary feminist who considers the realities of living in the margins of "a small Kentucky town." Like Domitila, hooks critiques the feminist theory that emerges "from privileged women who live at the center, whose perspectives on reality rarely include knowledge and awareness of the lives of women and men who live on the margin" (preface). For hooks, "the tracks" keep African Americans on the edge and on the margins, and they reinforce a double bind: "Across the tracks were paved streets, streets we could not enter, restaurants we could not eat in, and people we could not look directly in the face. Across the tracks was a world we could work in as maids, as janitors, as prostitutes, as long as it was in a service capacity. We could enter the world but we could not live there. We had always to return to the margin, to cross the tracks, to shacks and abandoned houses on the edge of town." For hooks, communities linked in oppositional worldviews generate the strength of resistance. Community mutually sustains and regenerates itself in the struggles against marginalization and exploitation: "The sense of wholeness, impressed upon or consciousness by the structure of our daily lives, provided us an oppositional world-view—a mode of seeing unknown to most of our oppressors, that sustained us, aided us in our struggle to transcend poverty and despair, strengthened our sense of self and our solidarity."

Likewise, in the final section of her first chapter, "La Travesía," Anzaldúa illuminates how members of the border patrol "stalk and track economic refugees," thereby reinforcing the status of the immigrants as dehumanized subjects who are literal and symbolic prey to the fluctuations of market demand in the United States and underdevelopment in Mexico. Anzaldúa understands the militaristic function of the INS, and she describes in vivid detail their high-tech and apocalyptic-like methods of waging war in the "frontline": "Hunters in army green uniforms stalk and track these economic refugees by powerful nightvision of electronic sensing devices planted in the ground or mounted on Border Patrol vans. Cornered by flashlights, frisked while their arms stretch over their heads, los mojados are handcuffed, locked in jeeps, and then kicked back across the border" (12).

Anzaldúa's testimony is made even more powerful by addressing how violence created by the border, even the border crossing itself, has greater impact on women, who not only contend with racism and economic exploitation but also sexual violence: "She may work as a live-in maid for white, Chicano, and Latino households . . . or work in a garment industry, do hotel work.[14] Isolated and worried about her family back home, afraid of getting caught and deported, living with as many as fifteen people in one room, the mexicana suffers serious health problems. *Se enferma de los nervios, de alta presión*" (13). In addition, women are sexually and economically exploited by the border crossing itself: "Often the coyote (smuggler) doesn't feed her for days or let her go to the bathroom. Often he rapes or sells her into prostitution" (13).

One need only go to the border towns of Tijuana and Mexicali to see the proliferation of economies that thrive on the violent sexual trafficking of Mexicanas and Latinas (Centro-Americanas) to understand the different effects that immigration and migration have on men and women.[15] In the final paragraph of the section, Anzaldúa poetically expresses the multiple marginalization of undocumented women:

> La mojada, la mujer indocumentada, is doubly threatened in this country. Not only does she have to contend with sexual violence, but like all women, she is prey to a sense of physical helplessness. As a refugee, she leaves the familiar and safe homeground to venture into unknown and possibly dangerous terrain.
> This is her home
>   this thin edge of
>   barbwire

Border Feminism: Struggles Against the Material and the Discursive

In "Feminism on the Border" (1991) Sonia Saldívar-Hull proposes a mode of analysis and resistance called "border feminism." Similar to bell hooks and other radical women theorists of color, Saldívar-Hull critiques such vanguard feminists as Elaine Showalter, Toril Moi, and Julia Kristeva for their unwillingness to see Chicana feminists as responding to material geopolitical issues. Saldívar-Hull maintains that "the Chicana feminist does not present 'signifying spaces,' but rather material geopolitical issues that redirect feminist discourse" (208).

Saldívar-Hull argues that the feminist agenda should no longer focus just on "issues of race, class, ethnicity and sexual orientation," but should challenge the divisions between third world women and women of color in the United States. Similar to Chandra Mohanty's views (1991) discussed in chapter 1, Saldívar-Hull argues that "we must examine and question the First versus Third world dichotomy before we accept the opposition as an inevitable fissure that separates women politically committed in different ways from any common cause" (208). For Saldívar-Hull, border feminism must be wedded to praxis—the deconstruction or dismantling of "geopolitical boundaries."

The ideas behind border feminism as both theoretical and political strategy were originally developed in Saldívar-Hull's dissertation "Feminism on the Border" (1990), which is condensed in the article discussed above (also titled "Feminism on the Border"). Saldívar-Hull's study argues that texts and stories such as Borderlands, Helena María Viramontes's "Cariboo Cafe" (1985), and Sandra Cisneros's Women Hollering Creek

(1990), among many other Chicana literary and theoretical works, bridge or situate themselves in the borders between first and third worlds, creating alliances between Chicanas and "the campesinas south of the U.S. border." In the case of *Borderlands,* Saldívar-Hull states: "In the poetry and prose of *Borderlands,* Anzaldúa redefines feminism. She complicates issues of "First World" versus "Third World" in ways that link the Chicana's struggles with the struggles of a Bolivian activist" (186).

For Saldívar-Hull, Anzaldúa epitomizes the border feminist project: "For Anzaldúa feminism emerges as the force that gives voice to her origins as 'the new *mestiza*' " (211). To be the new mestiza is to challenge racist conceptions of Mexicans, Indians, and Africans, patriarchal oppression of Chicanas, Mexicanas, and Indigenas, and homophobia both in Euro-American overculture and in Chicano/Latino culture: "Anzaldúa's project problematizes further still the traditions of Chicanismo, when as a lesbian Chicana, she forces the homophobes of the Chicano community to see their prejudice" (213).

The speaking subject located in the borders and interstices where numerous discourses and practices intersect is also in the position to "subvert old ways of being, rejecting the homophobic, sexist, racist, imperialist, and nationalist." The point is first discussed in Saldívar-Hull's dissertation (1990): "Through her relentless critique, Anzaldúa makes the feminist on the border's dialectical position clear: patriarchal traditions become co-conspirators with capitalism, imperialism, and white supremacy to keep the Chicana exploited, oppressed, and silent" (180). As such *Borderlands* is a counterhistory to six hundred years of patriarchal and Euro-American domination: "While Anzaldúa transgresses aesthetic boundaries in her text, transgresses gender boundaries in what she names her 'choice' to be a lesbian, transgresses ethnicity and race in her formulation of the new mestiza combining Indian, Spanish, African, and even Anglo 'blood' to form a mestizaje, her project is nonetheless articulated within the vital history of the Texas Chicana" (188).

Likewise, in "Anzaldúa's *Frontera:* Inscribing Gynetics," (1996) Norma Alarcón understands Anzaldúa's struggle for self-representation against a backdrop of racially and sexually coded colonial, neocolonial, and patriarchal violence. Alarcón argues that the moment the woman of color in the Americas "emerges as a 'speaking subject-in-process' the heretofore triadic manner in which the modern world has largely taken shape becomes endlessly heterogeneous, and ruptures the 'oedipal family romance' " (43).

Alarcón defines the oedipal family as "the underlying structure of the so-cial and cultural forms of the organization of Western societies." The oedi-pal family structure has been superimposed on preexisting indigenous social and cultural forms, many matrilineal, "by systems of domination — political, cultural and theoretical" (43). When mestiza speaking subjects enunciate their multiple subjectivities from the heterotopic interstices, discontinuities, and gaps of the U.S. nation-state, they disrupt the sym-bolic economies of phallocentric desire in homogenous nation-making processes.

Alarcón points out an irony in the differences between juridical and textual/symbolic discourses and the effects on Chicanas: "A Chicana may have better fortunes at representing herself or being represented textually than legally as a Chicana" (44). The juridical text is "generated by the ruling elite who have access to the state apparati" whereas the literary/symbolic text or "cultural text" at the interstices of the nation-state is "generated by herself" (44).

After framing the interplay of discursive forces that are "in the spirit" of *Borderlands*, Alarcón grounds her reading of *Borderlands* to a site-specific appreciation of the social and political dynamics of south Texas — El Valle. She states: "These *Borderlands* are spaces where, as a result of expansion-ary wars, colonization, juridico immigratory policing, coyote exploitation of emigrés and group-vigilante, formations of violence are continuously in the making" (44). Alarcón argues that violence was exacerbated after the Mexican-American War in 1848; peoples of Mexican descent were and are "dichotomized into Mexican/American," muting the "presence of indige-nous peoples" (45).

The New Mestiza and the Challenge to Internalized Colonialism

As a person, I as a people, we, Chicanos, blame ourselves, hate ourselves, terror-ize ourselves. Most of this goes on unconsciously; we know that we are hurting, we suspect that there is something "wrong" with us, something fundamentally "wrong."—Gloria Anzaldúa, *Borderlands/La Frontera*

Inspired by how Saldívar-Hull and Alarcón ground the enunciative force of mestiza consciousness to the materiality of patriarchal nation-state vio-lence, this section focuses on how *Borderlands* conceptualizes the complex issues of mestizaje (racial, ethnic, and cultural mixing) for Chicanas/os and Mexicanas/os and challenges the insidious processes of internalized colonialism violently driven by over five hundred brutal years of material and psychic colonialism. In the case of Mexico and other Latin American countries, internalized colonialism on a national level translates into an internalized colonialism on a personal level. Europeanized mestizos (ladinos) continue to denigrate and exploit contemporary peoples whose first language is Zapotec, Tzotzil, Yaqui, and Nahua, to name just a few.[16] As discussed in chapter 2, for Latino culture the Mesoamerican societies of the Aztec and Maya belong in the past; they are dead and only to be resuscitated for use as tourist traps. The Mexican tourist council encourages such Toltec and Maya "ruins" as Chichén Itzá, a ceremonial center of extreme sacred complexity, to have "spectacular sound and light shows." They want to dazzle foreign and national tourists with a blend of the "primitive" and the technological. The nearby Club Med complex (where the "beautiful" people of the world go to relax) sells itself as a jungle paradise built right next to the ancient, "primitive," and "mysterious" pyramids.

At the same time, Eurocentric canons of beauty are imposed and circulated by the popular media: the *güero* (blond) and the European are venerated. Products ranging from blond hair dye to contact lenses that make eyes blue are promoted and sold in great quantities. People save their limited wages to try to remove the indigenous and African by way of expensive nose operations. The logic is that the more one looks European the greater the likelihood of moving up in social rank and having access to higher-paying jobs.

In the chapter "An Other Tongue" (1994), Alfred Arteaga refers to the most extreme response to material and discursive colonialism as "autocolonialism." For Arteaga, autocolonialism occurs when the colonized subject made Other, or subaltern, "effaces or denigrates him/herself from within. In the endeavor to mimic the monologue of power, the Other harmonizes with it and suppresses difference" (77). The following concrete examples of autocolonialism come to mind: Hispanic border patrol agents who are hired to chase, detain, and deport "illegal aliens," keep the border "clean," the Other out, and preserve America for "real" Americans; and GOONS, Guardians of the Oglala Nation, assimilated Lakota peoples who are hired to harass and shoot militant and traditional Lakotas. The official purpose of the GOONS is to ensure that the Lakota nation at Pine Ridge has a "smooth" transition into progress and civilization (Matthiessen 1983). Similarly, during the death squad regimes of the 1960s to 1990s in Guatemala, Mayan soldiers captured, tortured, mutilated, and killed their own peoples in the name of freedom and democracy (Jonas 1991).

Arteaga's term autocolonialism echoes earlier discussions of the psychic or psychological effects of colonialism on the colonized. The foundational study *Black Skin, White Masks* (1967) by Antillean psychiatrist Frantz Fanon describes how internalized colonialism functions with peoples affected by colonialism. Fanon clarifies the dialectics of negotiating identity in a colonial context: "The colonized is elevated above the jungle status in proportion to his adoption of the mother country's cultural standards." Specifically, Fanon argues that "he becomes whiter as he renounces his blackness, his jungle" (18). Fanon gives the specific example of Senegalese officers of the "French colonial army" who are ordered to translate to the troops and "convey the master's orders to their fellows," gaining a "certain position of honor" as a result (19). Fanon's chapter "The Negro and Psychopathology" clarifies the effects of colonialism on the psychic makeup of subjects who are negotiating their identity in a colonial context. He provides a map to understanding the schizophrenia produced by the psychic violence of colonial relations. These effects of internalized colonialism cause a schism that equates "immorality" with blackness in African subjects: "Moral consciousness implies a kind of scission, a fracture of consciousness into a bright part and an opposing black part. In order to achieve morality, it is essential that the black, the dark, the Negro vanish from consciousness. Hence a Negro is forever in combat with his own image" (194).

In *Columbus and Other Cannibals* (1992) Jack Forbes interprets the colonially produced cultural schizophrenia in the Americas as the wétiko disease. Forbes states that the overriding characteristic of a wétiko, a Cree word literally meaning "cannibal," is "that he consumes other human beings for profit, that is, he is a cannibal" (55). Forbes ranges his discussion of violent wétiko systems from medieval Europe to the death squad repression of peoples in Central America. In the case of tribal reservations in the United States, Forbes considers how the wétiko disease drives "Indian agents" to sell out their people's land to business interests, as in the case of the Oklahoma oil rush. Forbes argues that the "secret of colonialism" lies in the internal divisions created by a colonial administration: "This is the secret of colonialism, how to divide the conquered masses (who are usually a majority population) into rival groups with a small sector (the *ladinos,* or *mestizos,* or light mulattoes in the plantation south of the United States) being used to kill, lash, and control their more oppressed relations" (68).

Forbes describes how ladinos, mestizos, and others who assimilate into the European value system, reenacting the denigration and exploitation of their own peoples, partake in the "profits." They are given the "privileges" of raping and beating their own peoples without "fear of prosecution" (69). However, Forbes argues that the wétikos, the ladinos, "are brutalized as they brutalize. They are steadily more corrupted until finally an Indian machete or bullet ends their career" (69).

In an earlier study of Chicano and Mexicano identity, *Aztecas del Norte* (1973), Forbes challenges the imposed divisions between mestizos and "Indians." Forbes defines Chicanos as follows: "The Aztecas del Norte (an Aztec is a person of Aztlán or 'the Southwest') compose the largest single tribe or nation of Anishinabe (Indians) found in the United States today. Like the other Native American groups, the Aztecas of Aztlán are not completely unified or homogenous people" (13). Obviously, there is no issue for Forbes to refer to Chicano/Mexicano peoples as detribalized Anishinabes (Indians of the Americas). In fact, Forbes argues that the "common denominator" between the diverse Chicano community is that "they all possess Mexican Anishinabe (Indian) descent to some degree" (13). Obviously, Forbes considers tribal identity to be something more profound than a precise percentage of "Indian" blood or having the family name in official tribal roles.[17]

For Forbes, the term mestizo is a colonially imposed "tactic of divide and conquer" that favors light skin and creates a caste system according to blood quantum and mixture: "To the Spaniards, the native generally was not *de razón,* but mixed-bloods could be!" (188). Forbes goes on to argue that the distinctions of coyote, lobo, pardo, and so on were invented to create hierarchies of privilege and to reinforce ruling-class dominance: "It is extremely doubtful if the differences between a coyote (three quarters Anishinabe), a mestizo (one half Anishinabe), a lobo (Anishinabe-African), pardo (Anishinabe-African-European), and so on were at all significant *except in as far as the Spanish rulers sought to make them significant"* (emphasis added; 189).[18]

In the United States, there are dual pressures for peoples of Mexican and Latino descent to assimilate into the mainstream Euro-American culture at the expense of losing their language and cultural identity. There is pressure to live in a state of enforced marginalization because of their identity as Chicana/o and Latina/o. This marginalization translates literally into few jobs, few educational opportunities, English language use only, police brutality, INS abuses, and incarceration, not to mention the denial of such human rights as education and medical attention to those perceived as "illegal aliens."

Anzaldúa's *Borderlands* asks: How do we challenge these forces of assimilation, marginalization, and internalized colonialism without suppressing issues of sexism and homophobia in our own communities? In her second essay, *"Movimientos de rebeldía y las culturas que traicionan,"* Anzaldúa is clearly prepared at all costs "to defend my race and culture when they are attacked by non-Mexicanos," but she also knows *"el malestar de mi cultura"* sexism and homophobia. She states: "But I will not glorify those aspects of my culture which have injured me in the name of protecting me" (22).

Identity, Mestizaje, and the Living Mesoamerican Past

The anthology *Without Discovery* edited by Ray Gonzalez (1992) brings together Chicana/o, Puerto Rican, and Native American poets, scholars, and novelists, such as Inés Hernandez, Diane Glancy, and Francisco Alarcón. Creative and testimonial in form, the anthology is an arena for alliance across difference, and it reorients the critical paradigm of American studies to studies of the Americas following an east-west and north-south axis. This anthology is a dialogue with other anthologies and book-length studies that offer a comparative inter-Americas focus: for example, *The Dialectics of Our America* (1991) by José David Saldívar; *Do the Americas Have a Common Literature?* (1990) edited by Gustavo Pérez Firmat; and *An Other Tongue* (1994) edited by Alfred Arteaga. However, what makes *Without Discovery* unique is that in addition to linking Chicanos with peoples of the Caribbean and Latin America, it links Chicanos with Native Americans. As Ray Gonzalez states in his preface: "Five hundred years have passed, and these writers know it. Five hundred years of native and foreign languages have already created voices of mixed cultures, the true sound of the Americas, as its artists and writers mark history with honest visions of what it means to be citizens of the Americas, not American citizens" (x). Gonzalez concludes his preface by arguing in support of the primacy of native writers and voices at "the final years of the twentieth century" who "prove the true mark of history," which Gonzalez states "comes from individuals living and writing their own stories."

The fifth essay of this anthology, "Reclaiming Ourselves, Reclaiming America," by poet and scholar Francisco Alarcón, considers the survival and persistence of the Mesoamerican culture in the contemporary politics of Chicana/o identity (1992). Alarcón considers how "for many of us, our America has been taken away from us. Our America has been invaded, occupied, whitewashed, gagged, suppressed, sanitized, and at best, ignored" (34). Furthermore, Alarcón celebrates the fact that "Mesoamerica has survived and is alive, well, and all around us." The vitality of Mesoamerica "cannot be reduced to museum artifacts, bones and stones," but rather it is found in the "flesh and spirit of many contemporary Native and Mestizo peoples" (35). Additionally, Alarcón argues, "one of the most pressing changes that needs to happen is our recognition and celebration of a cultural face of ours that has been suppressed and denied for so long: our living Mesoamerican heritage" (36).

In a way that challenges linear conceptions of history, Alarcón mandates that this "awareness of our Mesoamerican past should be projected into our present and our future in radically new ways" (36). Alarcón ends his essay by arguing that hegemonic America must engage with the *carne* and *hueso* (flesh and bones) of the Mesoamerican Chicano and native cultural worlds: "America must be able to see, hear, touch, taste, and smell this America" (37).

As discussed, Anzaldúa's *Borderlands* offers strategies for decolonization that not only challenge Euro-American, Spanish, and Mexican cultural hegemony, but also confront sexism and homophobia in the Anglo, Chicano, and Mexican communities as well as in the Aztec nation-state. Anzaldúa envisions a mestiza consciousness that not only charts how oppression strikes on the multiple registers of race, class, gender, and sexuality, but also engages with liberational strategies that (re)center women and gays in Brazilian theorist Paolo Freire's famous pedagogical praxis of the oppressed (1970).

In the chapter *"La conciencia de la mestiza/* Towards a New Consciousness" Anzaldúa considers how cultural denigration travels from Anglo institutions of power to the Chicano community, which in turn joins with the oppressor to denigrate indigenous cultures: "Within us and *la cultura chicana*, commonly held beliefs of the white culture attack commonly held beliefs of the Mexican culture, and both attack commonly held beliefs of the indigenous culture" (78). Anzaldúa calls for a plural subject that potently challenges the multiplicity of oppression in general and repels the multiple attacks on Mexican and indigenous cultures in particular. This rebellious subject of resistance is the "new *mestiza*": "The new *mestiza*, copes by developing a tolerance for contradictions, a tolerance for ambiguity. She learns to be an Indian in Mexican culture, to be Mexican from an Anglo point of view. She has a plural personality, she operates in a pluralistic mode" (79).

Anzaldúa writes from a subject-position of a working-class Chicana/ Tejana lesbian who actively embraces all aspects of her mestizaje. She counters the suppression of the African and indigenous by calling for a democratization of historical knowledge for peoples in all sectors of the Chicano/Mexicano community. Anzaldúa wants all Chicanas/os to "know their history" and celebrate the full range of their identity: "Our Mothers, our sisters and brothers, the guys who hang out on street corners, the children in the playgrounds, each of us must know our Indian lineage, our *afro-mestizaje*, our history of resistance" (86).

For Anzaldúa, to know her "Indian lineage" means to embrace the dualism of Azteca thought and explicate how Aztec dualism shapes her conceptualization as a new mestiza. In considering the role of gender and sexuality in the Aztec nation-state, *Borderlands* enters the duality of Nahuatl religious and philosophical thought and reconfigures the understanding of pre-Cortesian symbology to engage with the chthonic feminine forces of creation and destruction found in the expression of Coatlicue. By invoking Coatlicue, Anzaldúa challenges Chicano nationalist writings and their masculinist appropriations of the Azteca male *guerrero* (warrior) figures, such as Huitzilopochtli, as seen with Oscar Acosta, Alurista, and Luis Valdez.

Aztec dualism is guided by an appreciation of the primary spiritual force, Omeoteotl, who is the mother and father of gods and is neither masculine or feminine; Omeoteotl is the lady and lord of duality and maker of the world, the sun, and the stars.[19] Anzaldúa is entranced by Coatlicue. Coatlicue is the "Lady of the Serpent Skirt," an earth and fertility goddess who contains and balances the "dualities of male and female, light and dark, life and death" (32). According to the stories, Coatlicue is the mother of Coyolxauhqui (the Moon) and Centzon Huiznahua (the Stars). She was dismembered by her son, Huitzilopochtli, the god of war and blood and ruler of the fifth sun.[20] A stone sculpture of Coatlicue is in the National Anthropology Museum in Chapultepec Park, but rather than seeing Coatlicue as a dead statue, an archeological document of a bygone, strange, and brutal civilization, Anzaldúa is encircled, permeated, and enraptured by Coatlicue.

For Anzaldúa, Coatlicue is a living "incarnation of cosmic processes" that inhabits and travels through her psyche and sustains the articulation of an ancient psychic body that regenerates the wounded bodies of mestiza: "*Coatlicue* is one of the most powerful images or 'archetypes' that inhabits, or passes through my psyche. For me, the consuming internal whirlwind, the symbol of the underground aspects of the psyche. *Coatlicue* is the mountain, the Earth Mother who conceived all celestial beings out of her cavernous womb" (46) .By embracing the generative mythos of Coatlicue, Anzaldúa displaces the immanence of phallocentric desire that codes the reproduction of patriarchal dominance both in imperial nation-states and in cultural nationalist movements that are in opposition to these imperial powers.

In the same way that Anzaldúa charts the travel of oppression in systems of domination, she considers how discourses and practices of sexist violence emerge in various systems of patriarchal control, beginning with the dismemberment of Coatlicue. The notion of betrayal has been essentialized to all women of Mexican descent, starting with La Malinche at the time of the Conquest. La Malinche, or Malinali Tenepal, a young and brilliant linguist sold into slavery as a child, was given to Hernán Cortés to solidify alliances against the Aztec state.[21] However, Malinali, vulgarly known as la Chingada (the fucked one), is blamed for betraying or selling out the Mesoamerican peoples to the Spanish empire.[22] Unfortunately, La Malinche has become a pejorative adjective in Mexican and Chicano popular culture: to be called a *malinchista* is to be called a sellout or a betrayer of a people or cause. Anzaldúa reverses this notion of betrayal: "The worst kind of betrayal lies in making us believe that the Indian woman in us is the betrayer. We *indias y mestizas* police the Indian in us, brutalize and condemn her. Male culture has done a good job" (22). Again, Anzaldúa subverts the notion of betrayal to argue how patriarchal power, emerging in different cultural milieus and historical contexts, is the real betrayer of Mesoamerican women: "Not me sold my people but they me. Because of the color of my skin they betrayed me. The dark-skinned woman has been silenced, gagged, caged, bound into servitude with marriage, bludgeoned for 300 years, sterilized, and castrated in the twentieth century. For 300 years she has been a slave, a force of cheap labor, colonized by the Spaniard, the Anglo, by her own people (and in Mesoamerica her lot under the Indian patriarchs was not free of wounding)" (23).

With these words Anzaldúa considers the period of brutal oppression of women to be only three hundred years instead of five hundred years. Why? Weren't women brutalized from first contact? As qouted in Todorov (1989), Christopher Columbus's journal entry on December 11, 1492, gloats about how an Indian "harlot" was "thrashed" and raped by one of his officers (49). Perhaps Anzaldúa wants to draw attention to the fact that many tribal cultures that were (and are) matriarchal and matrilineal resisted the imposition of racist Spanish and Anglo systems of patriarchy (for two hundred years?) and were able to maintain more egalitarian gender roles. For example, the Zapotecas in Oaxaca, Mexico, are still a matrilineal culture (Castillo 1995).

For Anzaldúa, decolonization also means challenging male power over women. She declares that "mestizas should support each other in changing the sexist elements in the Mexican-Indian culture. As long as woman is put down, the Indian and the Black in all of us is put down" (84). However, liberation from the multiplicity of oppression is not entirely dependent on the conscientization of women, and Anzaldúa demands that the "men of our race" acknowledge "that they wound us, violate us, are afraid of us and our power" (84).

Decolonization also means confronting homophobia in men and women, and in all cultures. Anzaldúa considers that "women are the bottom of ladder one rung above deviants" (18). She defines "deviants" as the queer and the homosexual, and states that "most cultures have burned or beaten their homosexuals and others who deviate from the sexual common" (18), but she challenges the "despot duality" that forces people into rigid biologically determined sexual roles and identities: "But I, like other queer people, am two in one body, both male and female. I am the embodiment of the *hieros gamos:* the coming together of opposite qualities within" (19).[23] The price paid by Chicana and other women-of-color lesbians is rejection by the home community: "We're afraid of being abandoned by the mother, the culture, *la Raza,* for being unacceptable, faulty, damaged" (20). Anzaldúa describes how this multiple alienation pushes lesbians of color into "los intersticios, the spaces between the different worlds she inhabits" (20).

Alienation and oppression for the working-class lesbian of color registers on the multiple fronts of race, class, gender, and sexuality. Yet what makes *Borderlands* such an alchemical testimony is the way that Anzaldúa rebels against this multiple marginalization or victimization. Anzaldúa demands "the freedom to carve and chisel my own face" (22). As evidenced by the effective use of images such as "bricks," "mortar," and "lumber," Anzaldúa seizes control over all aspects of constructing her subjectivity: "And if going home is denied me then I will have to stand and claim my space, making a new culture—*una cultura mestiza*—with my own lumber, my own bricks and mortar and my own feminist architecture" (22).

Out of the painful interstices of multiple marginalization, Anzaldúa creates a way to account for the contradictory totality of the self in one's own terms—she has become *la nueva mestiza*. Mestizaje has become more than just a simple racial and cultural mixture between Spanish and Indian. Rather, it is an ethnic, sexual, and political challenge to revision systems of being that celebrate the multiplicity of consciousness. Anzaldúa creates what Yvonne Yarbro-Bejarano calls the "third space, the in-between, border, or interstice that allows contradictions to co-exist in the production of a new element (*mestizaje* or hybridity)" (11). In doing so, Anzaldúa articulates a psychic and political space that reaches deep into the nonbinary duality of premilitaristic Azteca philosophy and embodies what Emma Pérez (1999) calls "the decolonial imaginary": "The decolonial imaginary embodies the buried desires of the unconscious, living and breathing in between that which is colonialist and that which is colonized. Within that interstitial space, desire rubs against colonial repressions to construct resistant, oppositional, transformative, diasporic subjectivities that erupt and move into decolonial desires" (110). Like Coatlicue, *Borderlands* "plunges" into its "maw" and "devours" (46) the epistemological systems that reproduce binary (either/or) and hierarchical systems of subject-formation and political domination in the world.

To return to the questions of genre and subjectivity raised earlier, as well as to the discussion of the speaking subject-in-process and the politics of representation given in chapter 1, the multigenre, ritualistic, and polyphonic *Borderlands* has become less a description of mestizaje and more a vivid and intense evocation or performance of decolonial mestizaje that shatters the comfort zones and privileges of heterosexual, monolingual, and monocultural readers. In addition, by opposing the institutions of control and representation that continue to bear on the bodies of subaltern women and children in the Americas, *Borderlands* opens oppositional sites for alliance between Chicanas/os, Mexicanas/os, and Latinas/os in the United States and Latin America, and the emergent U.S. and international women-of-color political class, especially in the queer communities.

As such, *Borderlands* intersects Chicana/o, Latin American, and U.S. multiethnic and postcolonial critical discourse and challenges Chicana/o and transethnic comparative studies to move beyond the exclusive focus on singular issues and to bring intersections of gender, sexuality, race, and class to the forefront of epistemologies of knowledge, scholarship, and representation. As we are reminded by Sonia Saldívar-Hull's authoritative introduction to the 1999 edition of the "transfrontera, transdisciplinary" *Borderlands:* "It was—and remains—a defining statement on the inextricability of sexuality, gender, race, and class for Chicanas and changed the way we talked about difference in sexuality, race/ethnicity, and class in the U.S." (13).

Anzaldúa emerges as a speaking subject-in-process whose historicist recuperations of Chicana and indigena identity disrupt the racial and patriarchal metanarratives of nation-states and nationalisms. Anzaldúa grounds enunciatory discourse to the materiality of women's bodies traumatized by poverty and colonial, racial, and sexual violence and to the materiality of dispossessed territories to articulate the psychic processes of recovery and decolonization. By interrogating racialist and masculinist apparatuses of representation and material domination(s), Anzaldúa (re)centers and unshames desire for sexual and cultural decolonization into the "everyday resistance" of the lived, the living, and the present.

5

A Border Coda:
Dangerous Bodies, Liminality,
and the Reclamation of Space in
Star Maps by Miguel Arteta

Racial Imagery is central to the organization of the modern world. At what cost do regions and countries export their goods, whose voices are listened to at international gatherings, who bombs and who is bombed, who gets what jobs, housing, access to health care and education, what cultural activities are subsidized and sold, in what terms they are validated—these are largely inextricable from racial imagery.—Richard Dyer, *White*

In this age of corporate-driven multiculturalism, racialized panoptic regimes, and unequal social mobility and travel in the twenty-first century, citizen-subjects from imperial nation-states further enjoy the privileges of seeking refuge, "slumming," "rebelling," and finding their "humanity" and "soul" in controlled yet sometimes risky crossings, engagements, and appropriations of the ethnic and cultural Other.[1] These border crossings—excursions/incursions—into subaltern ethnic space provide an opportunity to "go native" and experience the "freedom" to express oneself without the confines of a culture burdened by the trappings of semibourgeois Eurocentric social codes and practices—a *Dances with Wolves/South of the Border* ritual and fantasy. In the case of the U.S. nation-state, these escapes into otherness recapitulate and build from what Owens (1998) calls the primal Western fantasy of "being inseminated with Indianness, of absorbing and appropriating everything of value in the indigenous world as a prelude to eradicating and replacing the actual Native" (123).

These privileged encounters with otherness, with risk factors built in, provide a source of controlled escape and immersion into "colorful," "primitive," and sexualized "ethnoscapes" (Appadurai 1996). Examples that come to mind include "salsa dancing" in the South Bronx, New York; "reveling" in the Dia de Los Muertos parade in the Mission district of San Francisco; crowding the sex bars of Tijuana, Mexico; or actually traveling to "do" Cancun, Mexico, "The Beach" in Thailand, "Carnaval" in Rio de Janeiro, and "find the groove" in the Bahamas. These journeys into the "exotic," the "primitive," and the "libidinal" are traditionally structured and marketed as temporary tourist jaunts; the subject—usually male—after spending himself can always return to the privilege and protection of his dominant community.[2]

However, in these colonially informed imaginaries and the attendant race, class, and gender hierarchies of the political economy, subjects who inhabit subaltern communities, barrios, and countries are faced with the incommensurability of symbolic transactions that predicate and truncate their mobility, movement, and access to the dominant social space.[3] For example, consider the case of Mexicanas/os and Chicanas/os in Los Angeles, especially dark-skinned monolingual Spanish speakers. Even though they can enter into the yards and homes of gated communities as gardeners and domestic servants, or as part of work crews with hats down and aprons tied, they must always return to their barrios, trailers, hotels, rented casitas, and dilapidated overcrowded apartments at sundown at the risk of being pulled over as suspected burglars, "wets," and gangbangers who will steal from and sully up "nice" neighborhoods.

As we begin the next millennium, cities have further become sites of bordered and contestatory ethnoscapes that are regulated, contained, and enforced by a growing militaristic presence of such formal state apparatus agencies as anti-gang task forces, the INS, the police and sheriff departments, and "white privilege" protectorate groups that range from mortgage-lending agencies to gated-community governance boards to neighborhood "citizen" groups to suburban teenage Nazi skinhead groups who rape, beat, and murder in the name of the "victimized" white race.[4] In the chapter "Fortress L.A." in his often cited City of Quartz (1992) Mike Davis comments on the increasing patterns of the militarized and cybernetic protection of segregated elite communities in the west side of Los Angeles, in the hills and canyons and sites of high-end retail commerce: "Welcome to post-liberal Los Angeles, where the defense of luxury lifestyles is translated into a proliferation of new repressions in space and

movement, undergirded by the ubiquitous 'armed response.' This obsession with physical security systems, and collaterally, with the architectural policing of social boundaries, has become a zeitgeist of urban re-
structuring, a master narrative in the emerging built environment of the
1990s" (223). On the cusp of the twenty-first century this racialized panoptic regime directs inward on the "domestic" terrorists of inner cities (*cho-
las/os* and gangbangers), poor people, and people of color, and also outward
at the edges of the U.S./Mexico border to survey, contain, and discipline
what Pat Buchanan calls "the invading" Latin hordes.

In thinking of the incommensurability of mobility, travel, and access/
exclusion and exchange in white privilege "protectionist" spatial economies, this chapter briefly traces a geneaology of how critical border studies
help us to understand the militarized U.S./Mexico border as a producer
and generator of liminality for Mexicanas/os in the United States, regard-
less of immigration status, generational ties, land grants that preexist the
Treaty of Guadalupe Hidalgo, and indigenous ancestries. My final analysis
will center on the 1997 film *Star Maps*, cowritten and directed by Miguel
Arteta, a young Latino director of Peruvian and Spanish descent born in
Puerto Rico, raised in Costa Rica and the United States. Contrary to seeing
liminality as a trendy accouterment of postmodern discourse, *Star Maps*
grounds subalternity, borders, mestizaje, machismo, and the decolonization of identity and sexuality to the materiality of bodies and dysfunctional
families negotiating space, time, and movement in a racialized panoptic
regime.[5]

In "Shifting Borders, Free Trade, and Frontier Narratives" (1994),
Pamela Maria Smorkaloff summarizes the movement of critical border
studies as it responds to specific geopolitical locations. Smorkaloff considers the ways in which theorists, writers, performance artists, and, I argue, filmmakers such as Arteta map transfrontier social space that challenges the myopia, amnesia, and exclusivity of a nation-state imaginary
built on territorial and cultural imperialism: "Transfrontier writers and
theorists are developing a kind of syncretism of the first and third worlds
in their writing that captures not only the complex reality of the border
zone, but also a more profound understanding of the contemporary U.S.
and the Latin America living within" (97).

In similar terms, *Border Writing* (1991) by D. Emily Hicks examines the
dialectics of transfrontier identity and border writing. Hicks uses the concept of border crossings as a metaphor and a tool to analyze the heteroge-

neity of identity in Latin American writing. Even though the bulk of the text focuses on two major Argentinean writers, Julio Cortázar and Luisa Valenzuela, Hicks begins her study by discussing the U.S./Mexico border region and concludes it by returning to the region to examine Chicano and Mexicano writing.

Hicks argues that border writing "emphasizes the differences in reference codes between two or more cultures" expressing the "bilingual, bicultural, bi-conceptual reality" of border crossers (xxv). However, Hicks is emphatic in positing that border writing is about crossing cultural borders not physical ones, and she disturbingly characterizes the U.S./Mexico border as a theater of "metaphors" where "actors" such as *pollos* (undocumented border crossers), la migra (INS), and coyotes act their daily "dramas." Hicks creates a universalizing model that moves beyond concrete historical understandings of subaltern Latina/o border crossers as "real people" responding to "real" geopolitical social realities and understands their experiences as a type of carnivalesque and postmodern theater. In doing so, Hicks deracinates the individuality of people—their specific histories and family and community ties—who negotiate the often violent border crossing for reasons such as poverty, hunger, political persecution, to reunite with loved ones, or a simple curiosity to see life *al otro lado* (on the other side).[6]

The foundational anthology *Criticism in the Borderlands* (1991), edited by Héctor Calderón and José David Saldívar, grounds the discussion of transfrontier ideology to a concrete geopolitical zone. This anthology challenges the exclusionary practices of the American literary academy and the formation of the canon by recovering "neglected authors and texts" in the "Southwest and the American West." The work also provides a sustained forum for presenting diverse theoretical perspectives: "Chicano/a theory and theorists in our global borderlands: from ethnographic to postmodernist, Marxist to feminist" (6). What renders the anthology even more significant to the growth of critical border studies is the argument by the critics that Chicano theoretical analyses can move from a regional understanding of relations of power to a global one without denying the historical specificities of each geopolitical locale.

In an earlier essay, "Limits of Cultural Studies" (1990), Saldívar articulates in more detail the cultural and border studies imperative, arguing that cultural studies must be both regional and global: "Finally, cultural studies, a border zone of conjunctures, must aspire to be regionally focused, and broadly comparative, a form of living and of travel in our global borderlands" (264). In this essay, Saldívar critiques the subjectifying forces that inferiorize and homogenize non-Western peoples in the social relations of power and how scholarly practices replicate these forces. Saldívar intervenes in the British cultural studies understanding of culture as a dynamic and heterogeneous site where tensions of domination and resistance compete, linking these principles to forge a greater understanding of borders, resistance, and mestizaje. By studying the "subordinate and dominant cultures like public schoolchildren in Great Britain or low riders and *cholos* in East Los Angeles," Saldívar argues that cultural studies is committed to "transforming any social order which exploits people on the grounds of race, class, and gender." Cultural studies and border theory challenge "the authority of canon theory and emergent practice" and the relations of power that sustain this authority (252).

After setting up his critique of monologic tendencies in anthropological practices, Saldívar surveys several key border writers, including "native informants" Rolando Hinojosa, Gloria Anzaldúa, Guillermo Gómez-Peña, and Renato Rosaldo. Saldívar argues that these writers offer counter-narratives to the master-narratives of nations that attempt to normalize identity and totalize cultural heterogeneity. Saldívar summarizes their writings as "cultural work" that "challenges the authority and even the future identity of monocultural America" (264).

Saldívar's *Border Matters* (1997), a dazzling and impressive study of border writers, artists, musicians, theorists, and scholars, dramatically builds on his critique of the master-narratives that author the hegemonization of "monocultural America" and analyzes how juridic, disciplinatory, and dominant cultural practices intersect to deny cultural and legal citizenship for peoples of Mexican descent: "The JAT border machine, moreover, positions its subjects in ways that dehumanize them. It often personalizes them as 'illegal aliens,' 'cases,' 'dirty,' 'amoral' and 'disease ridden,' and so militates against their collective identity" (96).

In similar terms, "Beasts and Jagged Strokes of Color" by Alfred Arteaga (*Chicano Poetics*, 1997) addresses the multidimensional intersection of real and discursive forces along the U.S./Mexico border—the border patrol and Tex-Mex Caló, for example—by discussing the formation of the Chicana/o subject in relation to tensions produced by the border. With reference to Chicano poet Juan Felipe Herrera's "Literary Asylums," a heteroglossia of voices subjectified by and resistant to competing discourses of the nation-state, Arteaga states: "'Literary Asylums'" and other Chicano poems play in a poetics of hybridization that calls to mind the quotidian cultural politics of hybridization in the material space of the frontier. What is at play is the formation of a Chicano subject coming to be amid the competing discourses of nation" (91). Arteaga continues his discussion of Chicano poetics of hybridization or dialogic poetics by grounding the discussion on the material border. He considers the purpose of the border as intended by the nations at stake—the United States and Mexico: "Consider the border: in the imagining of nation, it is the infinitely thin line that truly differentiates the U.S. from Mexico. The absolute certainty of its discrimination instills confidence in national definition, for it clearly marks the unequivocal edge of the nation. Its perceived thinness and keenness of edge are necessary for the predication of national subjectivity, which defines itself as occurring inside its border and not occurring outside" (92). Arteaga observes how "the thin borderline cleaves two national narratives, two national monologues of ideal and finalized selves" (92). Central to Arteaga's argument is the tension between the monologic tendencies of national narrative and the dialogic, interlingual, and hybridizing impulses of Chicana/o subjects and their literary expression. Arteaga locates the border zone as a site that is lived and expressed by those marginalized by the nationalizing forces and who reside in the physical/discursive interstices and margins generated by the border.

On a theoretical level, Arteaga locates the border as a site of power that selectively privileges and marginalizes, reinforcing social hierarchies along axes of race, class, nationality, and sexuality. To do this he compares the experience of elite Mexican bourgeois Octavio Paz—who knows himself to be fully Mexican when crossing the border, a line that reinforces his imagined singular self—with that of Gloria Anzaldúa, who argues that "borders are set up to define the places that are safe and unsafe, to distinguish us from them. The prohibited and the forbidden are its inhabitants" (94).

To consider the experience of Mexican immigrants crossing the border from the south, I assert a series of propositions that add to Arteaga's discussion of the multivalent nature of the U.S./Mexico border. At the outset, I need to clarify that these assertions on the effects of the border for Mexicans traveling north reflect the socioeconomic conditions of peoples who do not enjoy the privilege of national subjects such as Paz and other bourgeois elite who can demonstrate to the Visa-granting embassy in Mexico City, Ciudad Juárez, or Tijuana that they have sufficient economic ties to Mexico — bank accounts, businesses, and high-status occupations. As border performance artist and poet Gerardo Navarro (1995) states in his reference to the "apartheid" of the border, the tortilla curtain operates like "a valve that is closed or opened by the invisible hands of the market in accord with the fluctuations in Wall Street and in the global market." My propositions are as follows:

1. The border serves as a "free zone" for U.S. citizens and U.S. corporations (U.S. border crossers). The free zone applies to weekend tourists crowding the bars, drinking cheap beers, and seeking male and female prostitutes, and to U.S. companies exploiting "cheap" labor and lax environmental regulation controls; to name a few.[7]

2. Contrary to the free zone where all Euro-American taboos drop, the border is also a free zone of violence, a barrier to those trying to cross from the south, as evidenced by the border patrol, weekend vigilantism, bandits, and *coyotes* who, after collecting their fees, rob, rape, and denounce border crossers.

3. Even though the border is selectively open to those whose class positions confirm their tourist and student status, it forces a discourse of inferiorization onto Mexicans and other Latinos, especially those whose class position, ethnicity, and skin color emerges from the campesina/o and urban proletariat groups.

4. Finally, once crossed, the border is infinitely elastic and can serve as a barrier and zone of violence for Mexicanas/os, Centroamericanas/os, and other Latina/os confronted by racialist and gendered obstacles — material and discursive — anywhere they go in the United States. This means that the émigré/immigrant continually faces crossing the border even if s/he is in Chicago (or any other location in the United States) — a continual shifting from margin to margin.

In no way do these propositions give breadth to the infinite variety of experiences and struggles for Mexicans and other Latin American immigrants moving across and through this infinitely elastic border of the United States. The immediate questions that the border poses are: How can we chart the multiple vectors of forced liminalities produced by the U.S./Mexico border? Is it enough to say that no matter where a Mexican travels or lives in the United States, he or she always inhabits an economic, racial, and discursive status that is automatically secondary and perpetually liminal?[8]

Writing Chicanas/os into the Script

To illustrate the elasticity of the U.S./Mexico border where south-to-north Latina/o border crossers (or those perceived as such) continually negotiate violence-enforced borders/barriers through everyday resistances, my analysis focuses on the brutally stark depiction in *Star Maps* of the struggles of a dark-skinned Chicano teenager, Carlos Amaro (played by Douglas Spain), who is trying to cross the border into the citadel-like world of the Hollywood Film and Television Industry (HFTI) to land a role as an actor. As a cinematic border text, *Star Maps* provides dramatic insight into the power relations that drive the racial and (as we shall see) the sexual commodification of *recién llegado* (newly arrived) and first-generation immigrant Latina/o bodies in contemporary Los Angeles. These hegemonic processes of racial and sexual exploitation are conjoined, crystallized, and transmitted by Pepe, Carlos's father (played by veteran actor Efrain Figueroa) whose nascent and predatory machismo and pathological drive to "succeed" and "assimilate" into the leisure life of middle-class American (white picket fence, mid-week golf tee-offs, and all) represents the fruition of patriarchal and internally colonized practices at their extreme.

Pepe enacts emotional, psychic, and physical violence on all the women he has contact with (except his rich Anglo women clients). He runs a mainly male and teenage Latino prostitution ring, whose mainly male and all "white" clients are part of the elite Hollywood film industry. Pragmatically, Carlos justifies joining his father's ring on his return from Mexico as an opportunity to broker with a potential client his dreams for stardom in Hollywood. The results are an explosive and potent representation of a nonliberating breakdown of the Latino family structure due to a conflation of external forces (racism, the state, and colonialist consumption patterns) and internal factors (machismo, Americanization, active complicity) which take the longstanding sexist structures and processes of gender socialization to a grotesque extreme. By analyzing the intersection of forces that causes the distortion and dysfunction of already sexually violent rituals that inform the transmission of culture and power in the mestizo oedipal familia (father-son, father-daughter, mother-son, mother-daughter, and filial bonds), *Star Maps* offers a potent and explosive critique of Chicana/o subjects struggling for entitlement and sovereignty of body and social space and accessibility in the postmodern millennial urban flux of sexist and neocolonial power relations.[9] This is what George Lipsitz refers to as living in the "dangerous crossroads" of what I see as predatory and sexist global capitalism throwing *chingazos* (punches) of subaltern cultural resistance(s).

In addition to offering a powerful critique of racialized sexual appetites of the dominant culture for young brown and hard bodies, as well as of the complicit machismo, *Star Maps* offers a disparaging and accurate indictment of the schism between the HFTI and the surrounding Latina/o communities. The crucial and urgent issues of how Chicana/o and Mexicana/o subjects are either rendered invisible or criminalized by the dominant imaginary of the HFTI and its mammoth global apparatus of popular-culture representations are not only of concern to ethnic and feminist film scholars but also to a larger contingent of policy institutes and media advocates. According to a September 10, 1999, National Council of La Raza (NCLR) press release, a special coalition has been formed between "African American, Latino, Asian American, and Native American civil rights and media organizations" to increase "diversity in network television, both in front of the cameras and behind the scenes in decision making positions." The nineteen-member coalition, which includes NCLR, MALDEF, NAACP, American Indians in Film and Television, and the Media Action Network for Asian Americans, calls for a boycott of the fall 1999 premiere season.[10] A September 14, 1999, article in the *Los Angeles Times*, "Latinos: Pressure on Hollywood Urged," states: "The irony of Hollywood's white male dominance is hard to overlook, advocates noted: A famously liberal industry is headquartered among the largest concentration of Latinos, yet it fails to adequately represent them in hiring or programming" (22).

The Hollywood film and television community is situated in a state that according to a June 1999 report from the California Finance Demographic Research Unit has close to 10 million Hispanic residents in a state with a total population of 33.5 million, notwithstanding the recíen llegados who do not have driver's licenses or any of the other indicators of residency used in demographic studies. In addition, Los Angeles County itself is a huge Latina/o *cosmopolitas* of over 4 million residents of Latina/o descent in a population area of 9.7 million, and it has the largest concentration of Mexicanas/os outside of Mexico City. On a national level, according to U.S. Hispanic Chamber of Commerce market statistics, the Chicana/o and Latina/o peoples have a collective purchasing power of 477 billion dollars. Given these demographic and purchasing-power estimates, why do Latinas/os make up less than 1 percent of roles in the HFTI?

Unfortunately, even if Latinas/os are cast in television roles, the representations of Chicanas/os and Latinas/os are burdened by colonialist discourse and practices of racialization, criminalization, invisibilization, and sexualization of Chicana/o and Mexicana/o subjects, as seen with other ethnic subjects-turned-objects. The historical patterns of creating Mexicans and Latinas/os as Others in U.S. film are driven by a racialized gender formation that represents men as rapists, thieves, or knife-and-gun-wielding predators (and hence threats to racial and patriarchal order), or as childlike, chaotic, lazy drunks.[11] Chicanas/Latinas are cast as prostitutes, loose women, and the "señoritas" of Euro-American male colonialist fantasy who desire to be "plundered" or "rescued" from violent Mexican bandits and *pachucos*.[12] *The Chicano/Hispanic Image in American Film* (1995) by Frank Javier Garcia Berumen comments on the historical patterns of demonization of the Chicana/o image in film: "The stereotyping of Hispanic men and women on film is a cumulative perception evolving out of several historical and political events: the Black Legend, Manifest Destiny, the Monroe Doctrine, the mythology of the Alamo, the Mexican American War, and the racism implicit in the institutions of slavery and segregation" (1).

In similar terms, *Hispanics and United States Film* (1994) by Gary D. Keller, an encyclopedic study of the participation of Chicanas/os and Latinas/os in films from 1903 to the present, convincingly traces how the "stereotypical depictions of various outcast races, ethnicities, and cultures, often excruciatingly derogatory by contemporary standards" grew hand in hand with the "growing technology of film entertainment" dispersing and perpetuating the colonial gaze of the dominant culture. Keller argues that the "earliest films mostly catered to the dominant culture, usually the WASP power elite or sometimes farmers and ranchers, at the expense of out groups, which at the end of the century included not only blacks, Hispanics, American Indians, and Asians, but Irish, Italians, Jews, and Poles and others." (6). As the essay "Latino Sacrifice in the Discourse of Citizenship" (1992) by Kathleen Newman argues: "Despite the unflagging efforts of Chicano filmmakers from the 1960's onward to change the anglocentric

U.S. film industry . . . it is easy to find in the national media, particularly in the realm of entertainment, counterexamples of the devalorization of Latinos as citizens" (60).

Even though Miguel Arteta had unusual support for his directorial debut (shepherded by Jonathan Demme of the homophobic *Silence of the Lambs* fame), and the film was a Sundance audience favorite with later commercial release by Fox Searchlight, *Star Maps* is self-conscious of how Hollywood invisibilizes, demonizes, and sexualizes Chicanas/os. In fact, *Star Maps* parodies the "creative" processes by which Mexicans are written into a Hollywood script. In this case, Jennifer (played by Kandyce Jorden), who is the star of a popular daytime soap opera, *Carmel County*, and also one of Pepe's top clients, is impressed by Carlos's teenage sexual prowess. As a means to secure prolonged sexual favors from Carlos she asks her husband to cast him as an extra in an episode of the soap. Then, after Carlos recites the obviously ironic "Sweet Bird of Youth" in the afterglow of sex, Jennifer asks her husband to write a speaking part for Carlos, appealing to his "liberal" desire for social responsibility. Decrying the imaginative limits of the staff writers and producer who perpetuate the marketable perceptions of Mexicans by the dominant culture as uneducated, illegal, exploitable, replaceable, and vulgarly sexual, Carlos is cast as a leaf-blowing "wetback" gardener with a strong accent, who in the producer's eyes "looks the part." Even though Carlos regards his role with the utmost seriousness, the lines he is given, "I am like a matador with my leaf blower . . . I will mow your lawn like no other" are in the tradition of casting Mexican men as libidinous Latin lovers, tapping into the miscegenation taboos between men of color and white women (Takaki 1990).[13]

Highlighting Arteta's clever use of multilevel parody and social mimicry, the racialized vulgarity of Carlos's dialogue and his interaction with Jennifer mirrors the vulgarity of the libidinal exchange with Carlos. Her libertine drive fetishizes Carlos and his ability to "fuck" like "a poor hungry Mexican boy." In fact, right after Carlos is brought to the set and introduced to the production crew, Jennifer deflates his genuine elation of getting a speaking part by reminding him the reasons she did him a favor. Jennifer wants to reinforce her investment in Carlos's ability to provide sexual favors on request in exchange for giving him his first "break" by having him service her sexually on the set. Even though this scene reverses the historical trends of women having to endure sexual coercion and assault in the Hollywood industry by executives, producers, agents, lead actors, and so on, the mechanical nature of the libidinal exchange snuffs out any erotic liberation and highlights the sterility of the prostitute-client relationship. Meanwhile, Jennifer's successful television-producer husband is having an existential crisis about the lack of ethics and social responsibility; his desire to make meaningful films about social issues is met by casting Carlos in a role, even if it is as a buffoonish sex-hungry illegal. The irony of his angst is that he is blinded by the myopia of his privilege and self-absorption, and like many liberals he is unwilling to engage with his complicity in the roots, causes, and conditions of race, class, and gender subalternity in the United States.

Machismo and the Scission of the Body

Carlos's struggle for access to Hollywood, framed against a backdrop of disturbing patterns of racialization, is complicated further by the pathology, violence, and psychosis of his father Pepe. Pepe's desire to mimic in the Fanonian sense the elite dominant culture causes the attempted obliteration (psychic, physical, and emotional) of his immediate family and his mistress, brilliantly played by Annette Murphy. The now-famous work *Anti-Oedipus* (1983) by Gilles Deleuze and Félix Guattari argues that the nuclear family structure reproduces the "deterritorializations" and "reterritorializations" of capitalist productions in the social field of power relations (262–71). Fathers, they argue, become in microcosm the "despotic state or Urstaat" that attempts to regulate and constrain libidinal desire and enforce submission, obedience, and conformity to the hierarchical scripts and flows of capitalist production in the bourgeois family structure. The chapter "Ancient Roots of Machismo" in *Massacre of the Dreamers* (1995) by Ana Castillo clarifies how despotic patriarchal power travels from society to family to children, marked specifically by the imposition of colonialist and neocolonialist forms on some already patriarchal and matriarchal indigenous cultures in the Americas: "According to our social pyramid, all men who feel displaced racially, culturally, and/or because of economic hardships will turn on those whom they feel they can order and humiliate, usually women, children, and animals—just as they have been ordered and humiliated by those few privileged who are in power" (67).

Castillo accurately illuminates how male violence exists at all levels of race and class privilege and any justification is false. However, Pepe denies his nascent and displaced violence by arguing that his hard work and sacrifice is what gives his family their "nice" house in the "nice" neighborhood. With the profits of his prostitution ring, Pepe has moved his family to the suburbs to mimic the isolated nuclear Euro-American middle-class family structures that are disconnected from extended family, community, and land.[14] Free to rule his family with physical and psychological terror, the results are devastating: Pepe's wife (played by Martha Velez) is suicidal with a severe dissociative disorder; his daughter (played by Lysa Flores) is forced to cook and clean for the family while living in constant fear of physical and sexual assault. Pepe's other son, Carlos's brother (played by Vincent Chandler), displays abusive tendencies toward his sister, and suffers from acute depression as well as an eating disorder to keep chubby so that his father won't prostitute him further.[15] *Star Maps* draws into question how social dystopias of racial and gender power relations of the Los Angeles body politic intersect and inform the abuse and dysfunction that constitutes familial relations.

Carlos, like his mother, copes by creating alternate inner worlds. In the case of the mother, she develops a *cariñoso* (affectionate) relationship with Cantinflas, the famed Mexican pachuco-style comic famous for breaking class taboos in movies of bourgeois Mexican culture in the 1940s to 1970s. The tenderness and humor of her imagined relationship with Cantinflas offer her a psychic escape from years of enduring Pepe's emotional and physical brutality. For Carlos, escape is to create an alternate vision of himself as an Oscar-winning actor, adored by fans or, in another sequence, to see himself on the covers of *Spin, People, Time,* and other mainstream magazines that sustain the imaginary of the dominant culture and that rarely if ever feature Latinas/os. Warm enveloping color and triumphant music scores pervade the montage sequences of Carlos's imagining. And, in juxtaposition to his material liminality, Carlos stands centered in the top middle of the frame receiving adoration, respect, and recognition from all sides. Returning to Eisenstein's (1992) original propositions of montage as a "collision" of "incongruent" shots that creates dramatic tension (141–44), these montage dream sequences both motivate Carlos and offer him a dissociative escape from his "job" as a sex worker. To satisfy the racialized fetishes of his Anglo clients, Carlos offers up his body for manipulation and penetration: a passive bottom in the same-sex exchanges and a side-dominant top in the heterosexual couplings.[16] To invoke the "Bodies-Cities" analysis by feminist theorist Elizabeth Grosz (1995), Carlos's visions of media success provide a type of agency that helps him to protect his "interior psychic space" from the "inscriptions of social and familial" and, I add, racializing and sexualizing forces on his body.

In the denouement of the film, Carlos beats Pepe with a shovel for trying to steal his television role — the wounds send Pepe to a hospital (a recapitulation of the classic oedipal crisis). For Carlos, this event releases years of trauma, pain, fear, and anger from his father's longstanding abuse (brilliantly evoked throughout the film in orange gel-plate tone analeptic [flash back] scenes of his childhood). In *The Decolonial Imaginary* (1999) Emma Pérez argues that the official scripts of Mexican nationhood are driven by a "colonial imaginary" initiated "through the Oedipal Conquest Complex, one that we are forced to contend with and resist" (107). For Pérez, it is imperative that colonized subjects-turned-objects, especially women, reclaim, redefine, and enact their desire away from colonialist and patriarchal norms wedded in Oedipus: "The colonial object must defy Oedipus, must be anti-Oedipus to become decolonized, to become the decolonial subject . . . to challenge power relations . . .to move into liberatory terrain" (109–10). On an extant level, these scenes of oedipal struggle also speak to effects of institutional racism and longstanding systemic disenfranchisement where members of oppressed communities fight each other for limited resources while whites panic about crime.[17] After the fight with his father, Carlos refuses to allow his body to be used further by sex-addict Jennifer. He exits the set, thereby forsaking the privileged and protected space of the studio. The final scenes of the film show Carlos physically bruised but walking determinedly westward against traffic in a smoggy Los Angeles dusk.

Even though Carlos's *camino* (path) as a Chicano in the racialized state apparatus of "Fortress L.A." is precarious to say the least, he is free to negotiate space and movement away from the chains of his father's predatory machismo and to resist further the racialized and colonialist sexual addictions of the dominant culture. Struggling for autonomy over his body and space, Carlos begins to recover a new state of what Grosz (1995) refers to as a "psychic corporeality" and "embodied subjectivity" (22) that re-associates him into further ownership of his body.[18] The issues of sovereignty over one's body and territory are crucial to what Cherríe Moraga calls "la causa Chicana" in her *The Last Generation* (1993): "As a Chicana lesbian, I know that the struggle I share with all Chicanos and Indigenous peoples is truly one of sovereignty, the sovereign right to wholly inhabit oneself (*cuerpo y alma*) and one's territory (*pan y tierra*)" (171–72).

As a final note, *Star Maps* underscores the huge preponderance of children and youth who are coerced and forced into survival sex in the United States and elsewhere in the world.[19] According to the Children of the Night youth shelter services, there are over 1.4 million children on the streets in the United States, most of whom are escaping conditions of family violence and poverty. There are 20 thousand homeless youths in Hollywood alone, children who are lured by the tinseltown aura of false promises. In the case of Mexican and Central American youths, Santa Monica Boulevard is an area of young Latino sexual commerce. According to the in-depth interviews with young Latino male prostitutes on Santa Monica Boulevard in "Street of Broken Dreams" by Ricardo Rios of *qv Magazine*, West Hollywood is known as "Boystown" where married "rich guys used to put their boys up in apartments and condos" (24). San Diego's Balboa Park is also a gathering spot for undocumented homeless and malnourished youths as young as nine years old who trade sexual favors for food and lodging to rich men in "business suits" and "BMW's." In the 3 April 1993 *Los Angeles Times* article "Children of the Border," Carlitos, a fourteen year old who sleeps under a concrete bridge within walking distance to Balboa Park, describes the suburban house of a recent client: "'He has Super Nintendo, a video, big television, a pool' he exclaimed, black hair falling in his eyes. 'Like the movies.'"

As I have shown in this book, linguistic and discursive violence—the creation of the savage Other—interanimates violence on the body. However, this insight provokes further questioning. For example: How can we make the analysis of subalternity accountable to the increasing violence in which subaltern subjects negotiate their survival and resistance? Specifically, how do we (re)understand questions of essentialism, agency, and resistance when subjects are shot at, chased, detained, beaten, raped, bought and sold, and incarcerated because of their poverty and immigration status, and their ethnicity, gender, sexuality, religion, and language differences? How do we theorize on the social texts of racial, sexual, class, religious, and familial violence? Is violence the true language of social relations? If so, what is the *langue* and *parole* of violence? Is violence both the fringe and the center of social relations as well as the enforcer of the social order in a given historical and cultural context? How does the consideration of physical violence on the body impact the conceptions of race, class, ethnicity, gender, and sexuality?

Zillah Eisenstein, in *Hatreds* (1996), reminds us that "the physicality of the body becomes a horribly powerful resource for those who wish to conquer, violate, humiliate, and shame. The body's power—its intimacy, its creativity against systems of power, its physical dignity and integrity—is also its vulnerability" (33). In my future work I intend to focus directly on the interrelationship of discourse, violence, resistance, and the body. In particular, I aim to understand further how Chicana/o and Latina/o bodies—like other subaltern bodies—are raced, sexed, and othered by discourses and practices of abjection, and I want to examine as well how we Chicanas/os reclaim our bodies, enunciate our subjectivities, and articulate a resistance of the spirit and the flesh.

Notes

Preface

1 I am indebted to Norma Alarcón's (1996) bold epistemic theorizations on how the emergent "identity in difference" of Chicanas and women of color allows them to negotiate their everyday survival and enunciation of public and textual space in resistance to the intersections of nation-state, colonial, racial, sexist, and hetero-sexist oppressions. Also, I appreciate how *Disidentifications* (1999: 7–34) by José Esteban Muñoz deploys the emergent "identity in difference" paradigm to under-stand how "people of color/queers of color" negotiate strategies of resistance to racist discourses in the mainstream gay and lesbian community and homophobia in the Latina/o, Asian American, and African American communities.

2 My use of "we" assumes or imagines a community of readers who directly relate to or sympathize with the struggles for mestiza/o, Chicana/o, and Native American peoples to reclaim and articulate our identities, given a five hundred year his-tory of brutal invasions in the Americas, slavery, manifest destiny, institutional racism, sexism, human rights abuses, assassinations, the border patrol, police shootings, and poverty magnified by globalization.

3 See Emma Peréz, *The Decolonial Imaginary* (1999); José David Saldívar, *Border Matters* (1997), and *The Dialectics of Our America* (1991); Louis Owens, *Mixed-blood Messages* (1998); Alfred Arteaga, *Chicano Poetics* (1997); W. S. Penn, *As We Are Now* (1997); Tey Diana Rebolledo, *Women Singing in the Snow* (1995); and Carl Gutiérrez-Jones, *Rethinking the Borderlands* (1995).

4 For excellent discussion of resistant Chicana/o counterdiscourses, see Rafael Pérez-Torres, *Movements in Chicano Poetry* (1995: 23–55).

5 In the post-1910 revolutionary Mexican nation-state imaginary, the mestizo be-came the national subject. However, the official narration of mestizaje projects a patriarchal indignation at native women for allowing themselves to be colo-

nized by the Spaniards; an indignation that is also repeated in Chicano nationalist ideologies and sexist practices. To understand how this sexist nationalist logic is portrayed, see Octavio Paz, *The Labyrinth of Solitude* (1985: 78–89) and his discussion of Malintzin Tenepal as seen as La Chingada (the fucked one), the "Eve" of the Mexican people. For a brilliant counterhistory of Malintzin Tenepal, see Adelaida R. Del Castillo, "Malintzin Tenépal," in her *Between Borders* (1990; 124–47); and Emma Peréz, *The Decolonial Imaginary* (1999: xiv–xv).

6   See, Victor Turner, *Dramas, Fields, and Metaphors* (1974), which describes my ancestors, the Aldama brothers, in detail.

1. The Chicana/o and the Native American "Other" Talk Back: Theories of the Speaking Subject in a (Post?)Colonial Context

1   Although I agree with the reasons that Niranjana (1992) chooses the term "postcolonial" to support the indigent "forces against colonial and neocolonial domination in these societies" (8), I chose the term neocolonial over postcolonial because I want to emphasize that colonial-like relations of power are still operating in communities and nations that have supposedly liberated themselves from colonial rule. For example, see Ward Churchill, *The Struggle for the Land* (1993), which is a series of case studies on contemporary neocolonial encroachments and appropriation of tribal lands. Also, for discussion of how the term "postcolonial" creates an intellectual elite that denies the continued hyperexploitation of excolonials, see Aijaz Ahmad, "Politics, Literature, and Postcoloniality" (1995).

2   As mentioned in the preface, my use of "we" imagines a community of readers who directly relate to or sympathize with the struggles for mestiza/o, Chicana/o, and Native American identities in the context of colonialism in the Americas and neocolonialism in the U.S./Mexico borderlands.

3   See Pedro Ceinos, *Abya Yala* (1992). Ceinos explains that the use of the name Abya-Yala (the Americas), a term from the Cuna peoples of Panama that means the "Earth in its full maturity," spread to many indigenous peoples defending themselves against invasion by the Europeans. In ways similar to Eduardo Galeano's trilogy *Memory of Fire* (1985), this study chronicles over six hundred scenes of strategic resistance to the colonial invasion from first contact to the Mohawk takeover of 1990.

4   See Tzvetan Todorov, *The Conquest of America* (1984), which estimates that through murder (inside and outside of warfare), bad treatment, suicides, and diseases seventy million lives were lost between first contact and the middle of the sixteenth century (133–34).

5   For discussion of how tropes of the savage and civilized are embedded in humanistic discourse and the humanities, see Walter D. Mignolo, *The Darker Side of the Renaissance* (1995); Abdul R. JanMohamed and David Lloyd, eds., *The Nature and Context of Minority Discourse* (1990: 1–37); and Henry Louis Gates Jr., ed., *"Race," Writing, and Difference* (1986: 1–21).

6   For a discussion of how the notions of the libidinal are essentialized to race,

see Ronald Takaki, *Iron Cages* (1990); and Winthrop D. Jordan, *White over Black* (1968).

7   See Arthur O. Lovejoy, *The Great Chain of Being* (1936).

8   In the 1982 edition of *Ancient Society* published in Calcutta, Debiprasad Chatto-padhyaya's introduction illustrates the influence of Morgan on Marx and Engels (i–xxx), especially on their conceptualization of a primitive communist society. Chattopadhyaya compares the notions of cultural stages in ancient society with Marx's and Engel's discussion's of the progress of society from primitive, preclass, class, and classless society. Also, for extent of Morgan's influence, see Engels's now famous work *The Origin of the Family, Private Property and the State* (1884).

9   This issue is discussed further in chapter 3, where I consider how *Of Gramma-tology* (1976) by Derrida, along with Mignolo's *The Darker Side of the Renaissance* (1995), challenge the ethnocentrism involved in considering the phonetic alphabet as the summit of writing.

10   For discussions of the evolutionist mind-set and scientific racism as applied to Native American peoples, see Robert F. Berkhofer, *The White Man's Indian* (1978: 44–55).

11   See Lewis Hanke, *Aristotle and the American Indian* (1959) and *All Mankind is One* (1974), as well as Todorov, *The Conquest of America* (1984: 151–52), for fascinating studies that analyze how Sepúlveda used Aristotelian principles.

12   In another study it would be interesting to pursue the contradictory racial ideologies of Las Casas. For Las Casas, Mesoamerican peoples are noble savages who can be redeemed by the universality of the Christian faith. But how, then, does he justify having African slaves? Are they beyond redemption because of their race, according to Las Casas? In *The Conquest of America* (1984: 171–72) Todorov devotes some attention to these issues.

13   For discussions of colonialism in north America, see Richard Drinnon, *Facing West* (1990); Ronald Takaki, *Iron Cages* (1990); Richard Slotkin, *Regeneration Through Violence* (1973); Eric R. Wolf, *Europe and the People Without a History* (1982); and Olive Patricia Dickason, *The Myth of the Savage and the Beginnings of French Colonialism in the Americas* (1984).

14   There are several works that deal with the complexities of colonialism and post-colonialism in the United States in dialogue with such other sites of colonialism as India, Africa, Latin America, and China. These works include *An Other Tongue* (1994), edited by Alfred Arteaga; and *The Nature and Context of Minority Discourse* (1990), edited by Abdul R. JanMohamed and David Lloyd. Also see José David Saldívar, *The Dialectics of Our America* (1991), which locates Chicano literary/critical discourse in frameworks of colonialism and neocolonialism in the United States and Latin America.

15   See Frantz Fanon, *Black Skin, White Masks* (1967) for discussion of cultural schizophrenia produced by colonialism.

16   See Annette M. Jaimes, ed., *The State of Native America* (1992); and Ward Churchill, *The Struggle for the Land* (1993), which is a series of case studies on contemporary neocolonial encroachments and appropriation of tribal lands. Also, for

discussion of internal colonies, see Robert Blauner, *Racial Oppression in America* (1972), which describes how communities of color are segmented into internal colonies in the United States, providing cheap and unprotected labor. For discussion of how this segmentation of internal colonies applies to Chicano communities, see Mario Barrera, *Race and Class in the Southwest* (1979), and Rudolfo Acuña, *Occupied America* (1988).

17 I am indebted to such vanguard theorists and literary historians as Gayatri Spivak (e.g., *Outside the Teaching Machine*, and *In Other Worlds*), Homi Bhabha (e.g., *Location of Culture* and *Nation and Narration*), and Edward Said (e.g., *Orientalism* and *Culture and Imperialism*). However, in these works there is never more than a brief mention of U.S. minoritized subjects. This does not disturb me as much as how the academy in its desire to circumscribe fields considers issues of colonialism and postcolonialism everywhere but in the United States and countries affected by U.S. imperialism. At the same time, U.S. scholars of color take issues of coloniality as central to discussion of "minority" literature, culture, and subjectivity. Also, see François Lionett, *Postcolonial Representations* (1994), which uses Chicano/a border theory to discuss the hybridity in Caribbean women writers. Even though Lionett offers an intriguing discussion of writers in conditions of neocolonialism (what she calls "post-contact" writers), she does not mention the United States.

18 The source for the Mayan use of the cross is in the documentary *The Southern Cross* by Abímael Gúzman, which was shown at the Pacific Film Archive on May 7, 1993, as part of the San Francisco International Film Festival. In addition, for an intriguing discussion of symbolic translation in colonial cultures, see Michael Taussig, *Colonialism and the Wild Man* (1987).

19 For an interesting discussion of the semiotics and ideologies of torture, see Elaine Scarry, *The Body in Pain* (1985), which discusses the body as a site manipulated by direct extension of power relations in a particular society (27–60); and Bartolomé de Las Casas, *The Devastation of the Indies: A Brief Account* (Brevissima relación de ls destruycíon de las Indies), first published in Seville, 1522, which chronicles torture and brutality during the Conquest.

20 See Firdous Azim, *The Colonial Rise of the Novel* (1993), which brilliantly discusses the rise of the autonomous bourgeois subject and its complicity with the imperial project (1–34).

21 For a critique of Kristeva's orientalist tendencies toward Chinese women, see Gayatri Spivak, "French Feminism in an International Frame," in her *In Other Worlds* (1988: 134–54). Also see Lisa Lowe, *Critical Terrains* (1991: 144–52).

22 See Bruce Johansen, *Forgotten Founders* (1982), and his "Native American Societies and the Evolution of Democracy in America, 1600–1800," (1990).

23 See Ashis Nandy, *The Intimate Enemy* (1983), which discusses sexuality and imperialism in India; Trinh T. Minh-ha, *Women, Native, Other* (1989), which discusses colonialist attitudes toward third world women; Firdous Azim, *The Colonial Rise of the Novel* (1993: 34–60), which discusses Aphra Behn's *Oronooko* in light of the rise of the noble black savage and the taboo of miscegenation in Euro-

pean cultural and literary discourse; and Ronald Takaki, *Iron Cages* (1990: 49, 114–15), which discusses miscegenation laws in the United States. These laws promoted usually violent unions between Anglo men and African women as a means of increasing the slave stock, but violently punish the union of African men with women of European descent.

2. When Mexicans Talk, Who Listens? The Crisis of Ethnography in Situating Early Voices from the U.S./Mexico Borderlands

1 See Thomas L. Friedman, *The Lexus and the Olive Tree* (2000), which unabashedly celebrates the global access of privileged and technologically sophisticated consumers.

2 See Kevin Bales, *Disposable People* (1999), which estimates that in the recent global era there are over twenty-seven million people who are in a state of slavery.

3 See international relations scholars Alex Fernández Jilberto and André Mommen, eds., *Regionalization and Globalization in the Modern World Economy* (1998), which examines the hegemony of "private capital enterprises" on regional states and local economies in the creation of a "borderless" global community and provides evidentiary statistical data.

4 See Zygmunt Bauman, *Globalization* (1998) for discussion of the mobility and fixity of peoples depending on their positions within the global economy.

5 Scholars who contribute to the field of critical border studies include José David Saldívar, Vicki Ruiz, Sonia Saldívar-Hull, Ramon Gutiérrez, Teresa McKenna, Rafael Pérez-Torres, Norma Alarcón, Alfred Arteaga, Gloria Anzaldúa, Rolando Romero, and Alberto Ledesma.

6 To support the rise in refugees seeking political asylum in the United States resulting from the U.S.-backed wars in El Salvador and Nicaragua the Mission neighborhood area was given sanctuary status. However, immigrant-rights activists are dismayed by the attempts of the city administration to repeal the sanctuary status.

7 See Richard Rodriguez, "Across the Borders of History" (1987), which relates the commissioned accounts of his journey into Tijuana, where he would return from the poverty of the barrios to the comfort of the San Diego Hilton in *Harpers Magazine* (March 1987:42–53).

8 I say this thinking of ex-Governor Pete Wilson's racially charged reelection campaign ads. These ads depicted Latinos running en mass across the U.S./Mexico border. Clearly, the semiotic charge of the image plays into the nativist fears of being run over by the "invading Latin hordes."

9 This border was established after the defeat of General Santa Anna through the Treaty of Guadalupe Hidalgo in 1848. The border is literally a straight line over 2,300 miles that has no respect for natural ecosystem formations and tribal territories. For a solid multidisciplinary study of the U.S./Mexico border, see J. West, ed., *Borderlands Sourcebook* (1983).

10 See Ángeles Gamio-González, *Manuel Gamio: Una lucha sin final* (1987). This

work, written by Gamio's granddaughter, is the only biography on Gamio in print.

11 See the final chapter in Ruth Behar's, *Translated Woman* (1993: 320–45), which discusses crossing the border carrying stories from Mexico and translating them for a U.S. academic audience.

12 For discussion of the caste system in Mexico that equates social privilege with quanta of European blood, see Jack Forbes, *Aztecas del Norte* (1973: 188–205); Jacques Lafaye, "Historical Differences" (1990); and Alan Knight, "Racism, Revolution, and Indigenismo" (1990).

13 See John Hart, *Revolutionary Mexico* (1987).

14 See Gonzalo Aguirre Beltrán, *La población negra de Mexico* (1990).

15 In his later work *Consideraciones sobre el problema indigena* (1948) Gamio reveals a change in his attitudes toward indigenous peoples. He understands the conditions of their poverty as not a product of blood and mentality, but as a result of conquest, dispossession, and racism.

16 For discussion of anti-Mexican attitudes, see David Gutiérrez, *Walls and Mirrors* (1995); and Arnoldo de León, *They Called Them Greasers* (1983). See also the pro-manifest destiny doctrine in Walter Prescott Webb, *The Texas Rangers* (1935).

17 For discussion of the fluidity of resistance to colonialism, see Chandra Mohanty, "Cartographies of Struggle" in her edited volume *Third World Women and the Politics of Feminism* (1991: 1–47); and Homi Bhabha, *The Location of Culture* (1994), especially the chapter "Of Mimicry and Man" (85–93).

18 For discussion of power relations involved in the representation of culture, see James Clifford, *The Predicament of Culture* (1988); James Clifford and George Marcus, eds., *Writing Culture* (1986); Renato Rosaldo, *Culture and Truth* (1989); Trinh T. Minh-ha, *Woman, Native, Other* (1989); and Tejaswini Niranjana, *Siting Translation* (1992).

19 For discussion on colonialism and cultural simulations, see Neal Bowers and Charles L. P. Silet, "An Interview with Gerald Vizenor" (1981).

20 Niranjana (1992) discusses the site of translation as "a practice that shapes, and takes shape within, the asymmetrical relations of power that operate under colonialism" (2).

21 For discussion of humor in ethnographic encounters, see Keith Basso, *Portraits of "The Whiteman"* (1979); Jaime de Angullo, *Indians in Overalls* (1985); and the introduction to *Yaqui Deer Songs* (1987) by Larry Evers and Felipe Molina.

22 See Stanley Ross, *Francisco I. Madero, Apostle of Mexican Democracy;* John Womack, *Zapata and the Mexican Revolution* (1970); and Enrique Krauze, *Biografías del Poder* (1992), a popular series on male leaders of the Mexican Revolution such as Francisco Villa, Emiliano Zapata, and Francisco I. Madero.

23 See Elaine Scarry, *The Body in Pain* (1985), which argues that torture is the most extreme manifestation of ideology (27–62).

24 To see how Chinese workers were demonized in California in ways similar to that of Mexicans and other people of color, see the chapter "The 'Heathen Chinee' and American Technology" in Ronald Takaki, *Iron Cages* (1990: 215–40).

25 As a term, "immigrant" is problematic in understanding Mexican people. What is the status for Mexicans who lived in Mexican territories before they were annexed by the Treaty of 1848? See Acuña (1988); Gutiérrez (1995); and John Chavéz, *The Lost Land* (1984). For further discussion of immigration and questions of identity and liminality, see Roger Rouse, "Mexican Migration and the Social Space of Postmodernism" (1991).

26 See José David Saldívar, *The Dialectics of Our America* (1991), for discussion of oppositional pan-Latino alliances.

27 See Leo Chavez, *Shadowed Lives* (1991); and Renato Rosaldo, "Ideology, Place, and People without Culture" (1988).

28 There are other tensions in the text that exist beyond the immigrants' voices, the ethnographic apparatus, and the racially charged social-historical context. For example, the text provides many examples of interethnic tensions between the Mexican Americans and recently arrived Mexicans. See David Gutiérrez, *Walls and Mirrors* (1995: 61–68) where he analyzes the tensions between the Californios and other original residents of the Southwest, such as *Pochos* (people of Mexican descent "bleached" and assimilated in the Anglo culture), and the immigrants. Also, Gamio relates several instances where the narrators comment on their mistreatment by the Japanese, or the case of Wenceslao Iglesias who is appalled at being told to sit in the "colored section" of a restaurant (177).

29 See Emma Pérez (1999) for a discussion of patriarchal bias in Chicano labor histories.

30 For an overview of the Bracero Program see David Gutiérrez, *Walls and Mirrors* (1995: 133–51); and Rudolfo Acuña, *Occupied America* (1988).

3. Counting Coup: Narrative Acts of (Re)Claiming Identity in *Ceremony* by Leslie Marmon Silko

For a discussion of counting coup in narrative, see Catherine Rainwater, *Dreams of Fiery Stars* (1999: 33–34).

1 According to John Mason Hart in *Revolutionary Mexico* (1987), the racial caste system was abolished by the independence movements of 1810. For discussion of the racial caste system, see Jacques Lafaye, "Historical Differences" (1990); and Jack Forbes, *Aztecas del Norte* (1973), especially the chapter "The Mestizo Concept and the Strategy of Colonialism" (188–205). Also see Ronald Wright, *Stolen Continents* (1992), where he describes the Mayan Caste War of 1821 (255–63). Finally, see Alan Knight, "Racism, Revolution, and Indigenismo" (1990: 71–113).

2 See Ronald Takaki, *Iron Cages* (1990), which discusses the origins and justification for racial inequality in the United States. In contrast to the growth of mestizaje in Mexico, the politics of conquest in the United States are characterized by an overriding fear of miscegenation, especially concerning African peoples (59–60; 114–15).

3 For discussions of how "Indians" are invented and simulated in racially essentialist terms, see Robert Berkhofer, *The White Man's Indian* (1978); Louis Owens,

Other Destinies (1992: 3–32); Gerald Vizenor, *Manifest Manners* (1994); and W. S. Penn, *All My Sins Are Relatives* (1995: 185–216).

4 See Henry Louis Gates Jr. in his introduction to *"Race," Writing, and Difference* (1986), where he discusses how "writing" is considered solely the possession of the Europeans (9–19).

5 See Tobin Siebers's discussion of Rousseau's influence on contemporary cultural anthropology in *The Ethics of Criticism* (1988: 69–97). For discussions of the idea of the "savage" in European thought, see Antonello Gerbi, *The Dispute of the New World* (1973); Lewis Hanke, *Aristotle and the American Indians* (1959); and Olive Patricia Dickason, *The Myth of the Savage* (1984). In the case of the "savage" in Euro-American colonial thought and literary practice, see Roy Pearce's *Savagism and Civilization* (1988); and Robert Berkhofer, *The White Man's Indian* (1978).

6 In addition to the theorists already mentioned in these notes, I refer to the following theorists and their writings (to name a few) who repatriate subaltern cultural and literary production in the United States and other sites of postcoloniality and multiculturalism: Ngũgĩ Wa Thiong'o, Gayatri Spivak, Tejaswini Niranjana, Alfred Arteaga, Homi Bhabha, Gerald Vizenor, Trinh T. Minh-ha, Norma Alarcón, José David Saldívar, and Paul Gilroy.

7 The Mexica amoxtli and Mayan vuh are hand-painted "sacred texts" that encode, record, and facilitate the transmission of the genealogical, astronomic, and scientific knowledge in these civilizations.

8 Also see the following: Ian Watt, *The Rise of the Novel* (1957), which brilliantly locates the rise of novel with the rise of capitalism, the middle class, and the individual; Terry Eagleton, "The Rise of English" in *Literary Theory* (1983: 17–54), which considers how novels perpetuate models of the ideal bourgeois families in times of extreme alienation produced by the rise of industrialism; and Firdous Azim, *The Colonial Rise of the Novel* (1993).

9 See the discussion of the polyphonic syncretic, or postcolonial hybrid, in Bill Ashcroft et al., *The Empire Writes Back* (1989); and Robert Young, *Colonial Desire* (1995: 1–25). Also see the discussion of emergent significatory practices in African American literary production in Henry Louis Gates Jr., *The Signifying Monkey* (1988); and discussions of Chicano, Latin American, and postcolonial hybrid cultural production in José David Saldívar, *Border Matters* (1997) and *Dialectics of Our America* (1991: 121–49).

10 For examples of syncretic narrative sites, see Gerald Vizenor, *Bearheart* (1990); Ishmael Reed, *Mumbo Jumbo* (1985); and Gloria Anzaldúa, *Borderlands/La Frontera* (1987), who writes in languages that reflect the historical range of Chicana/o identities: English, Spanish, Caló, and Nahuatl.

11 See David Moore, "Myth, History, and Identity in Silko and Young Bear" (1993: 370–87) for an excellent discussion of relational and communal subjectivity.

12 See W. S. Penn, *All My Sins Are Relatives* (1995), which discusses the history of power relations in Native American writing using personal examples of his own novel (151–85). See also Arnold Krupat, *For Those Who Come After* (1985) for dis-

cussion of power relations between anthropologists and editors and the "native" informants.

13 For discussion on the importance of Thought-Woman in the Southwest, see Paula Gunn Allen, *The Sacred Hoop* (1986).

14 See Gerald Prince, "Introduction to the Study of the Narratee" (1980). Prince argues that within novels there is an internal dialogic relationship between the narrator and who that narrator addresses. In a lecture at Berkeley on November 10, 1992, Gerald Vizenor argued that "through trying to articulate the narrative possibilities surrounding the location of the narratee, we are able to appreciate the codes, humor, and language play of a particular narrator. This will reveal the given tribal or ethnic authenticity of a particular author without falling into the essentialist traps surrounding an author's marketed ethnicity."

15 For a general discussion of the effects of World War II on Native Americans, see Allison Bernstein, *American Indians and World War II* (1991). For a discussion of the role of the purification ceremonies for Navaho and Zuni soldiers before and after World War II, see John Adair and Evon Vogt, "Navaho and Zuni Veterans" (1949).

16 For an anthropological discussion of the specific phases of this journey home, see Edith Swann, "Healing via the Sunwise Cycle in Silko's *Ceremony*" (1988), and "Laguna Symbolic Geography in Silko's *Ceremony*" (1988). Note, however, that these readings are problematic in that they assume that Silko's text is a cultural artifact and representative of Laguna symbology, ceremony, and ritual, and thereby deny the imaginative play of the text.

17 See Wallace Martin, *Recent Theories of Narrative* (1986), which discusses Gustav Freytag's interpretive model of plot development (81–83).

18 For an interesting historical overview of the Marmon family and "how they all married Laguna women and formed a small colony," see Ellis Florence, *Handbook of North American Indians*, vol 9 (1979: 447). Also see Leslie Marmon Silko, *Storyteller* (1981), especially the stories of her grandmother.

19 For discussion of cultural schizophrenia produced through colonialism, see Frantz Fanon, *Black Skin, White Masks* (1967), and Homi Bhabha's foreword to the 1986 edition of that volume; and N'gúgí Wa Thiong'o, *Decolonising the Mind* (1988).

20 For a discussion of crossing between indigenous peoples and Europeans in the United States, see David Smits, "Abominable Mixture" (1987).

21 Here I am indebted to Deena Gonzalez. In her careful reading of a version of this chapter, she suggested that the name might come from the Spanish verb *tallar,* especially because Silko speaks Spanish.

22 For discussion of colonialist and neocolonialist functions through racial and sexual violence on women, see Norma Alarcón, "Chicana Feminism in the Tracks of 'The' Native Woman" (1990); Trinh T. Minh-ha, *Woman, Native, Other* (1989); and Chandra Mohanty, ed., *Third World Women and the Politics of Feminism* (1990: 1–51).

23 See Maria Campell, *Halfbreed* (1973).

24 See John Chávez, *The Lost Land* (1984), especially the first chapter. Also see Richard Parmentier in "The Mythological Triangle" (1979) where he examines stories of Montezuma. According to popular stories in the Southwest, Montezuma is a sorcerer who left the Pueblos for the valley of Mexico but prophesied one day to return.

25 See Jana Sequoya, "How(!) Is an Indian" (1993). Sequoya argues that Mexico and Latin America offer models of "stable" mestizo societies that contrast with the fragmentation of crossblood Native American identity. However, her argument is problematic because it denies how indigenous peoples are marginalized by mixedblood ladino hegemonies.

4. Toward a Hermeneutics of Decolonization: Reading Radical Subjectivities in *Borderlands/La Frontera: The New Mestiza* by Gloria Anzaldúa

1 See Emma Pérez, *The Decolonial Imaginary* (1999: 3–31).

2 See Arjun Appadurai, *Modernity at Large* (1996). See also Lourdes Torres, "The Construction of the Self in U.S. Latina Autobiographies" (1991). Torres argues that through "a mixture of genres," Latina autobiographers "marginalized by multiple discourses, and existing in a borderland" reject "prescriptive positions" and create "radical personal and collective identities" (275). For discussion of genres and the rise of Western civilization, see Alfred Arteaga, *Chicano Poetics* (1997: 126–57).

3 I am indebted to José David Saldívar for pointing out the term *autohistoriateoría,* which Gloria Anzaldúa shared with him during an interview.

4 In the Santeria traditions of Cuba, Yemaya is the Yoruban Orisha seen as the mother of all creation associated with the primordial force of the sea and wind. Anzaldúa acknowledges that she is the daughter of Yemaya.

5 See James Olney, ed., *Autobiography* (1980). Kaplan argues that "the placement of Gusdorf's essay at the head of Olney's anthology of autobiography criticism signifies the influence of Gusdorf in the field" (117).

6 Even though Jacques Derrida limits the majority of his critical work to European philosophy and theory, he reveals contradictions internal to the epistemologies from which European discourse draws its authority. See his "Law of Genre" (1980: 203–4). Derrida discusses the paradoxical nature of the term "genre." It is unclassifiable due to an intrinsic play of signifier-signified relationships—"the counterlaw." The "law," however, promotes its demarcation as "a norm" that "cannot risk impurity, anomaly or monstrosity" (204).

7 See Roy Harvey Pearce, *Savagism and Civilization* (1988); Richard Drinnon, *Facing West* (1980); Robert Berkhofer, *The White Man's Indian* (1978); and Richard Slotkin's *Regeneration through Violence* (1973).

8 See Walter Prescott Webb, *The Texas Rangers* (1935), and Arnoldo De León, *They Called Them Greasers* (1983). For discussions of the U.S. cavalry and "The Meta-

physics of Indian Hating," see Ronald Takaki, *Iron Cages* (1990); Richard Drinnon, *Facing West* (1980); and Richard Slotkin, *Regeneration through Violence* (1973).

9   For discussions of how traits such as immorality, bestiality, and criminality are
historically essentialized to race and skin color, see Winthrop Jordan, *White Over
Black* (1968). Also, for discussions of how bestiality, hypersexuality, and criminality are essentialized to race and gender, see Sander Gilman, "Black Bodies,
White Bodies" (1985).

10   To read the Black Panther "Ten Point Plan" along with historical analysis, see
Robert Allen, *Black Awakening in Capitalist America* (1990: 83–88). To read the
Chicano Movement Manifestos, see *Documents of the Chicano Struggle* (1971). To
see the "Plan de Santa Barbara: Manifesto," refer to Antonia Castañeda Shular,
Tomás Ybarra-Frausto, and Joseph Sommers, eds., *Literatura Chicana* (1972: 85–
87). Also see Armando Rendón, ed., *Chicano Manifesto* (1971). For historical analysis of the Chicano Movement Manifestos, see Carlos Muñoz Jr., *Youth, Identity,
and Power* (1989: 75–97, 191–202).

11   See Trinh T. Minh-ha, *Woman, Native, Other* (1989); Chandra Mohanty et al., eds.,
Third World Women and the Politics of Feminism (1990: 1–51); and Norma Alarcón,
"Chicana Feminism" (1990).

12   See Raymond Williams, *The Country and the City* (1973).

13   See Tobin Siebers's discussion of Rousseau's influence on contemporary cultural
anthropology in *The Ethics of Criticism* (1988: 69–97). For discussions of the
"noble savage" in European thought, see Antonello Gerbi, *The Dispute of the New
World* (1973); Lewis Hanke, *Aristotle and the American Indians* (1959); Olive Patricia Dickason, *The Myth of the Savage* (1984); and Robert Berkhofer "The Cult of
the Noble Savage" in *The White Man's Indian* (1978: 72–80).

14   See Teresa Córdova, ed., *Chicana Voices* (1993), especially Denise Segura, "Chicanas and the Triple Oppression in the Labor Force" (47–66). Also see Margarita Melville, ed., *Twice a Minority* (1980); and Elizabeth Martínez and Ed
McCaughan, "Chicanas and Mexicanas within a Transnational Working Class"
(1990).

15   See Leo Chavez, *Shadowed Lives* (1992: 30–55), which compiles testimonies of
exploitation and fears of crossing the border by "undocumented" women. Also
see Adelaida Del Castillo, ed., *Between Borders* (1990); and Wayne A. Cornelius,
Mexican Migration to the United States (1978).

16   The ladino hegemony in Mexico is currently being challenged by the Zapatista
rebellion. To read their communiqués and interviews, see Ben Clarke and Clifton
Ross, eds., *Voices of Fire* (1994).

17   See Terry Wilson, "Blood Quantum" (1992); and W. S. Penn, *All My Sins Are Relatives* (1995).

18   For discussion of the racial caste system in Mexico, see Jacques Lafaye, "Historical
Differences" (1990).

19   See Miguel León-Portilla, *Aztec Thought and Culture* (1963), which states: "In
short, Ometeotl was the cosmic energy upon which everything depended; the
world, the sun, and the stars" (31); and Jack Forbes, *Aztecas del Norte* (1973: 53–

54), which compares Omeoteotl with the spiritual concepts of the Creator and of the Great Mystery in North American tribes.

20 See Miguel León-Portilla, *Aztec Thought and Culture* (1963: 52–53).

21 See Adelaida Del Castillo, "Malintzin Tenépal" in her edited collection *Between Borders* (1990).

22 For discussion of Malintzin as La Chingada ('the fucked one," and the "Eve" of the Mexican people, see Octavio Paz, *The Labyrinth of Solitude* (1961: 78–89).

23 See William Roscoe, *The Zuni Man-Woman* (1991), which draws into question how much of violent homophobia is a product of colonialist cultures and their transported codes of gender, masculinity, and femininity. Also see Richard Trexler, *Sex and Conquest* (1995).

5. A Border Coda: Dangerous Bodies, Liminality, and the Reclamation of Space in *Star Maps* by Miguel Arteta

1 Two important "white" scholars engaging with the history and consequences of whiteness have enriched my thinking on white privilege: Richard Dyer, *White* (1997) and Ruth Frankenburg, ed., *Displacing Whiteness* (1997: 1–33). I also find bell hooks, *Killing Rage* (1995) crucial to recognizing how "white privilege" predicates the structural and "everyday" interactions between people of color and people in the dominant culture.

2 See Mary Louise Pratt, *Imperial Eyes* (1992). See also James Clifford's *Routes* (1997), where he struggles "to free" the term "travel" from the discourses and practices embedded in a "history of European, literary, male, bourgeois, scientific, heroic meanings and practices" (33–39). My thinking on travel, movement, and the negotiation of space is also influenced by Krista Comer's understanding of Western spatiality as "extremely laden with both an admission and a silencing of the historical fact of multicontinental genocide" (*Landscapes of the New West*, 1999: 37).

3 See Vickie Ruiz, " 'And Miles to Go . . .' " (1988), which charts systematically the low wage earnings of Chicanas. Also see David Maciel, ed., *Chicanas/Chicanos at the Crossroads* (1996: 52–81).

4 See George Lipsitz, *The Possessive Investment in Whiteness* (1999), which examines post-civil-rights era racial segregation in the labor and housing markets and the proliferation of legally protected white privilege communities. Also consider the evocative descriptions of Latina/o Los Angeles in Rubén Martínez, *The Other Side* (1993).

5 See Carl Gutiérrez-Jones, *Rethinking the Borderlands* (1995). For discussion of criminalization of the Chicano community and the resultant incarceration rates, see López, ed., *Criminal Justice and Latino Communities* (1995).

6 For a critique of Hicks's often-cited work, see Juan Bruce-Novoa (1996) and Maria Cordoba (1996).

7 For a discussion of how border cultures resist and subvert these tendencies, see

Guillermo Gómez-Peña's examination in "Border Culture" (1986) of hybridity and carnival along the border. See also his book, *Warrior for Gringostroika* (1993).

8 See Roger Rouse, "Mexican Migration and the Social Space of Postmodernism" (1991); and Renato Rosaldo, "Ideology, Place, and People Without Culture" (1988), which discusses the cultural invisibility of undocumented workers in the United States.

9 For a discussion of gender formation in Mexican and Chicano families, see Adelaida Del Castillo, "Gender and Its Discontinuities in Male/Female Domestic Relations" (1996: 207–31).

10 For a full description of the nineteen-member coalition, see the 10 September 1999 NCLR News Release, "NAACP, Latino, Asian American and Native American Groups Unite to Address Minority Underrepresentation at Television Networks."

11 For a discussion of how Chicanas/os have been vilified throughout the history of U.S. cinema, see Arthur Pettit, *Images of the Mexican American in Fiction and Film* (1980); Gary D. Keller, *Hispanics and United States Film* (1994); and Frank Javier Garcia Berumen, *The Chicano/Hispanic Image in American Film* (1995).

12 For a discussion of Chicana cinematic discourse that challenges the demonization of Chicana/o subjects as well as the positioning of women as passive and silent in male nationalist Chicano cinema, see "Chicana Film Practices" by Rosa Linda Fregoso in *Chicanos and Film*, ed., Chon Noriega (1992). Also see Aurelio de los Reyes's discussion of the "loose woman" and "suffering mother" archetypes in nationalist cinema in "El nacionalismo en el cine, 1910–1930" (1986).

13 For a discussion of the "Latin lover" image, see Keller (1994: 140); and Berumen (1995: 5–20).

14 For a discussion of the differences between the Euro-American family structure and the extended family, nonexclusive mothering activities in Chicanas/os and African American families, see Denise Segura and Jennifer Pierce, "Chicana/o Family Structure and Gender Personality" (1993).

15 See Yvette Flores-Ortiz, "The Broken Covenant" (1997); and Mónica Russel y Rodríguez, "(En)countering Domestic Violence, Complicity, and Definitions of Chicana Womanhood" (1997).

16 See Tomas Almaguer, "Chicano Men" (1991) for a discussion of how active and passive positions configure topographies of machismo, masculinity, and homosexuality in Mexico.

17 See Henry Giroux, "White Panic and the Racial Coding of Violence" in his *Fugitive Cultures* (1996: 27–55).

18 See Elizabeth Grosz, *Volatile Bodies* (1994) for an in-depth analysis of how social, juridical, cultural, medical, and familial apparatuses of power inscribe bodies.

19 For a discussion of globalization and child prostitution and slavery, see Kevin Bales, *Disposable People* (1999).

.

Selected Bibliography

Achebe, Chinua. *Things Fall Apart*. Greenwich, Conn.: Fawcett, 1959.

Acuña, Rodolfo. *Occupied America: A History of Chicanos*. 3rd ed. New York: Harper, 1988.

Adair, John, and Evon Vogt. "Navaho and Zuni Veterans: A Study of Contrasting Modes of Culture Change." *American Anthropologist* 51, 4 (1949): 547–61.

Aguirre Beltrán, Gonzalo. *La población negra de México: Estudio etnohistórico*. Mexico D. F.: Fondo de Cultura Económica, 1990.

Ahmad, Aijaz. "Politics, Literature, and Postcoloniality." *Race and Class* 36, 3 (1995): 1–21.

Alarcón, Norma. "Anzaldúa's *Frontera:* Inscribing Gynetics." In *Displacement, Diaspora, and Geographies of Identity*, ed. Lavie Smadar and Ted Swedenburg. Durham, N.C.: Duke University Press, 1997.

———. "Conjugating Subjects: The Heteroglossia of Essence and Resistance." In *An Other Tongue: Nation and Ethnicity in the Linguistic Borderlands*, ed. Alfred Arteaga. Durham, N.C.: Duke University Press, 1994.

———. "The Theoretical Subject(s) of *This Bridge Called My Back* and Anglo-American Feminism." In *Criticism in the Borderlands: Studies in Chicano Literature, Culture, and Ideology*, ed. Héctor Calderón and José David Saldívar. Durham, N.C.: Duke University Press, 1991.

———. "Chicana Feminism: In the Tracks of 'The' Native Woman." *Cultural Studies* 3, 4 (1990): 248–56.

———. "Chicanas Feminist Literature: A Re-vision Through Malintzin: Putting the Flesh Back on the Object." In *This Bridge Called My Back: Writings by Radical Women of Color*, ed. Gloria Anzaldúa and Cherríe Moraga. 2nd ed. New York: Kitchen Table/Women of Color, 1983.

Alcoff, Linda. "Cultural Feminism versus Poststructuralism: The Identity Crisis in Feminist Theory." *Signs* 13 (1988): 405–36.

Aldama, Arturo. "Sacred Breath, Sacred Life Dialogues." B.A. thesis, Evergreen State College, Special Collections Library, 1988.

Allen, Paula Gunn. "Special Problems in the Teaching of Leslie Marmon Silko's *Ceremony*." *American Indian Quarterly* 15 (1990): 379–86.

———. *The Sacred Hoop: Recovering the Feminine in American Indian Tradition.* Boston: Beacon, 1986.

———, ed. *Studies in American Indian Literature.* New York: Modern Language Association, 1983.

Allen, Robert L. *Black Awakening in Capitalist America: An Analytic History.* Trenton, N.J.: African World, 1990.

Almaguer, Tomas. "Chicano Men: A Cartography of Homosexual Identity and Behavior." *differences: A Journal of Feminist Cultural Studies* 3, 2 (1991): 15–100.

Althusser, Louis. "Ideology and the State." *Lenin and Philosophy and Other Essays.* Trans. Ben Brewster. New York: Monthly Review, 1971.

Anaya, Ruldolfo. *Albuquerque.* Albuquerque: University of New Mexico Press, 1992.

Anaya, Ruldolfo, and Francisco Lomeli, eds. *Aztlan: Essays on the Chicano Homeland.* Albuquerque, N. Mex.: El Norte, 1989.

Anderson, Benedict. *Imagined Communities: Reflections on the Origin and Spread of Nationalism.* London: Verso, 1987.

Anzaldúa, Gloria. *Borderlands/La Frontera: The New Mestiza.* 1987. 2nd ed., with introduction by Sonia Saldívar-Hull. San Francisco: Aunt Lute, 1999.

———, ed. *Haciendo Caras: Making Face, Making Soul: Creative and Critical Perspectives by Feminists of Color.* San Francisco: Spinsters/Aunt Lute, 1990.

Anzaldúa, Gloria, and Cherríe Moraga, eds. *This Bridge Called My Back: Writings by Radical Women of Color.* 2nd ed. New York: Kitchen Table/Women of Color, 1983.

Appadurai, Arjun. *Modernity at Large: Cultural Dimensions of Globalization.* Minneapolis: University of Minnesota Press, 1996.

Appiah, Kwama Anthony. "Is the Post- in Postmodernism the Post- in Postcolonial?" *Critical Inquiry* 17, 2 (1991): 336–57.

Arteaga, Alfred. *Chicano Poetics: Heterotexts and Hybridities.* Cambridge: Cambridge University Press, 1997.

———, ed. *An Other Tongue: Nation and Ethnicity in the Linguistic Borderlands.* Durham, N.C.: Duke University Press, 1994.

Asad, Talal. "The Concept of Cultural Translation in British Social Anthropology." In *Writing Culture: The Poetics and Politics of Ethnography,* ed. James Clifford and George Marcus. Berkeley: University of California Press, 1986.

Ashcroft, Bill, Gareth Griffiths, and Helen Tiffin. *The Empire Writes Back: Theory and Practice in Post-Colonial Literatures.* London: Routledge, 1989.

———, eds. *The Post-Colonial Studies Reader.* London: Routledge, 1994.

Azim, Firdous. *The Colonial Rise of the Novel.* London: Routledge, 1993.

Bahktin, M. Mikhail. *Speech Genres and Other Late Essays.* Ed. Caryl Emerson and Michael Holquist. Trans. Vern W. McGee. Austin: University of Texas Press, 1986.

———. *The Dialogic Imagination: Four Essays.* Ed. Michael Holquist. Trans. Caryl Emerson and Michael Holquist. Austin: University of Texas Press, 1981.

————. *Rabelais and His World*. Trans. Helene Iswolksy. Cambridge, Mass.: MIT Press, 1968.

Bahktin, M. Mikhail, and Pavel N. Medvedev. *The Formal Method in Literary Scholarship: A Critical Introduction to Sociological Poetics*. Trans. Albert J. Wehrle. Baltimore: Johns Hopkins University Press, 1978.

Baker, Houston A. Jr. "Caliban's Triple Play." In *"Race," Writing, and Difference*, ed. Henry Louis Gates Jr. Chicago: University of Chicago Press, 1986.

Balderrama, Francisco E., and Raymond Rodríguez. *Decade of Betrayal: Mexican Repatriation in the 1930s*. Albuquerque: University of New Mexico Press, 1995.

Bales, Kevin. *Disposable People: New Slavery in the Global Economy*. Berkeley: University of California Press, 1999.

Balibar, Etienne, and Immanuel Wallerstein. *Race, Nation, Class: Ambiguous Identities*. London: Verso, 1991.

Barrera, Mario. *Beyond Aztlán: Ethnic Autonomy in Comparative Perspective*. New York: Praeger, 1988.

————. *Race and Class in the Southwest: A Theory of Racial Inequality*. Notre Dame, Ind.: University of Notre Dame Press, 1979.

Barrios de Chungara, Domitila, and Moema Viezzer. *Let Me Speak! Testimony of Domitila, a Woman of the Bolivian Mines*. Trans. Victoria Ortiz. New York: Monthly Review, 1978.

Barth, Frederik, ed. *Ethnic Groups and Boundaries: The Social Organization of Culture Difference*. Boston: Little, Brown, 1969.

Basso, Keith. *Portraits of "The Whiteman": Linguistic Play and Cultural Symbols among the Western Apache*. Cambridge: Cambridge University Press, 1979.

Batalla, Guillermo Bonfil. *México Profundo: Reclaiming a Civilization*. Trans. Philip A. Denis. Austin: University of Texas Press, 1996.

Bauman, Zygmunt. *Globalization: The Human Consequences*. New York: Columbia University Press, 1998.

Behar, Ruth. *Translated Woman: Crossing the Border with Esperanza's Story*. Boston: Beacon, 1993.

Bejarano-Yarbo, Yvonne. "Gloria Anzaldúa's *Borderlands/La Frontera:* Cultural Studies, 'Difference,' and the Non-Unitary Subject." *Cultural Critique* 28 (1994): 5–29.

Benjamin, Walter. "On Language as Such and on the Language of Man." In *Reflections: Essays, Aphorisms, Autobiographical Writings*, ed. Peter Demetz. New York: Harcourt, 1978.

Bennett, Tony. *Outside Literature*. London: Routledge, 1990.

Benveniste, Emile. *Problems in General Linguistics*. Trans. by Mary Elizabeth Meek. Coral Gables, Fla.: University of Miami Press, 1971.

Berkhofer, Robert. *The White Man's Indian: Images of the American Indian from Columbus to the Present*. New York: Vintage, 1978.

Bernheimer, Richard. *Wild Men in the Middle Ages: A Study in Art, Sentiment, and Demonology*. Cambridge, Mass.: Harvard University Press, 1952.

Bernstein, Allison. *American Indians and World War II*. Norman: University of Oklahoma Press, 1991.

Berumen, Frank Javier Garcia. *The Chicano/Hispanic Image in American Film*. New York: Vantage Press, 1995.

Beverley, John. *Against Literature*. Minneapolis: University of Minnesota Press, 1993.

———. "The Margin at the Center: On Testimonio (Testimonial Narrative)." In *De/Colonizing the Subject: The Politics of Gender in Women's Autobiography*, ed. Sidonie Smith and Julia Watson. Minneapolis: University of Minnesota Press, 1992.

Bhabha, Homi K. *The Location of Culture*. London: Routledge, 1994.

Blauner, Robert. *Racial Oppression in America*. New York: Harper, 1972.

Blea, Irene I. *La Chicana and the Intersection of Race, Class, and Gender*. New York: Praeger, 1992.

Bowers, Neal, and Charles L. P. Silet. "An Interview with Gerald Vizenor." *MELUS* 8 (1981): 45–47.

Boyd, William. *Genetics and the Races of Man*. Chicago: Little, Brown, 1952.

Boyle, T. Coraghessan. *The Tortilla Curtain*. New York: Viking, 1995.

Bravebird, Mary, and Richard Erdoes. *Ohitka Woman*. New York: Grove, 1993.

———. *Lakota Woman*. New York: Grove, 1991.

Calderón, Héctor, and José David Saldívar, eds. *Criticism in the Borderlands: Studies in Chicano Literature and Ideology*. Durham, N.C.: Duke University Press, 1991.

Campell, Maria. *Halfbreed*. Lincoln: University of Nebraska Press, 1973.

Cardoso, Lawrence. *Mexican Emigration to the United States: Socio-Economic Patterns*. Tucson: University of Arizona Press, 1980.

Castillo, Ana. *Massacre of the Dreamers: Essays on Xicanisma*. New York: Penguin, 1995.

———. *So Far from God*. New York: W. W. Norton, 1994.

Castillo, Isidoro. *Indigenistas de México*. Mexico City: Secretaría de Educación Pública Dirección General de Asuntos Indígenas, 1968.

Ceinos, Pedro. *Abya Yala: Escenas de una historia India de América*. Madrid: Miraguano Ediciones, 1992.

Chabram-Dernersesian, Angie. "On the Social Construction of Whiteness within Selected Chicana/o Discourses." In *Displacing Whiteness: Essays in Social and Cultural Criticism*, ed. Ruth Frankenberg. Durham, N.C.: Duke University Press, 1997.

Chávez, John. *The Lost Land: The Chicano Image of the Southwest*. Albuquerque: University of New Mexico Press, 1984.

Chavez, Leo. *Shadowed Lives: Undocumented Immigrants in American Society*. Fort Worth, Tex.: Harcourt, 1992.

Churchill, Ward. *Struggle for the Land: Indigenous Resistance to Genocide, Ecocide, and Expropriation in Contemporary North America*. Monroe, Maine: Common Courage, 1993.

Churchill, Ward, and Jim Vander Wall. *Agents of Repression: The FBI's Secret War Against the Black Panther Party and the American Indian Movement*. Boston: South End, 1990.

Cisneros, Sandra. *Woman Hollering Creek and Other Stories*. New York: Random House, 1991.

————. *The House on Mango Street.* 2nd ed. Houston: Arte Público, 1988.

Clarke, Ben, and Clifton Ross. *Voices of Fire: Communiqués and Interviews from the Zapatista National Liberation Army.* Berkeley, Calif.: New Earth, 1994.

Clifford, James. *Routes: Travel and Representation in the Late Twentieth Century.* Cambridge: Harvard University Press, 1997.

————. *The Predicament of Culture: Twentieth Century Ethnography, Literature, and Art.* Cambridge: Harvard University Press, 1988.

————. "On Ethnographic Authority." *Representations* 2 (1983): 132–43.

Clifford, James, and George Marcus, eds. *Writing Culture: The Poetics and Politics of Ethnography.* Berkeley: University of California Press, 1986.

Comer, Krista. *Landscapes of the New West: Gender and Geography in Contemporary Women's Writing.* Chapel Hill: University of North Carolina Press, 1999.

Córdova, Teresa, ed. *Chicana Voices: Intersections of Race, Class and Gender.* Albuquerque: University of New Mexico Press, 1993.

Crow Dog, Mary, and Richard Erdoes. *Lakota Woman.* New York: Harper, 1991.

Davis, Marilyn P. *Mexican Voices/American Dreams: An Oral History of Mexican Immigration to the United States.* New York: Henry Holt, 1990.

Davis, Mike. *City of Quartz: Excavating the Future in Los Angeles.* New York: Vintage, 1992.

De la Peña, Guillermo. "Nationals and Foreigners in the History of Mexican Anthropology." In *The Conditions of Reciprocal Understanding,* ed. James W. Fernández and Milton B. Singer. Chicago: The Center for International Studies, University of Chicago, 1992.

De Lauretis, Teresa. *The Technologies of Gender: Essays on Theory, Film, and Fiction.* Bloomington: Indiana University Press, 1987.

Del Castillo, Adelaida R., ed. *Between Borders: Essays on Mexicana/Chicana History.* Encino, Calif.: Floricanto, 1990.

De León, Arnoldo. *They Called Them Greasers: Anglo Attitudes toward Mexicans in Texas, 1821–1900.* Austin: University of Texas Press, 1983.

Deleuze, Gilles, and Félix Guattari. *Anti Oedipus: Capitalism and Schizophrenia.* Trans. Robert Hurley, Mark Seem, and Helen R. Lane. Minneapolis: University of Minnesota Press, 1983.

Derrida, Jacques. "Law of Genre." Trans. Avital Ronel. *Glyph* 7 (1980): 203–4.

————. *Writing and Difference.* Trans. Allan Bass. Chicago: University of Chicago Press, 1978.

————. *Of Grammatology.* Trans. Gayatri Chakravorty Spivak. Baltimore: Johns Hopkins University Press, 1976.

Dickason, Olive Patricia. *The Myth of the Savage and the Beginnings of French Colonialism in the Americas.* Edmonton, Canada: University of Alberta Press, 1984.

Drinnon, Richard. *Facing West: The Metaphysics of Indian-Hating and Empire-Building.* New York: Schocken, 1980.

Dyer, Richard. *White.* London: Routledge, 1997.

Eagleton, Terry. *Literary Theory: An Introduction.* Minneapolis: University of Minnesota Press, 1983.

Eggan, Fred. *Social Organization of the Western Pueblos.* Chicago: University of Chicago Press, 1950.

Eisenstein, Sergei. "A Dialectic Approach to Film Form." In *Film Theory and Criticism: Introductory Reading,* ed. Gerald Mast, Marshall Cohen, and Leo Braudy. 4th ed. New York: Oxford University Press, 1992.

Eisenstein, Zillah. *Hatreds: Racialized and Sexualized Conflicts in the Twenty-first Century.* New York: Routledge, 1996.

Ellis, Florence Hawley. "The Laguna Pueblo." In *Handbook of North American Indians,* vol. 9. Ed. William C. Sturtevant. Washington, D.C.: Smithsonian, 1959.

———. "Keresan Patterns of Kinship and Social Organization." *American Anthropologist* 152 (1950): 499–513.

Fanon, Frantz. *Black Skin, White Masks.* Trans. Charles Lam Markmann. New York: Grove, 1967.

———. *The Wretched of the Earth.* Trans. Constance Farrington. New York: Grove, 1966.

Fernández-Kelly, María Patricia. *For We Are Sold, I and My People: Women and Industry in Mexico's Frontier.* Albany: State University of New York Press, 1983.

Fernández-Retamar, Roberto. *Caliban and Other Essays.* Trans. Edward Baker. Minneapolis: University of Minnesota Press, 1989.

Fisher, Michael M. J. "Ethnicity and the Post-Modern Arts of Memory." In *Writing Culture: The Poetics and Politics of Ethnography,* ed. James Clifford and George E. Marcus. Berkeley: University of California Press, 1986.

Flores-Ortiz, Yvette. "The Broken Covenant: Incest in the Latino Family." *Voces: A Journal of Chicana/Latina Studies* 1, 2 (1997): 48–70.

Forbes, Jack. *Columbus and Other Cannibals: The Wétiko Disease of Exploitation, Imperialism, and Terrorism.* Brooklyn, N.Y.: Autonomedia, 1992.

———. *Aztecas del Norte: The Chicanos of Aztlan.* Greenwich, Conn.: Fawcett, 1973.

Foucault, Michel. "Of Other Spaces." Trans. Jay Miskowiec. *Diacritics* 16, 1 (1986): 22–27.

———. *Discipline and Punish: The Birth of a Prison.* Trans. Alan Sheridan. New York: Vintage, 1979.

———. *The Archeology of Knowledge; and the Discourse on Language.* Trans. Alan Sheridan Smith. New York: Dorset by arrangement with Pantheon, 1972.

Frankenberg, Ruth, ed. *Displacing Whiteness: Essays in Social and Cultural Criticism.* Durham, N.C.: Duke University Press, 1997.

Fraser, Nancy. *Unruly Practices: Power, Discourse, and Gender in Contemporary Social Theory.* Minneapolis: University of Minnesota Press, 1989.

Fuss, Diana. *Essentially Speaking: Feminism, Nature, and Difference.* New York: Routledge, 1989.

Galeano, Eduardo. *Memory of Fire.* Trans. Cedric Belfrage. New York: Pantheon, 1985.

Gamio, Manuel. *The Mexican Immigrant: His Life Story.* Chicago: University of Chicago Press, 1931. Reprint, Salem, N.H.: Ayer, 1989.

———. *Consideraciones sobre el problema indigena.* 1948. 2nd ed. Mexico, D.F.: Ediciones del Instituto Indigenista Interamericano, 1966.

———. *Forjando Patria: Pro-nacionalismo.* 1916. 2nd ed. Mexico, D.F.: Editorial Porrúa, 1960.

———. *Mexican Immigration to the United States: A Study in Human Migration and Adjustment.* Chicago: University of Chicago Press, 1930.

———. *Aspects of Mexican Civilization.* Chicago: University of Chicago Press, 1926.

Gates, Henry Louis, Jr., ed. *"Race," Writing, and Difference.* Chicago: University of Chicago Press, 1986.

Gerbi, Antonello. *The Dispute of the New World: The History of a Polemic, 1750–1900.* Trans. Jeremy Moyle. Pittsburgh, Penn.: Pittsburgh University Press, 1973.

Gilman, Sander L. "Black Bodies, White Bodies: Toward an Iconography of Female Sexuality in Late-Nineteenth-Century Art, Medicine, and Literature." In *"Race," Writing, and Difference,* ed. Henry Louis Gates Jr. Chicago: University of Chicago Press, 1986.

Giroux, Henry. *Border Crossings: Cultural Workers and the Politics of Education.* New York: Routledge, 1992.

Gómez-Peña, Guillermo. *Warrior for Gringostroika: Essays, Performance, Texts, and Poetry.* Saint Paul, Minn.: Graywolf, 1993.

Gonzales, Ramón. *Between Two Cultures: The Life of an American-Mexican, as Told to John J. Poggie Jr.* Tucson: University of Arizona Press, 1973.

Gonzalez, Ray, ed. *Without Discovery: A Native Response to Columbus.* Seattle, Wash.: Broken Moon, 1992.

González-Gamio, Ángeles. *Manuel Gamio: Una Lucha sin Final.* México, D.F.: Universidad Nacional Autónoma de México, 1987.

Graham, Richard. *The Idea of Race in Latin America.* Austin: University of Texas Press, 1990.

Gramsci, Antonio. *Selections from the Prison Notebooks of Antonio Gramsci.* Ed. Quintin Hoare and Geoffrey Nowell Smith. New York: International, 1971.

Grant, Madison. *The Passing of the Great Race; or, The Racial Bias of European History.* New York: Scribner, 1918.

Grosz, Elizabeth. *Space, Time, and Perversion: Essays on the Politics of Bodies.* New York: Routledge, 1995.

———. *Volatile Bodies: Toward a Corporeal Feminism.* Bloomington: Indiana University Press, 1994.

Guerin-Gonzales, Camille. *Mexican Workers and American Dreams: Immigration, Repatriation, and California Farm Labor 1900–1939.* New Brunswick, N.J.: Rutgers University Press, 1994.

Gugelberger, Georg M., ed. *The Real Thing: Testimonial Discourse and Latin America.* Durham, N.C.: Duke University Press, 1997.

Gusdorf, Georges. "Conditions and Limit of Autobiography." In *Autobiography: Essays Theoretical and Critical.* Ed. and trans. James Olney. Princeton, N.J.: Princeton University Press, 1980.

Gutiérrez, David G. *Walls and Mirrors: Mexican Americans, Mexican Immigrants, and the Politics of Ethnicity.* Berkeley: University of California Press, 1995.

Gutiérrez-Jones, Carl. *Rethinking the Borderlands: Between Chicano Culture and Legal Discourse.* Berkeley: University of California Press, 1995.

Hagedorn, Jessica. *Dogeaters.* New York: Penguin: 1991.

Hanke, Lewis. *Aristotle and the American Indians: A Study of Race Prejudice in the Modern World.* Chicago: Regnery, 1959.

Harlow, Barbara. *Resistance Literature.* New York: Methuen, 1987.

Hart, John Mason. *Revolutionary Mexico: The Coming and Process of the Mexican Revolution.* Berkeley: University of California Press, 1987.

Hartman, Saidiya V. *Scenes of Subjection: Terror, Slavery, and Self-Making in Nineteenth-Century America.* New York: Oxford University Press, 1997.

Hawley, C. A. *Life Along the Border: A Personal Narrative of Events and Experiences Along the Mexican Border Between 1905 and 1913.* Spokane, 1955.

Hicks, D. Emily. *Border Writing: The Multidimensional Text.* Minneapolis: University of Minnesota Press, 1991.

Hilden, Patricia Penn. *When Nickels Were Indians: An Urban Mixed Blood Story.* Washington, D.C.: Smithsonian, 1995.

Hobson, Geary. "The Rise of the White Shaman as a New Version of Cultural Imperialism." In *The Remembered Earth,* ed. Geary Hobson. Albuquerque, N. Mex.: Red Earth Press, 1978.

———, ed. *The Remembered Earth: An Anthology of Contemporary Native American Literature.* Albuquerque: University of New Mexico Press, 1980.

Hoffman, Abraham. *Unwanted Mexican Americans.* Austin: University of Texas Press, 1974.

Holland, Sharon P. "If You Know I Have a History, You Will Respect Me: A Perspective on Afro-Native American Literature." *Callaloo* 17, 1 (1994): 334–50.

Holmes, Samuel J. "Perils of the Mexican Invasion." *North American Review* 227, 5 (1929): 615–23.

hooks, bell. *Feminist Theory from Margin to Center.* Boston: South End, 1984.

———. *Ain't I a Woman: Black Women and Feminism.* Boston: South End, 1981.

Hulme, Keri. *The Bone People.* Baton Rouge: Louisiana State University Press, 1983.

Huxley, Julian S. *We Europeans.* New York: Harper, 1936.

Iser, Wolfgang. *The Act of Reading: A Theory of Aesthetic Response.* Baltimore, Md.: Johns Hopkins University Press, 1978.

Jaimes, Annette M., ed. *The State of Native America: Genocide, Colonization, and Resistance.* Boston: South End, 1992.

Jameson, Fredric, and Masao Miyoshi, eds. *The Cultures of Globalization.* Durham, N.C.: Duke University Press, 1998.

JanMohamed, Abdul R., and David Lloyd, eds. *The Nature and Context of Minority Discourse.* New York: Oxford University Press, 1990.

Johansen, Bruce. "Native American Societies and the Evolution of Democracy in America, 1600–1800." *Ethnohistory* 37, 3 (1990): 279–90.

———. *Forgotten Founders.* Ipswich, Mass.: Gambit, 1982.

Jonas, Susanne. *The Battle for Guatemala: Rebels, Death Squads, and U.S. Power.* Boulder, Colo.: Westview, 1991.

Kaplan, Amy, and Donald Pease, eds. *Cultures of United States Imperialism*. Durham, N.C.: Duke University Press, 1993.

Kaplan, Caren. "Resisting Autobiography: Out-law Genres and Transnational Feminist Subjects." In *De/Colonizing the Subject: The Politics of Gender in Women's Autobiography*, ed. Sidonie Smith and Julia Watson. Minneapolis: University of Minnesota Press, 1992.

Katz, Friederich. "Labor Conditions on Haciendas in Porfirian Mexico." *Hispanic American Historical Review* 54, 1 (1974): 1–47.

Katz, Jane, ed. *This Song Remembers: Self-Portraits of Native Americans in the Arts*. Boston: Houghton Mifflin, 1980.

Keller, Gary D. *Hispanics and United States Film*. Tempe, Ariz.: Bilingual Press, 1994.

King, James. *The Biology of Race*. Berkeley: University of California Press, 1981.

Kingston, Maxine Hong. *The Woman Warrior: Memoirs of a Girlhood Among Ghosts*. New York: Vintage Books, 1976.

Knight, Alan. "Racism, Revolution, and Indigenisimo: Mexico, 1910–1940." In *The Idea of Race in Latin America*, ed. Richard Graham. Austin: University of Texas Press, 1990.

Kristeva, Julia. *The Kristeva Reader*. Ed. Toril Moi. New York: Columbia University Press, 1986.

——. *Powers of Horror: An Essay on Abjection*. Trans. Leon S. Roudiez. New York: Columbia University Press, 1982.

——. *Desire in Language: A Semiotic Approach to Literature and Art*. Ed. and trans. Leon S. Roudiez. New York: Columbia University Press, 1980.

Krupat, Arnold. *Ethnocriticism: Ethnography, History, Literature*. Berkeley: University of California Press, 1991.

——. "The Dialogic of Storyteller." In *Narrative Chance: Postmodern Discourse on Native American Indian Literatures*, ed. Gerald Vizenor. Albuquerque: University of New Mexico Press, 1989.

——. *For Those Who Come After: A Study of Native American Autobiography*. Berkeley: University of California, 1985.

——, ed. *New Voices in Native American Literary Criticism*. Washington, D.C.: Smithsonian, 1993.

Lacan, Jacques. *Ecrits: A Selection*. Trans. Alan Sheridan. New York: Norton, 1977.

Lafaye, Jacques. "Historical Differences: Caste Society in New Spain." *Artes de México: Nueva Epoca* 8 (summer 1990): 81–88.

Landry, Donna, and Gerald Maclean, eds. *The Spivak Reader: Selected Works of Gayatri Chakravorty Spivak*. New York: Routledge, 1996.

Las Casas, Bartolomé de. *The Devastation of the Indies: A Brief Account*. 1522. Reprint, Baltimore, Md.: Johns Hopkins University Press, 1992.

Lentricchia, Frank. *After the New Criticism*. Chicago: University of Chicago Press, 1980.

León-Portilla, Miguel. *Aztec Thought and Culture*. Trans. Jack Emory Davis. Norman: University of Oklahoma Press, 1963.

————. *The Broken Spears: The Aztec Account of the Conquest of Mexico.* Ed. Miguel León-Portilla. Trans. Lysander Kemp. Boston: Beacon, 1962.

————. *Five Families: Mexican Case Studies in the Culture of Poverty.* New York: Basic Books, 1959.

Lewis, Oscar. *The Children of Sánchez: Autobiography of a Mexican Family.* New York: Random House, 1961.

Limón, José E. *American Encounters: Greater Mexico, the United States, and the Erotics of Culture.* Boston: Beacon Press, 1998.

Lipschultz, Robert. *American Attitudes toward Mexican Immigration.* Chicago: University of Chicago Press, 1962.

Lipsitz, George. *Dangerous Crossroads: Popular Music, Postmodernism, and the Poetics of Place.* London: Verso, 1994.

Lodge, David, ed. *Modern Criticism and Theory: A Reader.* New York: Longman, 1988.

Lowe, Lisa. *Critical Terrains: French and British Orientalisms.* Ithaca, N.Y.: Cornell University Press, 1991.

Lucas, María Elena. *Forged Under the Sun/Forjada Bajo el Sol: The Life of María Elena Lucas.* Edited and with an introduction by Fran Leeper Buss. Ann Arbor: University of Michigan Press, 1993.

Lukacs, Gyorgy. *The Historical Novel.* New York: Humanities Press, 1965.

Mani, Lata. "Multiple Mediations: Feminist Scholarship in the Age of Multinational Reception." *Feminist Review* 35 (summer 1990): 25–41.

Marshall, Brenda K. *Teaching the Postmodern.* New Bunswick, N.J.: Rutgers University Press, 1992.

Martin, Wallace. *Recent Theories of Narrative.* Ithaca, N.Y.: Cornell University Press, 1986.

Martínez, Elizabeth, and Ed McCaughan. "Chicanas and Mexicanas within a Transnational Working Class." In *Between Borders: Essays on Mexicana/Chicana History,* ed. Adelaide Del Castillo. Encino, CA: Floricanto, 1988.

Martínez, Rubén. *The Other Side: Notes from the New L.A., Mexico City, and Beyond.* New York: Vintage, 1993.

Marx, Karl. *Capital.* vol. 1. New York: International, 1974.

Matthiessen, Peter. *In the Spirit of Crazy Horse.* New York: Viking, 1983.

Melville, Margarita B., ed. *Twice a Minority: Mexican American Women.* St. Louis, Mo.: Mosby, 1980.

Menchú, Rigoberta. *I, Rigoberta Menchú: An Indian Woman in Guatemala.* Ed. Elizabeth Burgos-Debray. Trans. Ann Wright. London: Verso, 1993.

Metz, Leon Claire. *Border: The U.S./Mexico Line.* El Paso, Tex.: Mangan, 1989.

Mignolo, Walter D. *The Darker Side of the Renaissance: Literacy, Territoriality, and Colonization.* Ann Arbor: University of Michigan Press, 1995.

Mirandé, Alfredo. *The Chicano Experience: An Alternative Perspective.* Notre Dame, Ind.: University of Notre Dame Press, 1985.

Mirandé, Alfredo, and Evangelina Enríquez. *La Chicana: The Mexican American Woman.* Chicago: University of Chicago Press, 1977.

Mohanty, Chandra Talpade, Ann Russo, and Lourdes Torres, eds. *Third World Women and the Politics of Feminism*. Bloomington: Indiana University Press, 1991.

Montejano, David. *Anglos and Mexicans in the Making of Texas, 1836–1986*. Austin: University of Texas Press, 1987.

Moore, David L. "Myth, History, and Identity in Silko and Young Bear: Postcolonial Praxis." In *New Voices in Native American Literary Criticism*, ed. Arnold Krupat. Washington, D.C.: Smithsonian, 1993.

———. "Material Meeting Points of Self and Other: Fetish Discourses and Leslie Marmon Silko's Evolving Conception of Cross-Cultural Narrative." In *Leslie Marmon Silko: A Collection of Critical Essays*, ed. Louise K. Barnett and James L. Thorson. Albuquerque: University of New Mexico Press, 1999.

Moraga, Cherríe. *The Last Generation: Prose and Poetry*. Boston: Beacon Press, 1993.

———. *Loving in the War Years: Lo que nunca pasó por sus labios*. Boston: South End, 1983.

Morgan, Lewis Henry. *Ancient Society: or, Researches in the Lines of Human Progress from Savagery through Barbarism to Civilization*. 1877. Reprint, with an introduction by Debiprasad Chattopadhyaya, Calcutta: K. P. Bagghi, 1982.

Muñoz, José Esteban. *Disidentifications: Queers of Color and the Performance of Politics*. Minneapolis: University of Minnesota Press, 1999.

Nakashima, Cindy L. "An Invisible Monster: The Creation and Denial of Mixed-Blood People in America." In *Racially Mixed People in America*, ed. Maria P. P. Root. Newbury Park, Calif.: Sage, 1992.

Nandy, Ashis. *The Intimate Enemy: Loss and Recovery of Self Under Colonialism*. Delhi: Oxford University Press, 1983.

Nathan, Debbie. *Women and Other Aliens: Essays from the U.S. Mexico Border*. El Paso: Cinco Puntos Press, 1991.

Nelson, Cary, and Lawrence Grossberg, eds. *Marxism and the Interpretation of Culture*. Urbana: University of Illinois Press, 1988.

Newman, Kathleen. "Latino Sacrifice in the Discourse of Citizenship: Acting against the 'Mainstream,' 1985–1988." In *Chicanos and Film: Representation and Resistance*, ed. Chon A. Noriega. Minneapolis: University of Minnesota Press, 1992.

Ngũgĩ wa Thiong'o. *Decolonising the Mind: The Politics of Language in African Literature*. London: Heinemann, 1981.

Niranjana, Tejaswini. *Siting Translation: History, Post-Structuralism, and the Colonial Context*. Berkeley: University of California Press, 1992.

Omi, Michael, and Howard Winant. *Racial Formation in the United States*. New York: Routledge, 1986.

Ortiz, Alfonso, ed. *Southwest. Handbook of North American Indians*. Vol. 9. Ser. ed. William C. Sturtevant. Washington, D.C.: Smithsonian, 1979.

———. *New Perspectives on the Pueblos*. Albuquerque: University of New Mexico Press, 1972.

Owens, Louis. *Mixblood Messages: Literature, Film, Family, Place*. Norman: University of Oklahoma Press, 1998.

————. *Other Destinies: Understanding the American Indian Novel.* Norman: University of Oklahoma Press, 1992.

Padilla, Genaro. *My History, Not Yours: The Formation of Mexican American Autobiography.* Madison: University of Wisconsin Press, 1993.

Paredes, Americo. *"With His Pistol in His Hand": A Border Ballad and Its Hero.* Austin: University of Texas Press, 1958.

Parkes, Henry B. *A History of Mexico.* Boston: Houghton, 1970.

Parmentier, Richard J. "The Mythological Triangle: Poseyemu, Montezuma, and Jesus in the Pueblos." *Handbook of North American Indians.* Vol. 9. Ed. Alfonso Ortiz Ser. ed. William Sturtevant. Washington, D.C.: Smithsonian, 1979.

Parsons, Elsie Clew. *Pueblo Indian Religion.* Chicago: University of Chicago Press, 1939.

————. "Early Relations between Hopi and Keres." *American Anthropologist* 38 (1936): 554–68.

————. "Laguna Genealogies." *Anthropological Papers of the American Museum of Natural History* 19 (1923).

————. "Notes on Ceremonialism at Laguna." *Anthropological Papers of the American Museum of Natural History* 19 (1920).

Paz, Octavio. *The Labyrinth of Solitude: Life and Thought in Mexico.* Trans. Lysander Kemp. New York: Grove, 1961.

Pearce, Roy Harvey. *Savagism and Civilization: A Study of the Indian and the American Mind.* Berkeley: University of California Press, 1988.

Penn, W. S. *All My Sins Are Relatives.* Lincoln: University of Nebraska Press, 1995.

Pérez, Emma. *The Decolonial Imaginary: Writing Chicanas into History.* Bloomington: Indiana University Press, 1999.

Pérez, Ramón. *Diary of an Undocumented Immigrant.* Houston: Arte Publico, 1991.

Pérez Firmat, Gustavo, ed. *Do the Americas Have a Common Literature?* Durham, N.C.: Duke University Press, 1990.

Pérez-Torres, Rafael. *Movements in Chicano Poetry: Against Myths, Against Margins.* Cambridge: Cambridge University Press, 1995.

Pratt, Mary Louise. *Imperial Eyes: Travel Writing and Transculturation.* London: Routledge, 1992.

Priestley, Herbert. *The Mexican Nation: A History.* New York: Macmillan, 1924.

Prince, Gerald. "Introduction to the Study of the Narratee." In *Reader-Response Criticism: From Formalism to Post-Structuralism,* ed. Jane P. Tompkins. Baltimore, Md.: Johns Hopkins University Press, 1980.

Rainwater, Catherine. *Dreams of Fiery Stars: The Transformation of Native American Fiction.* Philadelphia: University of Pennsylvania Press, 1999.

Rebolledo, Tey Diana. *Women Singing in the Snow: A Cultural Analysis of Chicana Literature.* Tucson: University of Arizona Press, 1995.

————. "The Politics of Poetics: or, What Am I, a Critic, Doing in His Text Anyhow?" In *Chicana Creativity and Criticism: Charting New Frontiers in American Literature,* ed. María Herrera-Sobek and Helena María Viramontes. Houston: Arte Publico, 1988.

Riley In the Woods, Patricia. "Standin' in the Middle of the Road: A Look at the Mixed-Blood Interpreter and Mythmaker in Leslie Marmon Silko's *Ceremony.*" *Cultural and Cross-Cultural Studies and the Teaching of Literature* (1992): 7–22.

Ríos, Ricardo. "Street of Broken Dreams." *qv Magazine* 2, 2 (November/December 1998): 24.

Rodriguez, Richard. "Across the Borders of History." *Harpers* (March 1987): 42–53.

Romero, Rolando. "Texts, Pre-Texts, Con-Texts: Gonzalo Guerrero in the Chronicles of the Indies." *Revista de Estudios Hispánicos* 26, 3 (1992): 347–64.

Ronnow, Gretchen. "Tayo, Death, and Desire: A Lacanian Reading of *Ceremony.*" In *Narrative Chance: Postmodern Discourse in Native American Indian Literatures,* ed. Gerald Vizenor. Albuquerque: University of New Mexico Press, 1989.

Root, Maria P. P. *Racially Mixed People in America.* Newbury Park, Calif.: Sage, 1992.

Rosaldo, Renato. *Culture and Truth: The Remaking of Social Analysis.* Boston: Beacon, 1989.

———. "Ideology, Place, and People without Culture." *Cultural Anthropology* 3, 1 (1988): 77–87.

Roscoe, William. *The Zuni Man-Woman.* Albuquerque: University of New Mexico Press, 1991.

Ross, Luana. *Inventing the Savage: The Social Construction of Native American Criminality.* Austin: University of Texas Press, 1998.

Rouse, Roger. "Mexican Migration and the Social Space of Postmodernism." *Diaspora* 1 (1991): 8–23.

Rousseau, Jean-Jacques. *The Confessions.* Trans. by W. Conyngham Mallory. New York: Tudor, 1928.

Ruiz, Vickie L. *From Out of the Shadows: Mexican Women in Twentieth-Century America.* New York: Oxford University Press, 1998.

———. "'And Miles to Go . . .': Mexicans and Work, 1930–1985." In *Western Women: Their Land, Their Lives,* ed. Lillian Schlissel, Vickie Ruiz, and Janice Monk. Albuquerque: University of New Mexico Press, 1988.

Ruoff, Lavonne Brown. *American Indian Literature: Redefining American Literary Arts.* New York: Modern Language Association, 1990.

Russel y Rodríguez, Mónica. "(En)countering Domestic Violence, Complicity, and Definitions of Chicana Womanhood." *Voces: A Journal of Chicana/Latina Studies* 1, 2 (1997): 104–42.

Said, Edward. *Orientalism.* New York: Pantheon, 1978.

Saldívar, José David. *Border Matters: Remapping American Cultural Studies.* Berkeley: University of California Press, 1997.

———. *The Dialectics of Our America: Genealogy, Cultural Critique, and Literary History.* Durham, N.C.: Duke University Press, 1991.

———. "Limits of Cultural Studies." *American Literary History* 2, 2 (1990): 251–66.

Saldívar, Ramón. *Chicano Narrative: The Dialectics of Difference.* Madison: University of Wisconsin Press, 1990.

Saldívar-Hull, Sonia. *Feminism on the Border: Chicana Gender Politics and Literature.* Berkeley: University of California Press, 2000.

————. "Feminism on the Border: From Gender Politics to Geopolitics." In *Criticism in the Borderlands,* ed. Héctor Caldéron and José David Saldívar. Durham, N.C.: Duke University Press, 1991.

Sandoval, Chela. *Methodology of the Oppressed.* Minneapolis: University of Minnesota Press, 2001.

Sanjinés, Javier C. "Beyond Testimonial Discourse: New Popular Trends in Bolivia (1995)." In *The Real Thing: Testimonial Discourse and Latin America,* ed. Georg M. Gugelberger. Durham, N.C.: Duke University Press, 1997.

Sarris, Greg. *Keeping Slug Woman Alive: A Holistic Approach to American Indian Texts.* Berkeley: University of California Press, 1993.

Scarry, Elaine. *The Body in Pain: The Making and Unmaking of the World.* New York: Oxford University Press, 1985.

Segura, Denise, and Jennifer L. Pierce. "Chicana/o Family Structure and Gender Personality: Chodorow, Familism, and Psychoanalytic Sociology Revisited." *Signs* (autumn 1993): 62–91.

Sequoya, Jana. "How (!) Is an Indian: A Contest of Stories." In *New Voices in Native American Literary Criticism,* ed. Arnold Krupat. Washington, D.C.: Smithsonian, 1993.

Siebers, Tobin. *The Ethics of Criticism.* Ithaca, N.Y.: Cornell University Press, 1988.

Silko, Leslie Marmon. *Yellow Woman and a Beauty of the Spirit: Essays on Native American Life Today.* New York: Touchstone, 1996.

————. *Almanac of the Dead.* New York: Simon and Schuster, 1991.

————. *Ceremony.* New York: Penguin, 1977.

Silverman, Kaja. *The Subject of Semiotics.* New York: Oxford University Press, 1983.

Smith, Sidonie. *Subjectivity, Identity, and the Body: Women's Autobiographical Practices in the Twentieth Century.* Bloomington: Indiana University Press, 1993.

Smith, Sidonie, and Julia Watson, eds. *De/Colonizing the Subject: The Politics of Gender in Women's Autobiography.* Minneapolis: University of Minnesota Press, 1992.

Smits, David. "The Abominable Mixture." *The Virginia Magazine of History and Biography* 95, 2 (1987): 227–61.

Spicer, Edward. *Cycles of Conquest.* Tucson: University of Arizona Press, 1962.

Spivak, Gayatri Chakravorty. "Can the Subaltern Speak?" In *Marxism and the Interpretation of Culture,* ed. Cary Nelson and Lawrence Grossberg. Urbana: University of Illinois Press, 1988.

————. *In Other Worlds: Essays in Cultural Politics.* New York: Routledge, 1988.

Swann, Edith. "Healing via the Sunwise Cycle in Silko's *Ceremony.*" *American Indian Quarterly* 12, 4 (1988): 313–29.

————. "Laguna Symbolic Geography and Silko's *Ceremony.*" *American Indian Quarterly* 12, 3 (1988): 229–51.

Takaki, Ronald. *Iron Cages: Race and Culture in Nineteenth-Century America.* New York: Oxford University Press, 1990.

————. *Strangers from a Different Shore.* New York: Penguin, 1989.

Taylor, Paul. *Mexican Labor in the United States.* Berkeley: University of California Press, 1932.

Tedlock, Dennis, trans. *Popol Vuh: The Mayan Book of the Dawn of Life*. New York: Simon and Schuster, 1985.

Todorov, Tzvetan. *The Conquest of America: The Question of the Other*. Trans. Richard Howard. New York: Harper, 1984.

Trinh T. Minh-ha. *Woman, Native, Other: Writing Postcoloniality and Feminism*. Bloomington: Indiana University Press, 1989.

Tula, María Teresa. *Hear my Testimony: María Teresa Tula, Human Rights Activist of El Salvador*. Ed. and trans. Lynn Stephen. Boston: South End, 1994.

Turner, Victor. *Dramas, Fields, and Metaphors: Symbolic Action in Human Society*. Ithaca, N.Y.: Cornell University Press, 1974.

TuSmith, Bonnie. *All My Relatives: Community in Contemporary Ethnic American Literatures*. Ann Arbor: University of Michigan Press, 1993.

Tylor, Edward Burnett. *Researches into the Early History of Mankind and the Development of Civilization*. London: J. Murray, 1865.

Vanderwood, Paul, and Frank Sampanaro. *Border Fury: A Picture Postcard Record of Mexico's Revolution and U.S. War Preparedness, 1910–1917*. Albuquerque: University of New Mexico Press, 1988.

Vasconcelos, José. *La Raza Cósmica: Misión de la raza iberoamericana*. 1925. Reprint, Mexico: Asociación Nacional de Libreros, 1983.

Villanueva, Tino. "Sobre el término 'Chicano.' " In *Chicanos: Antología historica y literaria*, ed. Tino Villanueva. Mexico: Fondo de Cultura Economica, 1980.

Vizenor, Gerald. *Manifest Manners: Postindian Warriors of Survivance*. Hanover, N.H.: University Press of New England, 1994.

———. *Crossbloods: Bone Courts, Bingo, and Other Reports*. Minneapolis: University of Minnesota Press, 1990.

———, ed. *Narrative Chance: Postmodern Discourse in Native American Indian Literatures*. Albuquerque: University of New Mexico Press, 1989.

Wei, William. *The Asian American Movement*. Philadelphia, Pa.: Temple University Press, 1993.

White, Hayden. *Tropics of Discourse: Essays in Cultural Criticism*. Baltimore, Md.: Johns Hopkins University Press, 1978.

Williams, Raymond. *The Country and the City*. New York: Oxford University Press, 1973.

Wilson, Terry. "Blood Quantum: Native American Mixed Bloods." In *Racially Mixed People in America*, ed. Maria P. P. Root. Newbury Park, Calif.: Sage, 1992.

Wong, Hertha. *Sending My Heart Back Across the Years: Tradition and Innovation in Native American Autobiography*. New York: Oxford University Press, 1992.

Wright, Ronald. *Stolen Continents: The "New World" Through Indian Eyes*. Boston: Houghton, 1992.

Young, Robert J. C. *Colonial Desire: Hybridity in Theory, Culture, and Race*. London: Routledge, 1995.

Index

Abject, the, 14, 106, 110, 113, 144. *See also* Kristeva, Julia

Abuse, 78, 107, 141–42; human rights, 36, 122

Abya Yala, 3, 4, 146 n.3. *See also* Resistance 500 events

African, 117; blood, 117; language, 98; men with European women, 149 n.22; women with Anglo men, 149

Afro-mestizo, 49

After the New Criticism (Lentricchia), 74

Against Literature (Beverley), 114

Alarcón, Francisco, 122–23. *See also* Mesoamerican

Alarcón, Norma, 29–33, 59, 96, 105, 117–18. *See also* Feminism

Albuquerque (Anaya), 88

Aldama, Juan, and Ignacio, xix, 146

All My Relatives (TuSmith), 78

All My Sins Are Relatives (Penn), 77, 152

Almanac of the Dead (Silko), 93

Althusser, Louis, 20–21, 23, 30, 59. *See also* Hailing; Interpellation

American Encounters (Limón), 50

American Indians, 4, 10, 12, 14, 17–18, 72, 76, 78–79, 90, 138, 146; activist, 4; in film and television, 137

American Southwest, 19, 52, 72, 86, 88, 102, 111, 121, 132, 151 n.28, 154 n.24

American West, 19, 106, 132

Ancestors, 7, 88

Ancient Society (Morgan), 11, 147

Anglo, 15, 37, 61, 88, 103, 126, 136, 141; based solidarity groups, 6; blood, 94, 117; centric U.S. film industry, 138; community, 97, 123; culture, 151 n.28; dominated political economy, 97; feminism, 30; identity, 77; immigrant, 104; institutions of power, 123; language centrism, 17; men, 149 n.22; patriarchal system, 126; point of view, 124; workers, 66

Anglo-American, xi, 107; culture, 18; democracy, 107; empire, 108–9; feminism, 29; racial superiority, 108; tradition, 97; in the U.S., 71

Anthropology, 12, 33, 44, 56–58, 87, 153; cultural, 57, 74, 152 n.5, 155 n.13; Euro-American, 45; European, 45; Mexican, 42–43; National Anthropology Museum in Chapultepec

Anthropology (*continued*)
Park, 125; practice, 133; structuralist, 75; writing, 87. *See also* Batalla, Guillermo Bonfil; Clifford, James; Gamio, Manuel; Rosaldo, Renato

Anti Oedipus (Deleuze and Guattari), 140

Anzaldúa, Gloria, 96–97, 100, 103–4, 108, 111, 115, 117–18, 123–28, 133–34; *Borderlands/La Frontera*, 84, 95–97, 99–100, 102, 109, 111, 116–18, 123–24, 127–28

Aristotle and the American Indians (Hanke), 3, 13

Arteaga, Alfred, 77, 104, 112, 119–20, 122, 133–34; *An Other Tongue*, 122; *Chicano Politics*, 104, 112, 133

Arteta, Miguel, 129, 131, 139; *Star Maps*, 129, 131, 136–37, 141, 143

Aspects of Mexican Civilization (Gamio), 50

Authority, 133; epistemological, 74; metaphysical, 74; of states, 105; postcolonial and poststructural interrogations of, 57

Autobiography, 33, 43, 58, 96, 100, 104–5, 112, 154 nn.2, 5; expression, 97; feminist, 104; practice, 105, 109; traditional, 105; Western, 104. *See also* Gusdorf, Georges; Kaplan, Caren

Autocolonialism, 119–20. *See also* Arteaga, Alfred

Autoethnography, 33. *See also* Pratt, Mary Louise

Autonomy, 32, 77, 109, 148; and autonomous agency, 24; self, 24; and autonomous subject, 24

Aztec, 121; as middle-status barbarians, 12; cultural system, 75; dualism, 124; nation-state, 110, 123–24; philosophy, 127; society, 119; state, 125; thought, 124. *See also* Forbes, Jack

Aztec Thought and Culture (León-Portilla), 155

Aztecas del Norte (Forbes), 102, 156 n.19

Bahktin, Mikhail, 57, 58, 77, 90; *Dialogic Imagination*, 57–58, 77

Benveniste, Emile: *Problems in General Linguistics*, 20, 24. *See also* Silverman, Kaja; Speaking subject

Beverley, John, xvii, 112, 114; *Against Literature*, 114; "Testimonios," xvii

Bhabha, Homi K., 9, 18, 83; *The Location of Culture*, 83

Bicultural composite composition, 45, 49. *See also* Krupat, Arnold

Black Skin, White Masks (Fanon), 120, 147, 153

Blood: African, 117; Anglo, 94, 117; cross-, 19, 77, 80, 84, 88, 106; European, 49, 150 n.13; full-, 72, 88; Indian, 94, 117, 121; mixed-, 72, 94, 121; quantum, 4, 54, 72, 81–83, 91, 94, 121; sorcery, 94; Spanish, 94, 117; white, 54, 94. *See also* Owens, Louis; Penn, W. S.; Root, Maria P. P.; Wilson, Terry

Boas, Franz, 43

Bodies: Latina/o, 136; raced and sexed, 32

Body in Pain, The (Scarry), 148

Border: and borderland, 32, 42; and borderlessness, 33, 35; crossing, 36, 38–40, 42, 47, 58, 102, 115, 129, 131–32, 134–36, 150 n.11; cultural, 132; culture, 157 n.7; feminism, 116; geopolitical, 100; global, 133; Mexican, 43, 102; militarized, xii; patrol, 36, 60, 115, 133, 135; power to, 88; purpose of, 134; as a site of power, 134; south of the, 38; studies, 132; Texas-Mexican, 96, 111; theory, 133, 148 n.17; U.S./Mexico, xi–xii, 33, 35–36, 41, 43, 59, 95, 100, 102–3, 108, 111–12, 131–36, 146 nn.8, 9, 149. *See also* Arteaga, Alfred; Globalization; Pérez-Torres, Rafael; Saldívar, José David; Saldívar-Hull, Sonia

Border Matters (Saldívar), xii, 133, 152

Border Writing (Hicks), 131
Borderlands/La Frontera (Anzaldúa), 84, 95–97, 99–100, 102, 109, 111, 116–18, 123–24, 127–28
Braceros, 52–53, 66–67, 104

Campesinas, 56, 117, 135
Capitalism, 7, 26, 82, 117, 152 n.8; anti-, 33; bourgeois, 109; global, 17, 33, 36, 90, 98, 137; investment, 35
Castillo, Ana: *Massacre of the Dreamers*, 140; *So Far from God*, 88
Ceremony (Silko), 72, 78, 80, 87
Chasqui March and Rally (San Francisco), 4
Chicana/o, xii, 8, 19, 47, 100, 118, 121, 128; community, 96–97, 117, 123–24; feminist, 5, 95, 116; identity, xvii, 104, 123–24; lesbian, 97; poetics, 134; subject, 133. *See also* Arteaga, Alfred
Chicano Poetics (Arteaga), 104, 112, 133
Chronotopes, 77, 88. *See also* Arteaga, Alfred; Bahktin, Mikhail
City of Quartz (Davis, M.), 130
Clan, 47
Class, 43, 116, 123, 128, 134; differences, 45; exploitation by, 133; inequities, 71; oppression, 17; position, 135
Clifford, James: *Predicament of Culture*, 46, 87, 156; *Routes*, 156 n.2. *See also* Writing: culture
Coatlicue, 110, 124–25, 127. *See also* Anzaldúa, Gloria; Arteaga, Alfred
Colonialism, xi–xii, 3–5, 7, 14, 16, 17, 19, 26–27, 31, 40, 76–77, 82, 91, 94, 120, 146–48, 153 n.19; absentee, 17; in the Americas, xii; anti-, 33; consciousness, 80; discourse, 56, 74; discursive, 119; domination and resistance, 45; European, 21, 88; imaginary, 142; imagination, 13; internalized, 3, 31, 51, 83–84, 86, 91, 94, 118–20, 122; in Mexico, 71; power, 33; practices, 100; resistance to, 150

n.17; subjection, 8; violence, 117. *See also* Mohanty, Chandra Talpade; Niranjana, Tejaswini
Colonial Rise of the Novel, The (Azim), 76, 148
Colonization, 96; religious, 73
Colony: internal, 17; U.S. as, 17
Columbus and Other Cannibals (Forbes), 84, 120
Columbus, Christopher, 4, 7, 9, 22, 126
Commodification: sexual, 136
Community: Chicana/o, 96, 117, 123–24; gay and lesbian, 145; global, 35; Mexican, 96, 124; oppressed, 142; queer, 128; subaltern, 35; ties, 132
Conquest, 5, 9, 15, 18, 22, 31, 73, 105; and Oedipal Conquest Complex, 142; politics of, 54, 151
Conquest of America, The (Todorov), 13, 146–47
Conquest of Mexico (1521), 15, 109–10, 148
Consciousness: mestiza/o, xii, 9, 98, 118, 123; of the Americas, 97
Corridos, 101, 104
Coyote, 88, 115, 132, 135
Critical Terrains (Lowe), 100
Criticism in the Borderlands (Calderón and Saldívar), 132
Culture: border, 157 n.7; Chicana/o, 103, 117; dominant, 133; Euro-American, 81, 121; Hispanic popular, 88; indigenous, 123, 124, 140; Laguna, 86; matrilineal, 126; Mexican, 124; native, 24; savage, 73; subordinate, 133; U.S., 107; white, 123
Culture and Truth (Rosaldo), 47, 58
Cycle of Conquests (Spicer), 88

Darker Side of the Renaissance, The (Mignolo), 21, 76, 146 n.5, 147 n.9
Decolonial Imaginary, The (Pérez), 95, 142

Decolonization, xii, 4, 16–18, 32, 33, 72, 77, 80, 90, 95–96, 123, 126, 128; of identity and sexuality, 131; sexual, 128. *See also* Fanon, Frantz; Moraga, Cherríe; Pérez, Emma

Democracy, 100

Deportation, xv, 36, 39, 67; of Latinos, 40; of Mexicans, 66–68

Derrida, Jacques, 9, 24, 74–76, 147 n.9, 154 n.6; *Of Grammatology*, 74–75, 147 n.9. *See also* Genre

Descent: Euro-American, 72; European, 149; Hispanic, 37; Indian, 108, 121; Laguna, 72; Latino, 108, 121, 137; Mexican, 66, 72, 108, 118, 121, 125, 133, 151; mixed racial, 80; white Spanish, 71

Devastation of the Indies, The (Las Casas), 148

Dia de Los Muertos (Day of the Dead), 130

Dialectics, 110, 120, 131; colonialist, 73; Hegelian, 32

Dialectics of Our America, The (Saldívar), 97, 122, 152

Diallo, Amadou, 21

Dialogic Imagination, The (Bahktin), 57–58, 77

Diary of an Undocumented Immigrant (Pérez), 63

Diaz, Porfirio, 55–56, 59–60

Discipline, xiv, 17, 28, 95, 97, 100, 108, 131

Discipline and Punish (Foucault), 108

Discourse, 30, 59; colonial, 8, 33, 56, 74; feminist, 28, 59, 116; heteroglossic, 103–4; history of, 24; of colonization, 46; of inferiorization, 135; of power, 46; of the nation-state, 133; racialist, 43, 59

Discrimination, 36, 42, 49, 58, 61, 134

Disempowerment, 35

Disenfranchisement, 142

Disidentifications (Muñoz), 145

Disposable People (Bales), 149 n.2, 157 n.19

Dispute in the New World (Gerbi), 10

Do the Americas Have a Common Literature? (Pérez Firmat), 122

Domination, 118, 133

Economy: cultural, 31, 43; patriarchal, 31; political, 46

Écriture, 74, 76

Eisenstein, Sergei, 141

El Norte, 38–39, 52. *See also* Border: U.S.-Mexico

Emigration, 52, 65

Émigrés, 21, 42, 43, 96, 118, 135

Empire Writes Back, The (Ashcroft), 152 n.9

Encounter, 14, 41, 45, 47, 56–58, 130, 150

English language, 45, 88, 98; and English-only, 100

Equality, 100

Essentialism, 83, 85, 143; racial, 72

Ethnicity, 43, 72, 116–17, 128, 135; affiliations, 37; differences, 45

Ethnocentrism, 30, 74–75, 147; and conceptualizations of writing, 74; and onerism, 75; and violence, 75

Ethnography, 42, 56, 59; auto-, 33; constructing, 57; project, 43–45; theory, 132; translation, 46, 56, 58. *See also* Behar, Ruth; Clifford, James; Colonial; Encounter; Rosaldo, Renato

Ethnohistorical writing, 87

Ethnoscapes, xvii, 130. *See also* Appadurai, Arjun

Euro-American, 10, 12, 41, 44–45, 52, 61, 78, 138; colonial thought, 152; cultural and political economy, 61; cultural hegemony, 123; culture, 81, 84, 85, 121; descent, 72, 80; domination, 117; family structure, 141, 157;

legal practices, 19; manifest destiny, 21; nation-state, 97; overculture, 117; subjectivities, 62; taboos, 135

Eurocentrism, xi, xvii, 30, 32, 48, 56, 73, 96, 105, 119, 129

Exploitation: coyote, 96; economic, 115; hyper-, 35; racial and sexual, 136

Family: Latino, 136; oedipal, 118, 137; ties, 132

Fanon, Frantz, 18, 83, 120, 140; *Black Skin, White Masks*, 120, 147 n.15, 153 n.19. *See also* Schizophrenia

Feminism, xvii, 9, 31–32, 57, 95–96, 105, 114, 116–17, 127, 137; Anglo-American, 29–30; Chicana, 5, 33, 116; discourse, 28; identity, xii, 36; post-colonial, 27; theory, 26, 32, 104, 114, 132, 141; third world, 32–33, 96

Feminism on the Border (Saldívar-Hull), 100, 116

Figueroa, Efrain, 136

Film industry, 33, 138; Hollywood, 136; U.S., 139

For Those Who Come After (Krupat), 45

Forbes, Jack, 84, 102, 120–21; *Aztecas del Norte*, 102, 156 n.19; *Columbus and Other Cannibals*, 84, 120

Foreigner, 66, 94, 104, 119

Foucault, Michel, 25, 100; *Discipline and Punish*, 108

Free zone, 36, 135

Freire, Paolo, 123

French Enlightenment, 24

From Out of the Shadows (Ruiz), 67

Gamio, Manuel, xv, 43–49, 51, 54–55, 59–60, 63–65, 150 nn.10, 15, 151 n.28; *Aspects of Mexican Civilization*, 50; *Consideraciones Sobre el Problema Indigena*, 150 n.15; *The Mexican Immigrant*, 36, 42, 49, 58, 71; *Mexican Immigration to the United States*, 42, 58

Gender, 43, 101, 123, 128; in the Aztec nation-state, 124; boundaries, 117; exploitation by, 133; oppression, 17

Genocide, xi, 3–4, 9, 14–15, 19, 32, 106, 156 n.2

Genre, 8, 33, 57, 95–97, 109, 112, 154 nn.2, 6; autobiographic, 104; boundaries, 100; cross-cultural literary, 77; disrupting, 100; limits of, 105; margins of, 105; multi-, 127; novel, 73, 76; pluri-, 96. *See also* Derrida, Jacques; Kaplan, Caren

Globalization, 5, 16–17, 27, 33, 35–36, 40, 56, 77, 90, 98, 104, 132–33, 137, 149 n.3, 157 n.19

Great Chain of Being, 11–12, 23

Great Depression, 65–66

Green card, 37

Grosz, Elizabeth, 9, 141–42

Guadalupe Hidalgo, Treaty of (1848), 19, 66, 103, 109, 149 n.19

Gusdorf, Georges, 104–5, 154 n.5. *See also* Autobiography

Hailing, 20–23. *See also* Althusser, Louis

Harassment: racial and sexual, 36

Hatreds (Eisenstein), 144

Heterogeneity: cultural, 133; of identity, 131

Heteroglossia, 77, 133. *See also* Bahktin, Mikhail

Heterotopia, 100, 118. *See also* Foucault, Michel

Hinojosa, Rolando, 133

Hispanics and United States Film (Keller), 138

History: revisionary, 104

Hollywood, 137, 139–40, 143; Hollywood Film and Television Industry (HFTI), 136

Homophobia, 97, 117

hooks, bell, 114–16, 156 n.1

Hopi, 87

Hybrid, xii, xvi, 11, 33, 36, 54, 72, 76–77, 87, 95, 127, 134, 148 n.17, 157 n.7; cultural and linguistic, xi; identity, xii; postcolonial, 152; subject, 112; subjectivities, 77; writing practice, 77

Identification, self-, 47
Identity, 58, 72, 128, 151; Anglo, 77; Anzaldúa's exploration of, 97; Chicana/o, xvii, 123–24; Chicano/Mexicano, 102, 121; collective, 133; crossblood, 80; cultural, 121; feminist, xii; indigenous, 104; lesbian, 97; mestiza/o, xii, xvii, 80, 84, 96; Native American, 154; poetics of, 72; politics of, 72; postmodern, 32; racialized, xii; subaltern, xii; transfrontier, 131; tribal, 121
Ideology: American progressivist, 45; of power, 46; transfrontier, 132
Iglesias, Wenceslao, 151
Imaginary: colonial, 8, 13, 142; decolonial, 127; Mexican nation-state, 145; nation-state, 131; nativist, 104; U.S. nation-state, xii
Immigration, 6, 21, 37, 41–43, 45, 47, 52–54, 56, 58, 62–63, 66–67, 99, 101, 103, 114–16, 118, 131, 135–36, 143, 149, 151; Anglo, 104; anti-, 41; Chinese, 62; European, 53; juridico-immigratory policing, 96; Latino, 41; Mexican, 19, 23, 36, 41–44, 46, 53–55, 61, 63, 65–67, 103, 134; subject, 45
Imperialism, xii, 4, 7, 18, 26, 46, 77, 88, 117, 148; dominance, 109; in Latin American, 63; nations, 13; over-cultures, 110; project, 24, 105; self, 24; territorial and cultural, 131; U.S., 17–18, 148
Indian, 46, 80, 104, 108–9, 117, 121, 127; blood, 117; language, 98; lineage, 124; Mexican, 94; patriarchal, 126; voice, 46
Indigenismo, xv, 9, 44, 50. See also

Batalla, Guillermo Bonfil; Gamio, Manuel
Indigenistas de México (Castillo), 44
Indigenous: communities, 49–51, 99; culture, 123–24, 140; identity, 104, 128–29; land, xi, 19, 88; people, 3–5, 9, 15–17, 22, 43–45, 56, 72, 96, 102, 110–11, 113, 117–19, 131, 142, 146 n.3, 150 n.15, 153 n.20, 154 n.25
Immigration and Naturalization Service (INS), 37, 39, 40, 67, 68, 100, 115, 130, 132. See also Migra, la
Intermarriage, 87
Interpellation, 9, 20, 22. See also Althusser, Louis
Inventing the Savage (Ross), 19
Iron Cages (Takaki), 149

Jameson, Fredric, 45

Kaplan, Caren, 105, 109. See also Autobiography; Genre
Kristeva, Julia, 14, 24–26, 116, 148 n.20. See also Abject, the
Krupat, Arnold, 45, 47, 89; "The Dialogic of Storyteller," 89; For Those Who Come After, 45

Ladinos, 51, 94, 119, 121, 154 n.25, 155 n.16. See also Forbes, Jack
Laguna Pueblo, 72, 82, 86–87; descent, 80; origins of, 87. See also Silko, Leslie Marmon; Spicer, Edward
Language, 72, 74, 78, 95, 101, 111, 121–22, 143; African, 98; Amerindian, 76; borders of, 7; dominant, 21; English, 73, 98, 100–101, 122; first, 119; forces in, 57; group, 21; Indian, 98; of interpellation, 22; invaders', 71; as a model, 25; multilingual, 10, 100, 103; Nahuatl, 100–101; play, 24; poetic, 25; Pueblo, 88–89; relationship to culture and power of, 74; relationship to subject and power of, 25; semiotic

meta-, 25; Spanish, 88, 98, 100–101; system, 77, 87; tribal, 48

La Raza Cósmica (Vasconcelos), 44

Las Casas, Bartolomé de, 13–14, 147 n.12; *The Devastation of the Indies*, 148 n.19

Last Generation, The (Moraga), 142

Latina/o, xviii, 5, 19, 37, 41, 54, 63, 115, 128, 135, 138–39, 141; anti-, 36, 42; autobiography, 154 n.2; bodies, 136, 144; border crossers, 132, 136, 149 n.8; civil rights, 137; community, 18, 137; cultural practices, 101; culture, 117, 119; deportation, 40; descent, 108, 121, 137; family, 136; in the film industry, 137, 138; identity, 122; immigrant, xvii, 41; neighborhood, 5; prostitution ring, 136; purchasing power, 138; sexual commerce, 143; writers, 78

Lesbian, 5, 30, 59, 105, 117, Chicana, 97, 117, 124, 142; of color, 126; identity, 97

Lévi-Strauss, Claude, 75

Life and Adventures of Joaquin Murieta (Yellow Bird), 106

Liminality, 36, 42, 60, 63, 102, 131, 141, 151. *See also* Border: crossing

Location of Culture, The (Bhabha), 83

Logocentrism, 16, 74, 76–77. *See also* Derrida, Jacques; Mignolo, Walter D.

Los Angeles (Calif.): contemporary, 136; East, 133

Los Tigres del Norte, 101–2. *See also* Corridos

Machismo, 9, 131, 136–37, 142, 157 n.16. *See also* Alarcón, Norma; Castillo, Ana; Saldívar-Hull, Sonia

Malinali Tenepal (La Malinche), 125, 146 n.5

Manifest Destiny, xi, 14, 19, 21, 94, 106, 109, 145, 150; in Texas, 108

Manifesto, 109–10. *See also* Smith, Sidonie

Marginalization, 43, 127; of Chicana/o and Mexicana/o peoples, 100

Market demand, 115

Massacre of the Dreamers (Castillo), 140

Matriarchy, 140

Mesoamerican, xvii, 13, 50, 97, 99, 119, 122–23, 125–26, 147 n.12. *See also* Alarcón, Francisco; Forbes, Jack; Mignolo, Walter D.

Mestiza/o, 4, 32–33, 36, 46, 47, 51, 54, 63–65, 72, 80, 88, 95, 121, 125–26, 137, 145 n.5, 154 n.25; bodies, 125; consciousness, 9, 98, 118, 123; culture, 127; Europeanized, 119; identity, xii, xvii, 80, 84, 96, 146 n.2; "new," 117–18, 124; poetics, 32; speaking subject, 118; subaltern subjectivity, 104; subject, 33, 71, 100, 103; subjectivity, 32, 99, 104

Mestizaje, xi, 6, 31, 98, 100, 117, 124, 127, 131, 133; afro-, 124; decolonial, 127; ethnic, 99; issues of, 119; linguistic, 99; in Mexico, 151; in Philippines, 77; sexual, 99. *See also* Alarcón, Norma

Methodologies: anticapitalist, 33; anticolonialist, 33

Methodology of the Oppressed (Sandoval), 32

Mexican: anti-, 36, 42; colonial regime, 99; community, 96–97, 106, 123–24; cultural economy, 97; culture, 49, 97, 124, 126, 141; deportation of, 66; descent, 66, 80, 108, 121, 133; exile of, 109; government, 51; hacienda, 55, 99; hegemony, 60, 123; identity, 104; immigrant, 41, 54–56, 101, 135; industrial control, 55; industrial instability, 54; labor, 53, 55, 97; land, 56, 62, 108; misrule, 108; nation, 54; nationality, 63–64; nationhood, 142; nation-state, 36, 97, 110; neighborhood, 5; point of view, 124; popular culture, 71, 125; products, 65; ruling-class, 59–60;

Mexican (*continued*)
  subject, 138; subjectivity, 110; terri-
  tory, 19; Texas, 54; tourist council,
  119; voices, 42; workers, 6, 53, 66,
  102
Mexican Emigration to the United States
  (Cardoso), 52, 56, 65
Mexican Immigrant, The (Gamio), 36,
  42–44, 49, 55, 58, 67, 71
Mexican Immigration to the United States
  (Gamio), 42, 58
Mexican Revolution (1910), 42, 47,
  51–52, 55, 59–60, 106, 150
Mexican Voices/American Dreams
  (Davis), 41
Mexican Workers and American Dreams
  (Guerin-Gonzales), 66
Mexican-American War (1848), 108, 118
México Profundo (Batalla), 44, 50
Middle class, 136
Mignolo, Walter D., 21, 76, 97, 101, 147;
  The Darker Side of the Renaissance, 21,
  76, 146 n.5, 147 n.9
Migra, la, 38–39, 67, 108, 132. *See also*
  Immigration and Naturalization
  Service (INS)
Migration, 102
Militarization, 82, 90
Miscegenation, 53, 151; laws, 149 n.22;
  taboos, 139. *See also* Mohanty, Chan-
  dra Talpade; Takaki, Ronald
Mixblood Messages (Owens), 18, 71
Modernity at Large (Appadurai), 154 n.2
Mohanty, Chandra Talpade, 27–30,
  32–33, 105, 116; "Cartographies of
  Struggle," 27
Moraga, Cherríe: *The Last Generation*,
  142. *See also* Sovereignty
Morgan, Lewis Henry, 11, 12, 147 n.8;
  Ancient Society, 11, 147 n.8
Movements in Chicano Poetry (Pérez-
  Torres), 103
Mulatto, 121
Murieta, Joaquin, 106

*Myth of the Savage and the Beginnings of
  French Colonialism in the Americas,
  The* (Dickason), 10, 14

Nahuatl tradition, 97
Narrative, 36, 57; acts, 88; autobiographical, 58; captivity, 41; counter-,
  87, 133; Gamio's, 47; hybrid, 95; master, xii, 7, 14, 95; meta-, 128; national,
  134; patriarchal nationalist, 97; syncretic, 152; terrain, 24; travel, 12;
  writing culture in, 57
Nationality, 134
Nationhood, 43
Nation-state, xi, xvi, 7, 14, 33, 37, 42, 97,
  103, 105; Aztec, 110, 123–24; building,
  47; colonial(ist), 105, 108; development, maintenance, and dominance
  of, 105; discourses of the, 133; formation, 46, 88; imaginary, 131; imperial,
  17, 129; intersections of, 145 n.1;
  interstices of the, 118; limits and
  margins of, 105; metanarratives, 128;
  Mexican, 36, 110, 145 n.5; militarized, 111; Spanish, 110; U.S., xii, 100,
  104–5, 110, 118, 129; violence, 118;
  Western, 35
Native, 104, 129
Native American, xii, 8, 18, 19, 72; autobiography, xvii, 97; identity, 154 n.25;
  novelist, 77
Neocolonial, 4, 7, 17, 19, 26–27, 76, 147
  n.14, 148 nn.16, 17, 153 n.22; consciousness, 80; educational systems,
  73; power, 33; scripts of subjection,
  46; in the U.S., xii; violence, 117
Nepantilism, 84
New Mexico: Hispano popular culture
  of, 88
Niranjana, Tejaswini, 8, 16, 17, 27, 46,
  146 n.18, 150; *Siting Translation*, 8, 16,
  46, 150 n.18. *See also* Postcolonialism
Novel, the, xiii, 72–73, 76–77, 79–
  80, 82, 85–86, 93–94, 112, 152 n.8,

153 n.14; *Colonial Rise of the Novel, The* (Azim), 76, 148 n.20; Native American, 77–79. *See also* Bahktin, Mikhail

Occupied America (Acuña), 107
Oedipal Conquest Complex, 142
Oedipus, 142
Of Grammatology (Derrida), 74–75, 147
Oppression, 65, 117, 125
Oral tradition, 72–73, 77–78, 89. *See also* Owens, Louis; Penn, W. S.
Orientalism, 100
Other Destinies (Owens), 78
Other Tongue, An (Arteaga), 122
Otherness, 14, 40–41, 61, 108, 110, 130, 138, 143
Owens, Louis, 18, 20, 71, 78–79, 81–82, 129; *Mixblood Messages*, 18, 71; *Other Destinies*, 78

Pastoral tradition, 111. *See also* Smith, Sidonie
Patriarchy, 136, 138, 140, 142, 145; bias, 151 n.21; control, 125; dominance, 25, 109, 117, 125; economy, 31; indigenous cultures, 140; narrative, 97, 128; nation-state, 118; oppression, 117; postmodernity, 98; power, 33, 65, 95, 125; project, 105; regulation of power, 97; subject, 30; subjection, xii, 4, 94, 104; tradition, 97, 117; violence, 32, 117
Penn, W. S.: *All My Sins Are Relatives*, 77–79, 152 n.12
Phallocentrism, 118, 125. *See also* Alarcón, Norma; Kaplan, Caren
Philippines: imperialism in, 17; mestizaje in, 77
Plantation slavery, 29
Poetics: of heterotopic space, 100; of identity, 72; mestiza/o, 32; politics of, 84
Poetry, 100, 103, 104

Politics: economy, 31; feminist, 32; of identity, 72; multilayered, 33; of poetics, 84; of representation, 42–43; system of domination, 118
Post-Colonial Studies Reader, The (Ashcroft), 18
Postcolonialism, 16–17, 147 n.14, 148 n.17; cultural studies, 74; discourse, 128; interrogations of authority, 57. *See also* Appadurai, Arjun; Bhabha, Homi K.; Mohanty, Chandra Talpade; Niranjana, Tejaswini
Postmodernism, xvi, 3, 6, 8, 26, 30, 32, 78, 98, 100, 104, 131–32, 137
Poverty, 35
Predicament of Culture, The (Clifford), 46
Problems in General Linguistics (Benveniste), 20
Proletariat, 135
Prostitution, 115, 135–36, 141, 157 n.19
Pueblos, 81–82, 87–88, 154

Quincentenary, 3–4. *See also* Resistance 500 events

Race: and blood quantum, 54; and class, 45, 49, 51, 59, 65, 71, 116, 134; class, and gender, xi, xiv, xvii, 19, 43, 59, 65, 96, 100, 110, 123, 127–28, 130, 133, 140, 143; consciousness, 47; crossing, 53–54, 85, 153 n.20; and culture, 122; differences, 45; and ethnicity, xii, xiv, 43, 45, 49, 59, 108, 116–17, 128, 143; eugenics, 49, 53–54, 108; exploitation by, 133; Gamio's views on, 49; and gender, 59, 155 n.9; inequities, 71; "inferior," 54; Mexican, 61; and notions of the libidinal, 146; outcast, 138; privilege, 140; relations, 47; and sexuality, 28, 116, 123, 127–28, 134, 143; and skin color, 155 n.9; white, 130
Race and Labor Immigration Debates, xv, 51–54

Racial: commodity, 46; discrimination, 49, 61, 134; essentialism, 72; exploitation, 136; identity, xii; imagery, 129; inequality, 151 n.2; oppression, 17; purity, 83, 98; and sexual, 20, 28, 36, 86, 106, 114, 136, 153 n.22; type, 47; violence, 20, 62, 86, 106, 111, 114, 117, 143

Racially Mixed People in America (Root), 80

Racism, 136; anti-, 32; and discrimination, 58; and exploitation, 49, 115; and institutional, 142; and poverty, 40, 150 n.15; scientific, 147 n.10; sexism, 26–27, 32, 36; slavery and segregation, 138

Recién llegado (newly arrived), xii, xvii, 136. *See also* Immigration

Redfield, Robert, 42–44, 46. *See also* Gamio, Manuel; *Mexican Immigrant, The* (Gamio)

Refugees: economic, 115

Regionalism, 47

Regulation: societal, 100

Relations: power, 17, 108, 136; representational, 100

Researches into the Early History of Mankind and the Development of Civilization (Tylor), 12

Resistance, 133

Resistance 500 events, 4–5, 7. *See also* San Francisco (Calif.)

Rosaldo, Renato, 47, 58, 87, 133; *Culture and Truth*, 47, 58. *See also* Ethnography: theory

Routes (Clifford), 156

Saldívar, José David, xii, 97, 122, 132–33, 152; *Border Matters*, xii, 133, 152 n.9; *The Dialectics of Our America*, 97, 122, 152 n.9

Saldívar-Hull, Sonia, 96, 100, 116, 118, 128; *Feminism on the Border*, 100, 116

San Francisco (Calif.), 4, 40, 47, 77, 130, 148. *See also* Resistance 500 events

Sandoval, Chela, 28, 32–33; *Methodology of the Oppressed*, 32

Santa Clara Pueblo et al. v. Julia Martinez et al., xvi, 82

Savage, xvi, 8–12, 14, 45, 86, 90, 108, 110, 143, 146 n.5, 152 n.5; noble and/or fierce, xiv, 3, 6–7, 13, 15–16, 28, 106, 111, 147 n.12, 155 n.13

Scenes of Subjection (Hartman), 23

Schizophrenia, 83, 84, 91, 120, 147 n.15, 153 n.191. *See also* Fanon, Frantz

Self-representation, 43, 96

Sepulveda, Juan Ginés de, 13–15

Sexism, 36, 97

Sexual: decolonization, 128; exploitation, 136; harassment, 36; orientation, 116

Sexuality, 100, 123, 128, 134; in the Aztec nation-state, 124

Silko, Leslie Marmon, 71–74, 76, 79–83, 85, 88–91, 93–95, 153 n.16; *Almanac of the Dead*, 93; *Ceremony*, 72, 78, 80, 84

Silverman, Kaja, 20, 23–24, 26; *The Subject of Semiotics*, 20, 23

Siting Translation (Niranjana), 8, 16, 46

Smith, Sidonie: *Subjectivity, Identity, and the Body*, 109–11

So Far From God (Castillo), 88

Sovereignty, 100, 137, 142. *See also* Moraga, Cherríe; Resistance 500 events

Spanish, 3, 13, 15–16, 22, 54, 87, 121; blood, 117; colonists, 15, 19, 76, 87–88, 94, 99, 126, 146 n.5; cultural hegemony, 123; descent, 131; empire, 125; hacienda system, 99; language, 5, 21, 37–38, 61–62, 85, 89, 98, 103, 130; literacy, 21; -Mexican, 63; nation-state, 97, 110; patriarchal system, 126; rulers, 121

Speaking subject, 9, 19, 20, 23–26, 30, 32, 59, 97, 103–4, 117, 127–28: mestiza/o, 118; Mexican, 36; subaltern, 33. See also Alarcón, Norma; Silverman, Kaja

Spicer, Edward, 87–89; Cycle of Conquests, 88. See also Pueblos

Star Maps (Arteta), 129, 131, 136–37, 139, 141, 143

Struggle for the Land (Churchill), 146. See also Neocolonialism

Subalternity, 61, 98, 113, 131, 140, 143; identity, xii. See also Border: theory; Postcolonialism

Subject: Anglo-American feminist, 30; autonomous, 24; Chicana/o, 133; Eurocentric, 30, 32; hybrid, 112; immigrant, 45; mestiza/o, 33, 71, 100, 103

Subject-in-process, 25–26, 32–33, 127–28; speaking, 117. See also Kristeva, Julia; Speaking subject

Subject of Semiotics, The (Silverman), 20, 23

Subjection, xii; colonial, 8; imperial, 94; patriarchal, xii, 4, 94, 104

Subjectivity, xi, 9, 24, 28, 31, 33, 58, 62, 77, 95, 96, 109, 118, 127, 144, 152 n.11; Chicana/o, 103; concept of, 24; diverse, xii; human, 44, 46; hybrid, 77; mestiza/o, 32, 99, 104; national, 134; personal, 32; subaltern, 33

Subjects: colonized, 8, 142; dehumanized, 115; indigenous, 15, 31–33; mestiza/o, 100; Mexican immigrant, 46; mixed-race, 33; national patriarchal, 104; racial, 84

Supremacy: white, 117

Taboo: class, 141; Euro-American, 135; of miscegenation, 149

Takaki, Ronald, 29, 62, 139, 149; Iron Cages, 149 n.22

Tayo, xvi, 78, 80–86, 88, 90–93, 95. See also Ceremony (Silko); Silko, Leslie Marmon

Teaching the Postmodern (Marshall), 8

Tel Quel Group, 25. See also Kristeva, Julia

"Testimonios" (Beverley), xvii

Texas-Mexican border, 96, 111

Theory: autohistory, 96; Chicano/a, 132; ethnographic, 132; feminist, 104, 132, 141; Marxist, 132; postmodernist, 132

They Called Them Greasers (de León), 108, 150 n.16

Third world, xiv, 27, 29, 112, 114, 116, 117, 131; feminist, 32, 33, 96; women, 27, 28, 29, 116, 148

Thought-Woman, 72–73, 79, 87, 91, 153 n.13. See also Ceremony (Silko); Silko, Leslie Marmon

Tijuana, Mexico, 37, 39, 41, 115, 130, 135

Todorov, Tzvetan, 13–15, 126, 146–47; The Conquest of America, 13, 146 n.4, 147 nn.11, 12

Torture, 9, 22–23, 120, 148 n.19, 150 n.23. See also Border: crossing; Conquest

Tourists, 38, 135

Translated Woman (Behar), 150 n.11

Translation: cultural, 56; studies, 46; symbolic, 148 n.18

Tribal consciousness, 47

Tropics of Discourse (White), 11

Underdevelopment: in Mexico, 115

Violence: anti-Mexicano/Latino, xii, 42; barbarous acts, 87, 106; border crossings, 115, 132, 135–36; cannibalistic, 84; colonial, 4, 6, 20, 23, 29, 32, 86, 91, 117, 120; corporeal, 23; of the Diaz regime, 55; disciplinatory, 106; domestic, 113; of domination, 28; ethnocentric, 75; family, 143; genocide, 14; imperial, 3; inflicted by the conquistadores, 22; intersection

Violence (*continued*)
   of power and, 8; male, 15, 140; material, 16; Mexican ruling-class, 60; military, 94; neocolonial, 20, 32, 117; patriarchal, 32, 117, 118, 140; physical acts of, 4, 136; police, 108; propensity for, 13; racial, 62, 111; racial and sexual, 20, 86, 106, 114, 117, 143, 153 n.22; sexual, 94, 107, 115, 116, 125, 128, 136; state, 36; unions between races, 149 n.23; vigilante, 106, 118; wetiko system, 120; of World War II, 81

Warrior for Gringostroika (Gómez-Peña), 133
Western Empire, 94
Wetiko psychosis, 84, 94, 120–21. *See also* Forbes, Jack
White (Dyer), 129
White Man's Indian, The (Berkhofer), 9–10

Whiteness, 94, 156 n.4
Wild men/women, xiv, 9, 11. See also *Myth of the Savage and the Beginnings of French Colonialism in America* (Dickason); *Tropics of Discourse* (White); *Wild Men in the Middle Ages* (Bernheimer)
Wild Men in the Middle Ages (Bernheimer), 11
Wilson, Terry, 81, 83, 85. *See also* Blood: quantum
Writing: agency of, 97; anthropological, 87; anthropological and ethnographic, 56; Aztec, 75; border, 131–33; Chicano, 132; culture, 57; decolonial, 72; ethnocentric conceptualizations of, 74; ethnohistorical, 87; Latin American, 132; Mayan, 75; Mexican, 132; Native American, 152 n.12; nonphonetic, 75; phonetic, 75; Western, 75

Arturo J. Aldama is Assistant Professor of Chicana/Chicano
Studies at Arizona State University.

Library of Congress Cataloging-in-Publication Data
Aldama, Arturo J.
Disrupting savagism : Chicana/o, Mexican immigrant, and Native
American struggles for self-representation / Arturo J. Aldama.
p. cm.
Includes bibliographical references and index.
ISBN 0-8223-2751-1 (cloth : alk. paper)
ISBN 0-8223-2748-1 (pbk. : alk. paper)
1. Mexican Americans—Mexican-American Border Region—
Ethnic identity.   2. Indians of North America—Mexican-American
Border Region—Ethnic identity.   3. Mestizos—Mexican-American
Border Region—Ethnic identity.   4. Mexican Americans in
literature.   5. Indians in literature.   6. Mestizaje in literature.
7. Ethnicity in literature.   8. Decolonization in literature.
9. Mexican-American Border Region—In literature.   10. Mexican-American
Border Region—Ethnic relations.   I. Title.
F787 .A43   2001
305.8'00973—dc21   2001033110